A
MIRROR
TO KATHLEEN'S
FACE

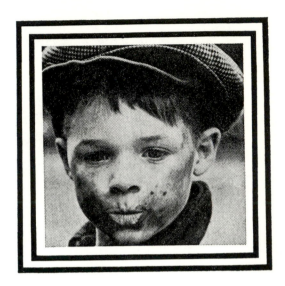

A Mirror to Kathleen's Face

Education in Independent Ireland
1922-1960

Donald Harman Akenson

McGill-Queen's University Press
MONTREAL AND LONDON

BY THE SAME AUTHOR

THE UNITED STATES AND IRELAND

EDUCATION AND ENMITY: THE CONTROL OF SCHOOLING IN
NORTHERN IRELAND, 1920-1950

THE CHURCH OF IRELAND: ECCLESIASTICAL REFORM AND REVOLUTION,
1800-1885

THE IRISH EDUCATION EXPERIMENT:
THE NATIONAL SYSTEM OF EDUCATION IN THE NINETEENTH CENTURY

THE CHANGING USES OF THE LIBERAL ARTS COLLEGE: AN ESSAY IN
RECENT EDUCATIONAL HISTORY *(with L. F. Stevens)*

© MCGILL-QUEEN'S UNIVERSITY PRESS 1975
International Standard Book Number 0 7735 0203 3
Legal Deposit third quarter 1975
Bibliothèque nationale du Québec

PHOTO BY *Saul Leiter*
DESIGN BY *Pat Gangnon*
PRINTED IN CANADA BY *The Bryant Press Ltd.*

*This book has been published with the help of a grant
from the Humanities Research Council of Canada using
funds provided by the Canada Council.*

To My Parents

CONTENTS

PREFACE

It is only fair to tell the reader that although this book completes my trilogy on Irish education in the nineteenth and twentieth centuries, it is an experiment and differs radically from the earlier studies in its approach to the subject.

As anyone who has had to read much educational history is aware, until roughly the time of the second world war writers of educational history in the British Isles were concerned mostly with describing the evolution of their educational institutions *in vacuo*. Educational and curricular systems were described as if they existed independent of the society from which they grew. These efforts should not be disparaged for at their best they gave us clear and precise descriptions which remain useful to this day. At their worst, however, they gave us self-righteous whiggish interpretations of the "inevitable" rise of educational democracy. For a considerable time now it has been a truism among educational historians that the history of educational institutions is the product of developments in the larger society and almost all recent work has encapsulated this point.

But systems of schooling not only are shaped by society, they in turn shape society. To ascertain the influence of the schools on a given social situation is a high risk venture. Not only are the forms of evidence about the effects of educational institutions very difficult to corral (even simple literacy statistics often say one thing and mean another) but on many issues (for example, the rise of a literate, politically-active working class) it is almost impossible to distinguish how much of any given effect is caused by the educational system and how much by other institutions and circumstances. And since the changes in the educational system cause changes in the general society, which in turn cause further change in the schooling system (and so on and on) the author of this kind of history runs the danger of being caught in a dizzying causal spiral; like a dog chasing his tail he may finish tired and exhausted, not knowing exactly where he is. Despite these dangers a few historians have attempted such analyses and the rewards have been great.

This brings us to the present experiment which involves, as it were, reading educational history backwards. That is, instead of studying the schools as something intrinsically interesting in themselves (either as administrative systems or as shapers of the national culture), I would like to approach the interrelations of Irish educational institutions and Irish society in a way such that the schools can be used as cultural litmus paper, telling us things about the Irish people which are otherwise apt to be overlooked. The manner in which people treat children is culturally diagnostic. The way a man responds to a crying child reveals as much about him in a moment as would be uncovered in a fortnight of phychoanalysis, and the way in which a society teaches children to face the pressures of the world tells us as much about that people as do all their statutes and parliamentary debates. Perhaps by focusing our probe on the Irish schools, light will be reflected on such simple but crucial issues as how deeply the Irish are concerned with their children's welfare, on whether minorities are really tolerated or are culturally harassed, on whether or not the Irish revolution was revolutionary and whether it led to a democratic or to an authoritarian state. In such a light both scars and beauty marks on the national countenance will be revealed. This approach explains the title of this book for the Irish schools are, indeed, a mirror to the face of Kathleen ni Houlihan.

During the writing of this book I received a great deal of help, always given generously and often entertainingly, from a wide variety of persons in Dublin, many of whom are in positions of considerable responsibility in educational affairs. I hope they will accept my thanks, which are no less heart-felt for being stated in general terms. This is a controversial book and some of those who helped me do not agree with all my points of interpretation. It would be unfair, I think, to associate them with views they may not accept. Equally, many of the views put forward here coincide only too precisely with the views of other of my sources and I defer to their quite understandable desire to preserve their careers by not mentioning them by name. I am grateful nonetheless.

The Bell Farm   Donald Harman Akenson
Gananoque
Ontario
1 September 1973

The Original Framework

Whether or not Ireland experienced a "Victorian Age" is a moot historical point, for Ireland in the nineteenth century was never bound fully by the assumptions about the constitutional, social, and moral order which prevailed in England and which were represented, as if in caricature, by the sovereign. Nevertheless, certain institutions in late nineteenth century Ireland were unmistakenly Victorian in the pejorative sense of the word, and none more so than the state educational systems. Like many quintessentially Victorian organizations and objects, the Irish school systems were elaborate, pious, and awkward. And like so many Victorian artifacts, the Irish school systems survived intact well into the twentieth century in this case into the 1920s. Obviously, to chart intelligently the history of education under the new government of southern Ireland, we must begin by discussing the all-Ireland educational structures that were inherited by the government in 1922 and subsequently modified according to the nation's peculiar circumstances. At the close of the nineteenth century there were, below the university level, three separate self-enclosed educational systems: national, intermediate, and technical education. The first provided primary schooling, the second academic secondary education, and the third vocational training.

The oldest and the most important of the three Irish educational systems was that of national education.[1] It had been founded in 1831 by Lord Stanley, then the chief secretary for Ireland. The basic structure was simple: an unpaid board of "commissioners of national education" in

Dublin made building and salary grants to local schools established under the management of some important local figure. The principle underlying the original arrangements was that the national system should not be denominational. Non-denominational in this context had three connotations: (1) at the local level schools should be managed jointly by Catholic and Protestant persons of repute; (2) the line between literary and religious instruction was to be drawn sharply so that there would be no chance of tampering with the children's religious beliefs during the hours of literary instruction when children of all denominations were to be taught together (during the time of separate religious instruction — at the beginning or end of the day or on a special day of the week — pastors of all faiths were to have access to the school to teach children of their respective flocks); and (3) the result of the first two precautions would be that the schools would have a "mixed" denominational population and persons of the different faiths would learn to live amicably with each other at a young age.

These ideals were noble but naive. To begin with, the commissioners of national education found that it was very difficult to secure applications for managerships jointly from Protestants and Catholics and, because the commissioners wanted the system to flourish quickly, they soon stopped seeking joint managerships. In actual practice they recognized as manager anyone of good character and by 1835 it was clearly established that Lord Stanley's first goal, inter-denominational managership, would not be reached. Of the 4,795 schools in operation in 1852 only 175 were under joint-managership.

Next, the line between literary and religious instruction, so clear in theory, was blurred increasingly in practice. Originally, religious instruction was to be conducted either at the beginning or the end of the school day or on a day set apart. By the late 1830s, however, the commissioners were allowing it to be given at any time of the day provided the period was announced in advance. Further, the set of textbooks sanctioned by the commissioners for common literary instruction was crammed with moral lessons and with references to Bible stories. Granted, the lessons and stories were neutral as between Christian denominations, but it was almost inevitable that a teacher would interpret these stories according to the tenets of his own persuasion.

The death blow to the idea of common literary and separate denominational education was administered by the Presbyterians. During the 1830s they campaigned against the national system of education on the grounds that the national schools mutilated the Bible. Also, they claimed that the requirement that the schools be open to clergy of all denominations during the time of separate religious instruction meant that even Presbyterian-financed schools could be used to advocate popery. The first grievance had no basis in fact and the second was the result of a remarkably selective sense of justice: the Catholic priests would be teaching only Catholic children, and in any case Presbyterian ministers were being granted the same access to all national schools that was granted to the Catholic clergy. Be that as it may, the Presbyterians burned national schools, harassed schoolmasters, and agitated furiously until finally in 1840 the commissioners of national education capitulated and redefined an existing category, that of the "non-vested" school, to mollify the attackers. Unlike all other national schools, these received no aid toward capital expenditure, receiving grants only for books and teachers' salaries. In return for accepting less state money than other school managers, those of the non-vested schools now could exclude clergymen of denominations other than their own from the school. Further, unlike the managers of other national schools they were not required to exclude children of a minority faith from religious instruction of the majority, but only to allow them to leave if they wished. Having gained these concessions the Presbyterians joined the system. The success of their agitation was fatal to Lord Stanley's ideals. They destroyed the two principles which had underlain the curriculum: (a) of excluding children from religious instruction of a faith other than their parents', and (b) of equality of access for clergy of all faiths during religious instruction periods. When those two principles were vitiated the scheme for combined literary and separate religious instruction became a faded illusion.

Simultaneously the Catholics and Anglicans acted in such a manner as to guarantee that most national schools would not be denominationally mixed. During the 1830s the Catholics accepted the national system and the Anglicans abstained. In the south of Ireland the Protestant population was sparse, a demographic fact which limited the degree of mixing that could take place. The Church of Ireland (Anglican) further reduced the potentialities for schools being mixed by denouncing the national schools and founding in 1839 a voluntary system of its own. Like the Presbyterians they had mistaken notions that the national schools were anti-Biblical, and in addition were perturbed that control of the national system was vested not solely in members of the Established Church, but shared by Anglicans, Catholics, and Presbyterians. Because of the Anglican abstention most rural schools in the south and west of Ireland contained only Catholic pupils.

As the century progressed the consequence of the combination of demographic factors, of the disappearance of the guarantees of denominational neutrality in the literary curriculum and of parity in religious instruction, and of the rarity of joint denominational managerships of schools, was a widening pattern of denominational segregation. In 1862 (the first year for which figures are available), 53.6% of the primary schools throughout Ireland were mixed, in the sense that they contained both Catholics and Protestants. In 1900 the figure was 35.6%.

To bring the discussion into the twentieth century, it should be noted that there were three problems, or failings, in the primary educational system with which successive governments grappled in the first two decades of the present century, in each case unsuccessfully: (1) the lack of local involvement by the Irish citizenry in educational affairs; (2) the small number of children in most Irish primary schools; and (3) the unnecessarily low proportion of children on the school rolls who attended school regularly. To note that none of these matters was adequately dealt with by the all-Ireland administration is to state that these problems were destined to be part of independent Ireland's educational inheritance.

From its earliest years the national system had effectively excluded parents and the majority of the local citizens from a voice in the management of the primary schools. Parents had almost no rights concerning their children's education and at the local level the manager of the national school was insulated from the citizen's influence by his being neither an elected official nor a representative of a local government body. Usually he was a cleric dependent only upon the good will of the commissioners of national education and of his religious superiors. Further, the citizenry were not required to aid the schools through the local rates; indeed they could not have done so legally even if they had so desired. A distinguished English school inspector reported after an extensive investigation of Irish primary education: "Except amongst the clergy, little or no local interest is manifest in the primary schools in Ireland. . . ."[2]

Although there was scant local interest in the schools, it cannot be demonstrated conclusively that this lack of interest was educationally dysfunctional. One can, however, suggest that the absence of parental and citizen involvement in all probability was harmful for two reasons. The first of these is that schools function most effectively when there is a connection between the home and the school. If parents are involved in the school in some way, they are more likely to be understanding of the school's methods and supportive of its objectives, so that the child's experience in school and at home complement each other. Second, on a purely financial level, if schools are underwritten in part by local taxation they will probably receive more money, and almost certainly receive it more regularly, than if they are dependent upon a combination of local charity and the arbitrary decision of treasury officials sitting in London. Sources of local charity dry up faster than rate-aid in times of depression, and the treasury authorities in London could divert Irish educational funds to pay for some other imperial venture any time they wished.

In suggesting that parental involvement in school activities would have been pedagogically beneficial and that local rate aid would have improved the schools' financial position, I am *not* making either of two arguments often made by contemporaries: that, as was maintained by many English Liberal party politicians, it was a constitutional necessity for the schools to be controlled by laymen representative of some local government body — or, as the civil servants of the Treasury tended to argue, that requiring support of the schools from the local rates would tie the citizens to their local schools as if by a golden cord, and that the aroused citizenry automatically would improve the management of the schools by mixing in what had been previously a clerical jurisdiction. The point at hand is much less contentious: that the existing arrangements deprived the child of educationally beneficial parental involvement in his schooling and that the absence of local rate aid left the schools unnecessarily vulnerable financially.

Given, then, that the problem was a real one, interested parties viewed it differently. The perceptions of four groups were important in determining the course of events: the educational professionals, the Catholic authorities, the Ulster Protestants, and the English Liberals. William Starkie, the resident commissioner of national education, was probably the most knowledgeable and certainly the most powerful of Irish professional educators. In September 1902 he delivered a controversial speech before the British Association in Belfast in which he adverted to the lack of local interest in elementary education.[3] Similarly, as noted above, F. H. Dale, the English H.M.I. who was seconded to Ireland to survey the Irish primary school situation, reported in 1904 that local interest in education was lacking.[4] It is clear that at the highest level the educational professionals recognized that the two problems, too small schools and the absence of local involvement, did indeed exist and that steps should be taken to deal therewith.

In contrast to the educational professionals, the authorities of the Catholic church failed to perceive (or refused to admit) that the problem was significant. The Catholic authorities perceived the national system as a moral, rather than as a strictly educational, structure. They viewed the system of clerical control over each local national school as a moral necessity: "The managerial system in our primary schools means, in reality, that legitimate and necessary control which the local pastors rightfully exercise over the national schools attended by the youth of their flocks, a control which is designed not merely to promote the general efficiency of the schools, but, above all, to safeguard the faith and morals of the pupils at the most perilous period of their lives."[5] Therefore, the Catholic authorities did not see the lack of local parental and civic interest in the schools as a problem, since such involvement would undermine the educational authority of the clergy. The Catholic bishops resolved in June 1904 that, "any limitation or restriction of the control which is now exercised by managers over the schools of the national system would be so injurious to the religious interests of our people as to make it imperative on us to resist the introduction of such a measure, and, in case it were adopted to reconsider our whole position in relation to those schools."[6] Accordingly, the Catholic school managers and bishops refused to consider throwing any portion of school expenses on the local rates, because such a policy would imply that local civic authorities would gain some control over the local schools.[7]

Leaders of the Ulster Protestants (and especially of the Presbyterians) perceived the matter differently. They were deeply concerned about the lack of local involvement in primary education. Significantly, however, the northern Protestants viewed the absence of local involvement not so much as a condition which hindered the effective functioning of the schools, but as an indication of clerical dictatorship in political matters. They demanded the introduction of local control of education, rate aid to schools, etc., as part of a policy of rescuing Irish democracy from the evil influence of the Catholic priesthood. Thus, neither the Catholic authorities nor the northern Protestant leaders realized that the absence of local involvement was an educational problem. The Catholics viewed the situation as a moral exercise and were thereby precluded from understanding that an educational problem existed; the northern Protestants viewed the situation as a case of democracy-versus-clericalism and they responded to the situation as a sectarian and political challenge, rather than as a matter of educational policy.[8]

The perceptions of the English leaders of the Liberal party were as important as those of any Irish group. These men saw the Irish situation through a lens originally shaped to suit the English situation. It is well to remember that the Liberals had opposed strongly the passage of the Balfour Education Act of 1902 which gave rate aid to English denominational schools without, the Liberals felt, providing a commensurate amount of governmental control over those schools. The Liberals stood united behind the principle of English educational institutions being controlled by local civic authorities and underwritten in considerable measure from local rates. When transposed to Ireland these English educational attitudes meant that the Liberal government would try to moderate the denominational and clerical control of the national schools and that it would press for rate aid to local schools and for the creation of local school boards.[9] Significantly, the tie between English events and Irish policies was guaranteed by the appointment in 1907 of Augustine Birrell as chief secretary for Ireland; Birrell had been president of the Board of Education in England from 1905 to 1907. His appointment meant that the gold-cord theory of educational reform would be invoked, whereby it was held that requiring local districts to vote rate aid for their schools would lead to local civic control of the schools, which would in turn lead to increased parental involvement and would thereby greatly facilitate educational improvements.

Despite their commitment to the principle of civic involvement in educational affairs, the Liberals accomplished little. After some minor skirmishes during the early years of the Liberal administration about the issue of local control, Birrell attempted to solve Irish educational problems and, perhaps, the home rule question in one measure. This was through his famous Irish Council Bill, introduced into the Commons in May 1907. The bill called for the establishment of an Irish council of eighty-two elected and twenty-four nominated members, plus the under secretary *ex officio*. This council was to assume control over eight existing departments. It was to assume direct control over the Department of Agriculture and Technical Instruction, and to merge the work of the commissioners of national education and the commissioners of intermediate education into a single department. The Irish council was not to have taxing powers but was to administer parliamentary grants.[10]

Notice here both what was explicitly proposed and what was left unsaid. The bill provided that control of Irish education would be placed in the hands of an assembly most of whose members were popularly elected, but nothing was said about local control of the schools or rate aid or about various forms of parental involvement. Nevertheless, the explicit provisions for popular control at the central level were almost perfectly designed to provoke the ire of the Catholic bishops, while Birrell's past record was enough to cast suspicions about his future intentions on the local level. Birrell as president of the Board of Education in England had shown himself to be a thorough-going advocate of local civic control of educational institutions and an opponent of denominational interests. It was natural to infer that once the council bill was passed, rules requiring substantial rate aid to schools and at least a modicum of local civic control would follow.

Therefore, it is not surprising that the Catholic bishops led a national agitation against the Irish council bill. At first the bill was approved by nationalists with such divergent views as John Redmond and Patrick Pearse, but the convention of the United Irish League, to which the Irish parliamentary party was effectively responsible on this matter, rejected the bill. It was precipitously dropped, and no English politician dared revive the question.[11]

Turning now to the second major problem that was eventually inherited by the new Irish government, the predominance of small schools, the dimensions of the matter are indicated in the following figures: in the school year 1904 more than three-fifths of the schools receiving grants from the commissioners of national education had an average daily attendance of less than fifty pupils.[12] Under the commissioners' rules, a school with less than fifty pupils in average attendance was entitled to only one teacher and, hence, the majority of Irish primary schools were small one-teacher schools. These schools, although now often enshrined in nostalgic memoirs, were educationally deficient by their very size. Whereas a school with three or four teachers allowed a teacher to concentrate on the educational problems of one or two age groups and allowed the pooling of resources for the purchasing of special equipment, the master of a one-teacher school was stretched thin, tending to six or seven standards simultaneously, with few pedagogic aids, such as maps, murals, or scientific demonstrating equipment to make his job easier. Further, ill-equipped as most tiny national schools were, they were expensive to build and to maintain. One well-equipped three room school was much cheaper to construct than three one-room schools and in most cases served as well or better.

In practical terms the issue of school size was a contest between the educational professionals led by William Starkie, resident commissioner of national education, and the Catholic authorities. Given the Catholic church's concern with each priest's oversight of the children of his own flock, it is hardly surprising that the church authorities refused to recognize that the proliferation of small schools was an educational problem, or that they fought hard against school amalgamations. It was a rare parish priest who was willing to give up his prerogatives and allow children of his parish to be educated in a school not under his sole supervision. The Catholic opposition to amalgamations was reinforced by the bishops' reluctance to merge boys' and girls' schools even when each was pathetically small: "Apart altogether from moral considerations, we believe that the mixing of boys and girls in the same school is injurious to the delicacy of feeling, reserve, and modesty of demeanour which should characterize young girls."[13]

Conflict became unavoidable when, in June 1903, the commissioners of national education unanimously requested that resident commissioner Starkie provide a report on the excessive expenditure incurred by the multiplication of small schools and that he prepare a plan to solve the problem. Starkie's answer to the problem was published as part of a revised set of rules and regulations adopted by the commissioners in December 1904. Starkie intended to solve the small schools problem by three rules: (1) rule 186 stating that separate boys and girls schools near to each other and under the same management had to be amalgamated unless both had an average attendance of at least thirty students; (2) rule 187 requiring that in the case of new applications for recognizing boys and girls schools in the same locality in place of an existing co-educational school, no aid would be granted unless there was strong evidence that each school would have an average attendance of at least fifty pupils; (3) rule 127b stating that boys under eight years of age were ineligible for enrollment in a boys school where there was not an assistant mistress on hand for their education, except in the case of there being no suitable girls school in the locality. On the surface this last rule seems strange, but actually it was ingenious. The idea was to transfer young boys to girls schools where they would be better taught by the school mistresses, and thereby let the masters of boys schools concentrate on teaching boys in the higher grades. This plan would not, of course, increase the average size of the schools (the loss in numbers in the boys schools was a gain in the girls) but would nevertheless yield one of the advantages sought in amalgamation: allowing some degree of specialization by grade levels instead of requiring the teachers in all small schools to teach children from first standard through the higher grades.[14]

Immediately upon publication of these rules a furor arose. Teachers were concerned about losing their jobs as the result of amalgamations. More important, the Catholic hierarchy and clergy were incensed. Starkie attempted to defuse the Catholic opposition by judicious compromise. Patrick Foley, bishop of Kildare and Leighlin, had become a commissioner of national education in January 1905, and Starkie attempted to negotiate with him a bargain which would be acceptable to the entire Catholic hierarchy. Starkie, with the unanimous approval of the commissioners of national education, made three concessions to the bishops as represented by Foley: first, rule 127b was amended to deal with boys under seven years of age instead of eight years as originally framed. Second, a further amendment of rule 127b provided that in cases where transfer of the young boys to a girls school would result in the boys school losing an assistant master (through attendance dropping below the level required for an assistant master to be maintained), special exceptions could be made and the young boys could continue in the boys school until the assistant master had found another appointment. Third, rule 186, the amalgamation rule, was modified to state "this rule shall not apply to any boys school, the average attendance of which, but for the operation of rule 127b would, in the opinion of the commissioners, be over thirty."[15] What would Bishop Foley provide in return for these concessions? According to the commissioners' minutes, the Most Reverend Dr. Foley stated that in his opinion the amendment went "some way" to meet the objections of the Catholic hierarchy and school managers, "and that as far as his influence went, he would exert it to obviate these objections."[16]

There is no reason to think that Foley acted in bad faith, but in the actual course of events his episcopal colleagues repudiated the bargain. In May 1905, Foley had the humiliating task of reporting to his fellow education commissioners that the standing committee of the bishops had considered the amendments and that although the bishops "heard with satisfaction" the amendments in the commissioners rules, "since these rules were part of a large scheme of amalgamation of boys and girls schools to which they (the bishops) had insuperable objections on moral grounds, they would feel it their duty to oppose them by every legitimate means in their power. . . ."[17]

How acute the conflict between the commissioners and the Catholic bishops might have become is impossible to say because at this point the bishops' anger shifted away from the commissioners and the amalgamation question towards the Irish administration and the question of local involvement in the schools (discussed above).

What were the results of the amalgamation campaign? In 1904, the year before the imposition of the new rules, the average number in daily attendance in Irish national schools was fifty-six. The corresponding figure for 1919 was sixty-one.[18] Some progress had been made, but obviously many schools were still too small, a problem which eventually would have to be faced by the government of southern Ireland.

A third educational problem that also went unresolved during the first two decades of the twentieth century and eventually had to be faced by the Irish Free State authorities was the low proportion of children on the primary school rolls who attended school regularly. The Compulsory Attendance Act of 1892, the operative statute until the 1920s, was a net with more gaps than webbing. This act, which was an attempt to bring Irish standards up to those of the English act of 1880, required parents to send children between the ages of six and fourteen to school for at least seventy-five days a year. It operated, however, only in towns wherein school attendance committees of local citizens and school managers were formed to enforce attendance by issuing legally binding school attendance orders. The most important local government bodies (such as the Dublin, Cork, Limerick, and Waterford corporations) refused to cooperate. One reason for their refusal was that the Catholic hierarchy was opposed to compulsory education as an infringement of parental rights. Further, some bishops and those on the municipal corporations who shared their views, were piqued at the government for its continual refusal to provide financial aid to the Christian brothers schools. As a result, average daily attendance in Irish primary schools in the years 1910–19 stayed near the seventy percent mark, instead of the eighty-five to ninety percent level which effective compulsory attendance laws would have yielded.[19]

When we turn to the system of intermediate education we are dealing with a network of more recent foundation than the national schools.[20] It was the Intermediate Education Act, 1878, which introduced a modicum of financial support and a magnum of regulation into the intermediate educational scene.

The intermediate education system was simplicity itself. It was the Victorian commercial code applied to education. A seven member unpaid board was appointed to distribute money to school managers according to the performance of their individual students on annual examinations set by the commissioners. The board of intermediate education was endowed with one million pounds from property formerly belonging to the late Established Church in Ireland and was allowed to spend annually the interest on this sum which amounted to £32,500. Most of this income annually went to the managers of schools who educated students successful in the examinations. A smaller portion of the commissioners' annual income was awarded in prizes and exhibitionships directly to the pupils with the most outstanding examination performances.[21]

Unlike the commissioners of national education, the commissioners of intermediate education were precluded by statute from aiding construction of new schools or enlarging old ones (and in any case their limited resources would have made such expenditure almost impossible). The necessity of working through existing institutions meant that the intermediate educational system was automatically a denominational one, for almost all of the schools efficient enough to earn grants were of this sort.

Undeniably, the inflow of money was beneficial to the Irish intermediate schools, especially because it was allocated by the commissioners according to high academic standards. Nevertheless, the mercenary mechanism used by the commissioners to adjudicate distribution of money often cramped individual schools. Because departures from the syllabus prescribed for the examinations cost the school examination fees, teachers were not encouraged to adapt the curriculum to their classes' individual situations. Thus, many intermediate schools became cramming establishments which spent all their energy trying to satisfy the intermediate education commissioners in Dublin.[22]

The harsh edges of the examination system could have been softened by replacing some of the emphasis upon external examinations with actual visits to schools by inspectors and this the commissioners attempted to do in the early twentieth century. After a long and involved battle with the Treasury and with the Dublin Castle administration lasting most of the century's opening decade, the commissioners established their right to provide a bonus grant of up to twenty percent upon the basis of inspections.[23] Then in 1913 the commissioners won the right to compute school grants for children in the preparatory grade (ages twelve and thirteen) on a capitation basis rather than upon examination results.[24] Five years later, in 1918, the commissioners gained an incremental £50,000 a year which they were allowed to distribute on a capitation basis in accordance with the inspectors' reports.[25]

But all these were minor changes; the examination system remained the bulwark of the intermediate school system. In August 1918 a vice-regal committee was appointed to inquire into the intermediate system. It concluded that dependence upon examinations produced a rigid, undesirable curriculum and recommended that the payment by results scheme be abolished and a flat capitation rate, subject to inspection, substituted.[26] Nothing came of these recommendations and the government of the Irish Free State inherited a high-pressure, examination-bound network of intermediate schools.

If curricular rigidity induced by the examination system was the primary problem facing those who wished to improve the intermediate educational system, the unsatisfactory physical condition of many schools was nearly as pressing. An investigation of 1904 found that ninety Irish intermediate schools (of which there were then 275 in operation) [27] had inadequate schoolrooms, cloakrooms, and playgrounds, or insufficient lighting and ventilation, or inadequate sanitary facilities.[28] Except for science equipment the intermediate commissioners were prevented by statute from making loans, much less grants, for capital improvements. Clearly, after 1922 the new Free State government would need to do a considerable amount of reconstruction of physical facilities before intermediate education could be set on a sound footing.

The 1904 investigations, which were conducted by two senior inspectors from England, revealed a third problem, namely that many intermediate schools were too small for educational efficiency. One hundred and ten schools had fewer than fifty pupils.[29] The problem was especially acute in the case of Protestant schools. For example, we find in 1917 that the average size of the Catholic intermediate schools was fifty-eight, that of Protestant schools, forty-nine.[30]

Behind the problems of curricular rigidity, inadequate facilities, and proliferation of small schools lay the fact of inadequate financial resources. Most, if not all, of the problems blighting intermediate education could have been solved if enough money had been available. The financial position of the commissioners of intermediate education was singularly unsatisfactory: their resources were fixed by law but their expenses were continually increasing. One reason for the elasticity of expenditure was that the number of children under the commissioners' aegis increased markedly during the first decade of the twentieth century. In 1901, 8,117 pupils sat for the commissioners' examinations; in 1910, 11,900 sat.[31] Second, the administrative costs of the intermediate system rose with the introduction of the inspectorial scheme which was discussed above. Third, and most important, the value of money decreased sharply during the first two decades of the twentieth century. One pound sterling worth twenty shillings in 1900 was worth nineteen shillings in 1911, sixteen shillings in 1915 and ten shillings in 1919.[32]

Through 1913 the intermediate commissioners' corporate income consisted solely of fixed resources: the interest on the million pounds allocated to the board in 1878 (procuring now about £30,900 annually), plus an annual grant under the Revenue Act of 1911, in lieu of the "whiskey money" granted earlier by Parliament (this yielded roughly £46,600 a year) and various miscellaneous revenues, such as school fees and interest on past savings, the total income being about £84,700.[33] The commissioners were voted an annual grant of £40,000 in 1914, an additional annual grant of £50,000 in 1918, and one of £50,000 in 1920.[34] These sums were not enough. In their report for 1920 the intermediate commissioners stated that "the whole edifice of secondary education in Ireland is toppling to destruction." They continued, "if something is not done immediately to place Irish secondary education in the position of financial equality with that of Great Britain, it is impossible to see how the complete disruption of the system can be avoided."[35]

The only part of the Irish educational structure which was prospering in the early twentieth century was the system of vocational training. Until the close of the nineteenth century technical education of post-primary standard had been the poor orphan of the Irish educational world. For example, Ireland received only the paltry sum of £3,840 in the year 1900 for technical education granted through the Department of Science and Art in London, a body not notably responsive to Irish needs.[36] Only near the century's end was a sequence of events initiated by Horace Plunkett (Sir Horace, 1903) which led to the creation in 1899 of an Irish Department of Agriculture and Technical Instruction.[37] "The department" (as it was called by staff) directly controlled four schools of its own and also carried on a good deal of agricultural extension work, but neither of these responsibilities was as important as its making grants to intermediate schools wherein practical science and/or drawing were taught. Because the intermediate education commissioners were very short of funds, they permitted science and drawing in the intermediate schools to be taught under the hegemony of the Department of Agriculture and Technical Instruction. This lasted until 1915 when friction led the intermediate board to reintroduce its own examinations. Perhaps most important of all, the new department granted funds to local civic bodies to establish and supervise local technical instruction institutes.[38]

The success of the department in prosecuting the activities specified above was astounding. "The programme of experimental sciences has been adopted with greater readiness and success by the Irish secondary school than the department ventured to anticipate," the annual report for 1901–02 stated. "The number of schools which carried out the first year of the programme was 152," the report continued, "and the number of pupils who worked during the course . . . was 6,412."[39] Grants that first year for the sciences and drawing programme totalled £9,575. By 1918–19 the number of students involved was 16,870 and the grants distributed, £33,450.[40] Similarly, the local civic authorities were quick to form their own technical education schemes. The school year 1902–03, only the second full year of the department's operation, saw the formulation of twenty-seven county and twenty-four urban schemes, plus six plans for the large county boroughs.[41]

Significantly, the department was remarkably adept at garnering parliamentary funds. Its original charter gave it £55,000 a year for technical instruction. Yet in the year 1918–19 the amount available for the science and art classes and the technical schools was: £114,210 from the parliamentary vote, plus an additional £65,867 from the board's annual endowment which also was allocated for technical instruction.[42] These funds were in addition to the sums granted for the maintenance of the central institutions and for agricultural extension work.

Why were the authorities of the Department of Agriculture and Technical Instruction so successful in obtaining money for their program, when the intermediate education commissioners were unsuccessful? Part of the explanation lies in the forces which led to the establishment of the department. Its creation was the result of agitation by Irish nationalist M.P.s (with some unionist involvement, most notably by Plunkett) who demanded that Irish technical education cease being controlled from South Kensington, London. This guaranteed that Irish M.P.s would press the department's case, particularly as the department's highest officials took great pains to establish that theirs was not a "Castle board."[43]

Equally important, the procedures followed the constitutional contours annunciated by English politicians and treasury mandarins, most particularly local involvement in all important activities. Many British M.P.s and most financial experts baulked at supporting any activity that did not have a degree of support from local rates and some element of local civic control. Neither the national nor the intermediate systems of education possessed these characteristics. The great good fortune of the Department of Agriculture and Technical Instruction was that it was formed *de nouveau* on the eve of the twentieth century and accordingly fitted into the constitutional template which United Kingdom governments of the time demanded. Also fortunate for the department was that having been established through the efforts of the Irish nationalist M.P.s it was propelled past clerical objections to its secularist characteristics with an ease unimaginable if it had been broached by either of the British parliamentary parties.

Let us briefly examine what local involvement actually meant in Irish technical education. Under the Irish Local Government Act of 1898, a complete system of local government had been established in Ireland for the first time. As in England, a network of county councils, county borough councils, and urban district councils blanketed the country. The Agricultural and Technical Instruction Act of 1899 built upon these local civic institutions by empowering the various councils to form committees composed of their members and other competent citizens to plan programs of technical and, if appropriate, agricultural instruction in the local areas. In the usual case a high official of the Department of Agriculture and Technical Instruction met with the local committee, offering suggestions and providing guidelines. Eventually, a plan was submitted formally to the department for its approval. Under these schemes each local government body voted a rate in support of technical education, usually the penny in the pound allowed by law, but occasionally less.[44] The department, after having approved the scheme, made a grant from its own funds to aid the local authority which directly supervised its own technical schools.[45]

This marked the first time in Irish educational history that local civic agencies controlled schools. The clerical authorities were extremely suspicious of these developments because local technical schools were avowedly secular institutions, but there was little they could do. Local civic leaders embraced the new system with enthusiasm. In the fiscal year 1914–15, for example, 135 separate local governing bodies participated under the Agriculture and Technical Instruction Act and raised through local rates over £62,000 for educational purposes.[46]

Yet another reason the Department of Agriculture and Technical Instruction was so successful was that its educational policies possessed a simple, but rare, virtue: they made sense. When granting money to intermediate schools for the teaching of science and drawing, the department made its grants to an individual school not on the basis of annual examinations but instead had each school carefully inspected and then made its grants on a capitation basis. Hence, the anxiety among students and the academic rigidity among the teachers which so marred the intermediate system were blessedly absent in the science classes conducted under the department's auspices. Further, the method of framing local technical instruction schemes was admirably flexible and responsive to local needs. The department refused to establish an architectonic scheme and instead each local authority planned what was best for the local area.

Much of the credit for the department's sensible methods must go to two men, Sir Horace Plunkett and T. P. Gill. The former was the original vice-president of the department, the latter the secretary. The chief secretary for Ireland, although in title the president of the department, was otherwise engaged, so these two men effectively controlled the department. Plunkett set policy and performed high-level negotiations, while Gill ruled the day-to-day administration. Plunkett left the vice-presidency in 1907 but Gill continued until the very last.[47] Both men had reason to be proud, for their department had established that a lay-controlled, nonsectarian educational system could function effectively in Ireland.

An acute observer of the Irish educational systems, writing in 1882, concluded, "I think I have said enough not only to prove the necessity for reorganizing our education department, but also to establish the proposition that it is expedient to appoint a supreme education department presided over by a minister of education."[48] Granted, in the early twentieth century efforts at coordination of the three Irish educational systems were made. There was a representative of both the intermediate and of the national education boards upon the consultative committee of the Department of Agriculture and Technical Instruction, and upon the Board of Technical Instruction. W. J. M. Starkie, resident commissioner of national education from 1899 until his death in 1920, was also chairman of the intermediate education board for the last ten of those years.

But these efforts were ineffective. The relationship of the primary and intermediate schools remained muddled. Most children stayed on too long at primary school, with the result that they entered intermediate school at an age when it was too late to begin with advantage the intermediate course.[49] Moreover, there was no public provision for scholarships to enable children to pass from primary to intermediate school. The intermediate schools were financed less generously by the government than were the elementary schools, which meant that there was severe social class discrimination in Irish education, with only the very exceptionally talented child of the working class being able to pass beyond the elementary school. Augustine Birrell had framed a modest scholarship program to help to meet this problem in 1911. It would have cost only £10,000 per year, but the Treasury refused to sanction it.[50]

Attempts at coordination of the systems of primary education and of technical education also were ineffective. Here the problem was that when students left the primary schools at age fourteen they were too young to benefit fully from the technical school classes. To bridge this gap many technical schools had to establish preparatory classes to teach the children lessons which, the technical authorities thought, should have been taught in elementary school.[51]

Snarled as were the interrelations of the three Irish educational systems, the problem of untangling them was a stimulating and beneficial task: in trying to remodel the systems, policy makers had the opportunity of confronting the multiplicity of educational difficulties which were detailed earlier in this chapter. Thus a major commission on intermediate education under the distinguished Catholic Lord Chief Justice Molony recommended in March 1919 not only the establishment of a single department of education but sweeping changes in the structure of intermediate education, especially local involvement in controlling and financing the schools.[52] Another vice-regal commission, this one on primary education under the well-known Catholic peer Lord Killanin, although precluded by its terms of reference from discussing the idea of a single national education ministry, prescribed fundamental changes in the local administration of the primary system.[53] In response to these reports the government formed a committee in May 1919 to draft a sweeping education bill which would, it was hoped, solve most of Ireland's educational problems.[54]

The resulting bill, completed in July 1919, was as educationally desirable as it was politically unpalatable: it provided logical, inclusive, and efficient solutions for most of the educational problems bedevilling

Ireland; but it stood no chance of success because it aroused the ire of the Catholic bishops. The bill's most important provisions were as follows. First, it provided for the establishment of a department of education, under the presidency of the chief secretary for Ireland, that would take control of all primary, secondary, and technical instruction. Second, an advisory board of education was to be established consisting of three senior governmental education officials, sixteen representatives appointed by county councils and county borough councils, nine representatives of the national schools, five of the secondary schools, two from the technical schools, and sixteen persons appointed by the lord lieutenant. Almost inevitably, this board of education would have a lay majority. Third, local education committees were to be established in each county and county borough to deal with primary, intermediate, and technical educa-tion. These committees were to have power to provide rate aid for primary, intermediate, and technical schools. They were to assume the duties of the existing local technical education committees in controlling tech-nical education in the local districts. Because of the controversy which was later to surround the bill it is important to realize that the local education committees were *not* to have any right to interfere with the existing managerial system in the elementary and intermediate schools or to become involved with the appointment of teachers in those schools. Arrangements for religious instruction were not to be tampered with in any way. Fourth, the bill proposed that the payment of grants to inter-mediate schools on the basis of examinations should cease, and that a full inspectorial system be introduced.[55]

This bill elicited the opposition of vested interests, both educational and clerical. While the bill was being drafted, T. P. Gill, secretary of the Department of Agriculture and Technical Instruction, addressed the Irish Technical Instruction Congress, stating that a crisis was taking place for technical education and that the proper course was not to legislate for his department but simply to give it more money.[56] After the bill was in-troduced the standing council of the Irish Technical Instruction Associa-tion argued that the bill would disturb the existing technical system and, by implication, impair its efficiency.[57] Similarly the commissioners of national education had reservations. They approved of the bill in most details, but objected to the establishment of a single department of education.[58]

The real opposition, however, came not from educationists, but from the Catholic bishops. They used the same technique which had been successful in blocking Augustine Birrell's Irish Council Bill in 1907. They fought the threat of lay involvement at the local level and lay control at the centre by pointing to the unrepresentative and un-Irish character of the proposed new education department. In later April 1919, even before the bill was drafted, the standing committee of the bishops issued a statement condemning the creation of a department of education under the control of a minister who would be responsible not to Irish but to British public opinion. This, they stated, "would be an altogether retrograde proceeding at variance no less with Irish feeling and Irish national rights than with Irish educational interests."[59] On the ninth of December 1919, after the bill was published, the standing committee of the Irish Catholic bishops, chaired by Cardinal Logue, stated that "the only department which the vast majority of the Irish people will tolerate is one which shall be set up by its own parliament. . . ."[60] The polarity of Irish denominations on educational issues is well indicated by the appearance in December 1919, almost simultaneously with the Catholic bishops' denunciation of the bill, of a resolution by the education board of the general synod of the church of Ireland expressing "hearty approval of the main principles of the Irish education bill."[61]

Under the crush of parliamentary business the original bill of 1919 was withdrawn without a second reading in late December,[62] but during the next session in late February, 1920 an almost identical bill was introduced.[63] Even before it was introduced the Catholic bishops, meeting at Maynooth, issued a declaration dated 27 January 1920, in which they said that the education bill was "the most demoralizing scheme since the Act of Union"; that "until Ireland is governed by her own Parliament, we shall resist by every means in our power any attempt to abolish the boards of primary, intermediate, and technical education"; that "the bill is an attempt on the part of the British government to grip the mind of the people of Ireland and form it according to its own wishes"; that if the bill is forced upon the country their lordships will issue instructions to Catholic parents on how to proceed "in such a deplorable crisis"; that rate aid to education was unacceptable; and the bishops expressed their "intense sympathy" with the teachers.[64] If there was any lingering doubt of the hierarchy's position it was dispelled by Cardinal Logue's condemnation of the bill in his lenten pastoral,[65] and by a condemnation read in each Catholic church in Ireland on Passion Sunday, 1920.[66]

The United Kingdom government, already engaged in passing the "Partition Act," was unwilling to become involved in another contentious

Irish measure. This reluctance to engage in Irish combat was reinforced in April 1920, when it was necessary to replace James Macpherson as chief secretary for Ireland with Sir Hamar Greenwood. (According to one inside observer Macpherson had suffered a breakdown;[67] considering the state of Ireland at the time, it is only surprising that it did not occur sooner.) Hence, the ministry simply ignored the Irish education bill for the entire session and in mid-December it was withdrawn without having received a second reading.[68]

The frustration among educators can easily be imagined. In May of 1920 A. N. Bonaparte Wyse, a highly placed Catholic education official framed a memorandum summarizing the flaws in the Irish educational structure. His observations, which were presented in uncompromising outline form, are summarized below:

Primary education. Outstanding deficiencies are:
A. Insufficiency of teachers' salaries leading to a great dearth of qualified teachers and consequent inefficiency of school work.
B. Bad schoolhouses and insufficiency of accommodation for pupils, the latter chiefly in Belfast.
C. Want of local interest in education and of provision of local aid for upkeep and maintenance of schools.
D. Laxity of school attendance and lowness of school leaving age.
E. Inadequacy of pension system.

Secondary Education. "If the state of Irish primary education is unsatisfactory, that of secondary education is deplorable." The great deficiencies are:
A. Low salaries of secondary teachers, absence of pensions, and insecurity of tenure.
B. The results system.
C. Insufficiency of government grants.
Overall lack of coordination of the primary and intermediate system.[69]

The continued existence of these problems was both an indictment of the United Kingdom government and a mandate for the future educational activities of the government of the Irish Free State. In evading a question concerning Irish secondary education, Sir Hamar Greenwood, the chief secretary for Ireland, uttered what well could be taken as the marching orders for the new government: "Under the Government of Ireland Act, 1920, questions of secondary and other education in Ireland pass under the jurisdiction of the Irish Parliaments, to which the final solution of these questions must now be left."[70]

THE REVOLUTIONARY INHERITANCE

Tinkering With The Machinery

"Next to our pillar boxes," an Irish educationist wrote in 1955, "probably the most distinctive monument recalling English rule in Ireland is the system of education."[1] As far as the structure of Irish education is concerned, as distinct from the curriculum, this statement errs by understatement, for Irish pillar boxes are less centrally located and are harder to find than are the schools. In most matters of public policy the Irish revolution was less a revolution than a change in management and in no area was the essential conservatism of the revolution more clearly exemplified than in the refusal of the new government to change fundamentally the school systems inherited from the imperial administration. Granted, the old machinery was tuned and tinkered with, but basic matters such as the existing arrangements for the control and financing of each of the three major school networks were accepted as axiomatic.

The honouring of United Kingdom precedents by the new Free State government was not the result of a considered appreciation of their virtues but rather of a failure on the part of most Irish revolutionary leaders to consider seriously matters of education. With the exception of the fragmented, and nearly powerless, socialist wing of the revolutionary movement, which had been led until 1916 by James Connolly, Irish revolutionaries were notable for their distaste both for ideology and thorough social planning. The near absence of ideology and social thought gave the revolutionaries a terrible purity, for all efforts could be directed at the clear, simple goal of freeing Ireland from the English. But their incandescent negativism precluded subtle analyses of cultural issues and in the field of education predisposed the revolutionaries to accept existing structures.

Here a well-drilled veteran of the national schools' history lessons might rise and say, "wait — wasn't Patrick Pearse a radical critic of the intermediate school system and wasn't Eamon de Valera a former school teacher and didn't many national teachers join the movement?" True. But let us look at the overall record (at the same time noting that Pearse died in 1916, his advice later being ignored by the new Irish government, that de Valera was such an educational conservative that when in office in the 1930s and 40s he reintroduced the British scheme of set texts which had been abolished in the 1920s, and noting too that the national teachers did not join the revolutionary movement to think about the educational system, but to escape it). The record shows that the constitution of Dail Eireann, as approved in January 1919, did not include provision for a minister for education.[2] This omission was understandable in view of the first Dail cabinet's comprising only five members, but it is significant that when the revolutionary Dail was expanded in April 1919 no education minister was named and when questioned later about the possibility of such an appointment, Cathal Brugha, minister for national defence, responded ambiguously that President de Valera, who was at that time in America, had some definite reasons for not appointing an educational minister when forming his cabinet.[3] Yet at the same time the Dail ministry responded to a resolution of the ard-fheis of the Gaelic league by creating a ministership for the Irish language.[4] The Irish language question is discussed in the next chapter, but at this juncture the point to be emphasized is that, in the revolutionary Dail, educational policy was subsumed by the plan for reviving the Irish language. As a result, what little thought there was about educational policy was an incidental offshoot of language concerns.[5]

Whatever attention the Irish language ministry could have given to larger educational issues was impeded by the minister J. J. O'Kelly's being on the run and subsequently being arrested.[6] In fact, in September 1920, the Dail had found it necessary to name an assistant secretary, "owing to the inability of the secretary [minister] for Irish to devote sufficient time to the duties of the position."[7] Then, in late August 1921, de Valera created a ministership for education and appointed the peripatetic Mr. O'Kelly to the post.[8] (The available Dail records do not make it clear whether or not the ministership for the Irish language was abolished or simply merged with the new education post; the question is a moot one in any case because the same man who had headed the language ministry was now heading education.) Whatever consideration O'Kelly may have been giving to education was cut short by the great debate on the Anglo-Irish treaty. O'Kelly voted with de Valera's minority against the treaty[9] and, as a result, in early January 1922, he was no longer in office.

Then ensued a year of confusion which precluded a serious assessment of the educational structure even if one had been contemplated. During the first five-and-a-half months of 1922 the provisional government was struggling desperately to stem the slide into civil war and thereafter the pro- and anti-treaty forces were locked in combat. Moreover, on the pro-treaty side ministerial confusion was rife; there were not one, but two ministers for education: Fionan Lynch for the provisional government and Michael Hayes for the Dail! (A full list of ministers for education in Ireland, from the first Dail to the present, is found in the Appendix.) This duplication was part of the extraordinary dualism that pervaded the entire structure of the new government. Under the Anglo-Irish treaty the powers of government were to be transformed to a provisional government of Ireland, the provisional government being headed by Michael Collins. But the theory of government to which many Irish nationalists ascribed postulated that Ireland was an autochthonous nation, its sovereignty stemming from the self-constituted Dail Eireann. After the split on the Anglo-Irish treaty the pro-treaty forces kept in existence a Dail cabinet, headed by Arthur Griffith, thus satisfying the demands of nationalist metaphysics and keeping open the door to rapprochement with the de Valera wing of the anti-treaty movement (this group recognized the Dail's legitimacy but not that of the provisional government formed under the treaty with the United Kingdom).

Within the sphere of education, as within the government as a whole, it is clear that all major functions were taken over by the officials of the provisional government.[10] But imagine the confusion of school teachers and managers who read the reports of the simultaneous appearance before the Irish national teachers' organisation of the Dail minister for education, Professor Michael Hayes, and the provisional government minister, Mr. Fionan Lynch![11] Only in the last quarter of the year 1922 was a single man, Professor Eoin MacNeill, given unfettered control of the state's educational machinery.

But even if the control of educational affairs had been unified immediately after the Anglo-Irish treaty was approved, it is doubtful if any root-and-branch examination of educational structures would have been possible, for the leaders of the pro-treaty administration were involved in endlessly complex negotiations about the as-yet-undrafted Free State constitution.[12] The formulating of the document which would be the foundation stone of the new Irish government precluded all other policy considerations and educational matters received scant attention in the deliberations. The constitution as finally enacted contained very little on social policy, including in the field of education only a statement of the right of all citizens to a free primary education.

Disasterously, during the summer of 1922, southern Ireland slid into a brutal civil war. Naturally enough the strife absorbed most of the new government's efforts. Many of the high ranking national leaders reverted to their earlier roles as military commanders. In mid-July Fionan Lynch, provisional government minister of education, was appointed vice-commandant of the southwestern division with the rank of commandant-general.[13] The war did education scant good, although a cynical observer reported: "one benefit, however, the rebellion has conferred on Irish education. It has furnished a new interest to the student of Irish geography. Few boys, until the other day, could have found Kilmallock. . . ."[14] Implicitly the civil war served to reinforce the status quo as far as educational structures were concerned. The drafting of cabinet personnel into the military left the establishment of the new Free State machinery in the hands of civil servants who had been trained under the imperial regime and who were predisposed to perpetuate existing institutions. Further, on a more general level, the civil war forced the new government to seek allies wherever it could find them. Chief among these was the hierarchy of the Catholic church, a group with an immense investment in protecting its existing educational prerogatives.

The transfer of day-to-day control of Irish educational institutions from the United Kingdom administrators to the provisional government's civil servants was a clumsy process. Not all of the awkwardness was the fault of the southern Irish officials. The chief impediment to a smooth transfer of powers to the southern government was the fact that under the Government of Ireland Act, 1920 (usually called the "Partition Act") the United Kingdom government was already involved in transferring many powers to the northern government well before the southern provisional government was established. Thus, what ideally should have been a clean, simultaneous transfer of power from Westminster to the two Irish governments instead was an unseemly scrimmage.

The Parliament of Northern Ireland had been established in May 1921 and a full cabinet named, with the Marquess of Londonderry as minister of education, in June 1921. Full powers over the educational institutions in Northern Ireland were transferred to the northern ministry on 1 February 1922, when the southern provisional government was less than a month in existence.[15] To simplify the transfer of power from the United Kingdom authorities, a provisional government order of 19 January 1922 reduced the number of governmental departments to nine, one of the nine being the Department of Education.[16] By joint order of the United Kingdom and provisional Irish governments, the Irish government as of 1 April took over control of the various government departments functioning in the twenty-six counties. The minister for education assumed control of national and intermediate education (as well as the much less important task of supervising the endowed schools), but did not take control of the technical schools which were placed under the jurisdiction of the minister for agriculture.[17]

Under the United Kingdom administration, policies for the primary schools had been set by the commissioners of national education, an unpaid board of distinguished citizens. Everyday control had been in the hands of the "resident commissioner" who was a permanent civil servant, and his subordinates. The resident commissioner, for two decades Dr. William Starkie, had died in mid-1920 and the imperial authorities had not appointed a replacement. (One educational journalist complained: "in appointing the resident commissioner of national education, as in admitting a candidate for holy orders, it is no doubt desirable that the authorities should 'lay hands suddenly on no man,' but six months, one would think, ought to give time enough for the necessary deliberation.")[18] This delay meant that the administrative staff of the national school system had been without effective leadership for a long time, but presented an off-setting advantage: that the provisional government could appoint its own man to fill the highest post without having to displace any permanent official.

But the commissioners of national education themselves were another story, for they had to be abolished if the new provisional government wanted its own civil staff to control directly and completely the primary school establishment. Thus, on the 31st of January 1922 the commissioners of national education were told to assemble in order to listen to a statement by Patrick Bradley, who held office under the new government as the "chief executive officer for national education." "I propose . . .," Bradley told them, "to take full control of, and responsibility for, primary education in Ireland including the full administrative and executive functions of the board."[19] Bradley was acting on behalf of the provisional government's minister for education, Fionan Lynch, who was said to be unavoidably absent. The commissioners were relieved of their policy making duties, but to soften the blow Bradley promised that "the minister will be anxious to avail himself of your long and varied experience. . . ."[20] Of course neither the minister nor the higher civil servants had any intention of taking advice from the commissioners and in June 1923 the board of commissioners, which had been in continuous existence since 1831, was discharged. A new board was constituted of two members: Bradley and another civil servant, Joseph O'Neill.[21]

Much the same thing happened in intermediate education, although somewhat more gently. Control of the intermediate schools was divided between northern and southern governments as of 1 February 1922,[22] and in mid-June 1923 the board of commissioners of intermediate education were superseded by two commissioners, one of whom was the same Joseph O'Neill mentioned above.[23]

Reflect for a moment on what had taken place. The new government of southern Ireland had taken full, unfettered control of the central administrative apparatus for education and had concentrated effective control of that apparatus in the hands of a small number of civil servants. That was reasonable and probably necessary. It was neither necessary nor reasonable, however, to abolish the former commissioners of national and intermediate education without providing for substitutes. Whatever their flaws,[24] the two boards had been independent bodies of intelligent citizens, concerned with education and not dependent upon the educational system for their own livelihoods. At their best they served a representative function, protecting the interests of the child and the layman against the pressures of aggrandising interests — religious, political, and bureaucratic. Granted that the two boards had serious flaws — they included too few educationists, they were often supine when they should have been truculent, and, having been appointed by the former Dublin Castle administration their membership was inappropriate to an independent Ireland — it does not follow that representative institutions of some sort were of no value.

For a time after the official establishment of the new state (the provisional government was replaced by the government of the Irish Free State on 6 December 1922) there were optimistic reports that the minister for education would set up an advisory council on education, comprising teachers and other qualified citizens, to advise him on all levels of education, from primary school to the university.[25] Actually, however, the Cosgrave government was far from enthusiastic about the establishment of any independent critical agency, and although de Valera and Fianna Fail favoured the establishment of such a body while they were in opposition,[26] they blocked its establishment once they were in power. Only in 1950, under considerable pressure from the Irish national teachers' organization[27] and the commission on vocational organization,[28] was an advisory "council of education" formed and it was a singularly tame body (its willow-like stance will be discussed in later chapters). But even this was far in the future. In its early days the new Irish government was content to replace the intermediate and national education commissioners with civil servants, thus substituting for an academic and professional oligarchy, an unfettered bureaucracy.

And who were the civil servants who were gaining such powers in the new Irish government? Almost all of them were former functionaries of the United Kingdom. Between 21,100 and 21,200 civil servants were transferred to control of the new state. Of these only 131 had been personnel of the revolutionary Dail. All the rest were formerly United Kingdom staff.[29] Not surprisingly, the Free State government took over not only the former United Kingdom personnel, but imperial civil service structures and procedures as well, only slightly modified to correspond to the abolition of the chief- and under-secretaryships for Ireland by the new constitution. The honouring of United Kingdom precedents and policies proved satisfactory to most Irishmen and the only investigation into the civil service conducted before the late 1960s, the Brennan commission of the mid 'thirties, concluded that there was no reason for any major change.[30]

Perhaps a vigorous minister could have jogged the educational service out of its old patterns, but the available evidence suggests that Eoin MacNeill, first minister for education in the Irish Free State was not such a man.[31] A brilliant scholar in early Irish history, he possessed the judicious, balanced temper which marks the mature scholar, but makes an indecisive political administrator. MacNeill's watchword in Dail discussions of education was not "reform" but "coordination," implying an automatic preservation with only slight modifications of the status quo. But even the task of coordination was accomplished slowly. As late as October 1924 MacNeill was forced to admit that, despite national and intermediate education being under a single ministry, the two divisions would have to publish separate reports for, "we have the different departments and it is hard to see how the reports can be other than separate."[32]

Then, in November 1924 MacNeill was appointed to the boundary commission to study and possibly revise the territorial limits of northern and southern Ireland. From the commission's first meeting in early November 1924 until MacNeill's resignation in disarray from the commission in mid-November 1925, and soon thereafter from the Cabinet, the Free State was effectively without a minister for education. Members of the Dail complained often that the minister rarely attended the Dail to deal with educational matters,[33] but to no avail. To a modern observer it is not surprising that the Free State government felt the boundary to be more important than educational affairs; what is surprising is that the government did not feel that educational affairs were important enough to warrant the appointment of a new minister for education once Mac-Neill's time was absorbed elsewhere.

During the MacNeill era, however, certain useful changes occurred. The Ministers and Secretaries Act of 1924 reorganized the Irish government into eleven departments. Significantly, the Department of Education assumed control of technical education, thus bringing the three chief branches of education, primary, secondary, and technical, under one minister.[34] (In the Act the former national schools were called "primary schools," the former intermediate schools became "secondary schools"; this usage became common but not universal in official circles; among teachers and journalists the old terminology prevailed; hereafter the two sets of terms are used interchangeably.)

Under the new act the Department of Education was able to coordinate educational services so that there were no curricular gaps between the various systems, but no real change was made in the basic structure of any of the three branches. As in the days of the imperial administration the primary schools continued to be managed in most cases by the Catholic parish priest or Protestant clergyman; he appointed the teacher and from local sources provided one third of capital construction costs and all maintenance expenses; the state paid two thirds of the capital costs and full teachers' salaries. The academic secondary schools were even more particularistic. Almost all of the secondary schools had been built at private expense and continued under private, almost always denominational, control; the private managers appointed the teachers and paid their basic salaries; the state paid incremental salaries to the teachers, and a grant to each school according to the number of approved pupils on the rolls (these last two practices were innovations), but still refused to put forward money for the construction or physical improvement of the schools. As for the technical schools, they continued to be controlled by local education committees and to receive grants both from local rates and from state sources.[35] Thus, the establishment of a department of education merely provided an umbrella for the maintenance unchanged of structures, policies, and powers which had been defined in the imperial era. By no stretch of the imagination was a unified nationwide system of education created, for the three systems remained distinct and administratively incompatible entities, only one of which (the technical school arm) was amenable to local civic influences.

A most significant alteration in Irish educational practice introduced by the new government was the abolition, in 1924, of the system of allocating grants to academic secondary schools according to their pupils' examination scores. Payments-by-results were replaced by a capitation grant paid for each child following an approved course. Simultaneously, the government began to provide increments to the salaries of teachers in recognized schools, thus making the teachers less dependent upon the whim of their school governors.[36] Equally to the credit of the Free State government was the passage in 1926 of an act which made fully effective the requirement that children between the ages of six and fourteen attend school regularly.[37]

Later, in 1930, near the end of the Cosgrave administration, a vocational education statute was passed. Although not the radical revision of the entire technical education system it was claimed to be, the new act actually did three things of note (I do not count the renaming of technical schools as "vocational schools" or the minor alterations in the composition of the technical education committees as significant changes). First, a network of vocational education authorities was created to cover the entire Free State. This was a signal improvement over the former permissive system under which the larger municipal corporations took advantage of the opportunity of creating technical educational committees, but rural committees did not. Second, each vocational education authority, a group appointed by the appropriate local government unit, was required, not merely permitted, to strike a local rate in aid of vocational schooling.

Third, the realm of vocational schooling was expanded to cover not only full time study but part time "continuation" education as well.[38]

What has our mirror shown us thus far about modern Ireland? In the first place it has reflected the fact that the Irish revolution was not revolutionary. Irish politicians replaced United Kingdom politicians in control of the state, but the basic institutions of government remained unchanged. Indeed, below the top level, even the civil service personnel stayed the same. In the field of education there was no fundamental questioning of the three systems of schooling, and thus no questioning of the nature and legitimacy of the powers which controlled those systems. If radical revolutions are concerned with the reorientation of systems of power, then the Irish revolution was a very superficial revolution indeed.

Next, if the field of education can be taken as typical, it appears that the new government of Ireland was somewhat authoritarian and distrustful of representative institutions. Developments in the 1920s strengthened the hand of the central bureaucracy against the teachers and lay citizens. The abolition of the commissioners of national education and the commissioners of intermediate education, when combined with the refusal to create an independent advisory council on education, meant that there was no effective forum for educators or concerned citizens to air their misgivings about government educational policy or seek redress for injustices inflicted by the state bureaucracy.

Third, one is left with the feeling that the new government was not greatly concerned with education (it was, as is discussed in the next chapter, concerned with the propagation of the Irish language, but that was more a political than an educational commitment). The first minister for education under the provisional government simply disappeared from the education office to fight the republicans; the first minister under the Free State government was out of effective control of his ministry for nearly an entire year which he spent negotiating with the British about the border. In the Dail, precious little time was spent discussing education (this at the very time the Northern Ireland Parliament was radically reconstructing its school system) and no fundamental studies of Irish education were commissioned by the Dail (and this at the time the English consultative committee under Sir W. H. Hadow was producing the monumental study upon which all subsequent British arrangements are based). No one would deny that the new government of Ireland had a great deal to think about, but one must still be struck by its spending so little energy reflecting upon the educational needs of the nation's children.

The Magic Of Words

If the Irish revolution changed little in the structure and control of Irish education, it yielded a vast change in one part of the school curriculum, namely in the position of the Irish language. From being just one subject of the school curriculum it became, overnight, the dominant subject. Two threads run through the discussion which follows. The first is that the language was given high priority, not for intellectual or educational reasons, but for nationalistic ones. Second, the politicians' affirmation of the value of the Irish tongue and their insistence upon its becoming the central subject in the curriculum is not amenable to rational explanation. The embracing of Irish was an intuitive act. Irish was seen as a national panacea. The Irish language came to have mystical, nearly-magical properties, and in dealing with the educational aspect of the Irish language revival one has to treat it sympathetically, on its own terms. One can do so if one realizes from the beginning that we are dealing with a phenomenon which must be explained not by logic, but by psycho-logic.

The foundation of the psycho-logic which led to the radical curriculum revision was the Free State leaders' awareness of the indisputable fact that their nation's ethnic language (Irish) had long ceased to be its native language (which now was English). Given below are the numbers of Irish speakers in the area which eventually became the Irish Free State:[1]

NUMBER OF IRISH SPEAKERS		PERCENTAGE OF POPULATION
1861	1,077,087	24.5%
1871	804,547	19.8
1881	924,781	23.9
1891	664,387	19.2
1901	619,710	19.2
1911	553,717	17.6

This trend, the leaders of the new state declared, had to be reversed.

Why? The reasons were articulated with varying degrees of subtlety, but the common thread binding almost all the Irish language revivalists was an equation of national identity with the ethnic language. Listen to a few statements. The taoiseach W. T. Cosgrave: "The possession of a cultivated national language is known by every people who have it to be a secure guarantee of the national future."[2] Eamon de Valera told the Gaelic league: "It is my opinion that Ireland with its language and without freedom is preferable to Ireland with freedom and without its language."[3] Eoin MacNeill, first minister for education of the Irish Free State, declared that for the members of the government to abandon the attempt to revive Irish would be to abandon their own nation.[4] Among politically influential persons the belief that the nation's identity hinges on the Irish language persists. "The Irish language is the most distinctive sign of our nationality," was categorically stated in a 1965 government white paper on the restoration of the language.[5] Such quotations could be multiplied almost endlessly, each one having the ring of a sincere evangelical faith.

It is easy to see how this equation of Irish nationality and preservation of the language developed. The Irish revolutionaries were neither ideological nor programmatic in their thinking and instead of specific plans for the future government of their country they filled their minds with a romantic idealization of Ireland's Gaelic past.[6] Ireland free and Ireland Gaelic became synonymous phrases, so that when the former revolutionaries came to power it was virtually automatic for them to try to reincarnate the virtues of the old Celtic order — and the Irish language they believed had been the lynch-pin of that order.

Even if the affirmation of the need to restore the Irish language had not been an automatic response, the men who formed the Free State government would have had to embrace it through political necessity. Their opponents in the post-treaty divide accused them of having sold the pass to the British, and affirmation of the language revivalists' ideals was one way in which the new government could establish that it was Irish to the hilt.

Further, in the three decades before independence the movement to revive the Irish language had played an important role in establishing a sense of national identity and it was a natural act to affirm the beliefs of those who had helped rouse the national spirit.[7] This sense of historical obligation was based on an overestimation of the importance of the language movement (one critic snorted: " . . . the driving force behind the scenes the whole time was this secret society which had as much to do with antiquity as a Mills bomb")[8] but that is beside the point. The sense of gratitude and obligation to the language movement was real and that reality determined the government's actions.

All this was reinforced by a very clever twist in terminology (whether consciously calculated or unconsciously motivated is unclear) whereby in the early twentieth century the language revivalists stopped talking about the Gaelic language and began pressing for the revival of the *Irish* language. This simple maneuver won for them the field because one now had a set of natural opposites: the English and the Irish languages which, by false but convincing analogy, were depicted as being as antagonistic as English soldiers and Irish heroes. The emotion attached to these linguistic antitheses precluded rational debate, for how could a patriotic Irishman be anti-Irish? That the native language of most Irishmen was English and thus part of the Irish nation's culture was a fact that was almost totally obfuscated by the English-Irish antithesis. The intellectually acute could perceive the rhetorical gambit which had been played ("The language commission by asserting that one-fifth of the people in this state speak Irish," a professor of Irish wrote in the mid '60s, "might as well have asserted that I am a Chinaman")[9] but even to the present day the polarities are affirmed unquestioningly by most Irish politicians.

That the revival of the Irish language and the flowering of the national identity were equated is clear; what is not clear is precisely what revival meant. To the more extreme revivalists the goal was to drive out English and to make Ireland a monolingual country.[10] Others, probably the majority, desired the country to become truly bilingual, with Irish serving as the ordinary home language of the majority of Irishmen, who would also retain English as a useful tool in dealing with outsiders.[11]

Given that the political leaders of the new nation were committed to reviving the Irish language, one must explain why they came to rely upon the schools as their chief instrument of linguistic resuscitation. In reality the Irish language was dying because the whole process of cultural transmission within the Gaelic speaking community had broken down,[12] but this was too terrifying a fact to deal with directly. Instead, the national leaders fell into a simple, comforting mélange of false history and bad logic. The false history declared that the national schools had been founded in 1831 as an intentional and successful attack by the British on the Irish language. From its early days the Gaelic league incorporated this belief in its pamphlets. "The real decadence of the Irish language," one pamphlet by the Reverend Michael Hickey stated:

began with the establishment in Ireland of the so-called national system of primary education. . . . The system as it was actually carried out made the parents spies upon the children; made the teacher a brutal tyrant; made the school a torture chamber to the pupil; sent the children forth into the world, when their school days had ended, without education and almost without a language.[13]

According to Douglas Hyde, founder of the league:

This extinguishing of the Irish language has not been the result of a natural process of decay, but has been chiefly caused by the definite policy of the board of "national education," as it is called, backed by the expenditure every year of many hundreds of thousands of pounds. This board, evidently actuated by a false sense of imperialism, and by an overmastering desire to centralise and being itself appointed by government chiefly from a class of Irishmen who have been steadily hostile to the natives, and being perfectly ignorant of the language and literature of the Irish have pursued from the first with unvarying pertinacity the great aim of utterly exterminating this fine Aryan language.[14]

As I have argued in detail elsewhere,[15] this belief bore little relation to the historical fact. First of all, the national schools were not decisive in destroying Irish because, in all probability, English had become the native language of most Irishmen even before the primary school system was established in 1831. Second, the commissioners of the national system were not so much hostile to the Irish language as unaware of it. That a proper education could occur in any language other than English never seems to have occurred to the education commissioners and thus they could not conceive of the Irish language as a serious rival to English; therefore they did not attack Irish, they merely ignored it. Third, shocking as this ignoring of the language was on pedagogical grounds, it met with the tacit approval of the great majority of the Irish people, the parents of the children and their natural leaders, the Catholic priests. This is not to deny that the primary schools were the mechanism whereby many thousands of Irish children learned the English with which to replace their ancestral tongue, but this displacement occurred with, not against, the will of the people.

Even had the historical basis of the revivalist argument been true it still would not have followed that the schools should, and could, be the chief instrument of the language's revival. The revivalists' social illogic was similar to the medical illogic of a doctor saying that since a man had been cut with one end of a knife the surgeon could perform the necessary corrective surgery with the other. It is bad logic indeed to assume that causality in cultural matters is a simple, reversible sequence.

But these considerations were irrelevant because a faith-state was crystallizing. "The chief function of Irish educational policy is to conserve and develop Irish nationality," wrote Eoin MacNeill. "Education, then, is either nationality in its making or in its undoing."[16] In the Dail MacNeill said that "the business and main function of the Department of Education in this country are to conserve and to build up our nationality. . . ."[17] As discussed in the early part of this chapter the building of Irish nationality automatically implied the revival of the Irish language, so in declaring that the schools were designed to build Irish nationality, it followed that the schools would be the agents of the Irish language revival. The psycho-logic which yielded this conclusion was, from an emotional point of view, a nearly seamless web. It tied into a single pattern empirical facts, historical myths, and cultural affirmations, thus providing a simple emotionally satisfying explanation of the language's decline and a clear, uncomplicated prescription for its resuscitation.

The web of belief was strengthened by a general phenomenon prevailing in Ireland during the 1920s, '30s, and '40s: the country underwent a cultural implosion. Cultural, religious, and economic factors combined to make Ireland shrink increasingly from interchange with the outside world. This was a retreat from the cultural lapses and moral sins of those outside. During this era the strict, religiously-dominated censorship code was introduced and most things foreign, books, films, and wireless transmissions, were seen as potentially dangerous — on moral grounds by the clergy and religious devotees and on cultural grounds by the Gaelic advocates. During the 1930s, economic parochialism was interwoven, as exemplified in the following statement taken from an address made by Archbishop Gilmartin of Tuam:

Now is the time for us all, young and old, to build up a real Irish

Ireland. To succeed in this noble task, Irish land must be made more productive. Irish people should buy and use Irish goods. Irish boys and their sisters ought to see that all their new clothes are going to be of Irish manufacture.

Let us cultivate our own games, our own amusements, our own language, and our own music.[18]

Some educated and influential Irishmen went so far as to declare that because they wrote in English, such writers as Yeats and O'Casey were not Irish writers at all, but merely Anglo-Irish and therefore not of stature.[19] As for those Irishmen, such as James Joyce, who went abroad, well, Daniel Corkery an important literary critic queried, "can expatriates, writing for an alien market, produce national literature?"[20] Of course his own answer was "no." Zealots denounced all English literature. The following is from the *Catholic Bulletin:*

Bilingualism is for them [Irish students] a practical necessity, both for religious ends and for national security against England. This in no way implies... that English literature should be at all studied, still less absorbed, in our schools by any general body of pupils. It will be well to have some few specialist students of university rank . . . but they should be few. . . . English literature in the mass, even as done in our schools and university colleges today is a poisonous substance nationally and religiously considered. . . . Its whole line of writers from Bacon to Macauley, and from Spenser to Wordsworth, Tennyson, Masefield, drips at every pore with intellectual and moral poisons.[21]

Fear of the culture of the outside world and the belief that the old Gaelic culture had been destroyed by an alien force were emotionally consonant. W. T. Cosgrave stated:

Our language has been waylaid, beaten and robbed, and left for dead by the wayside, and we have to ask ourselves if it is to be allowed to lie there, or if we are to heal its wounds, place it in safety and proper care and have it restored to health and vigour.[22]

Compare the tones of that statement with the following about the contemporary situation made by Thomas Derrig, minister of education in 1942:

We in this country are threatened to be engulfed by the seas of English speech washing our shores, so to speak, not alone from one side, but from the other, not alone through the newspapers, but through films and through the radio. I do not know how anybody can maintain that the unequal struggle can be maintained by the protagonists of Irish, unless we try to regard this as a matter in which we must have wholehearted effort. . . . We are trying to set up these embankments of Irish, these dykes, in order to keep out the tide of anglicisation and it is a very urgent matter indeed that we should get these embankments up.[23]

The congruence is obvious. Conceptions of the present reinforced understandings of the past and in so doing reinforced the psycho-logic syllogism which placed such great stress on the schools as the chief instrument in the future revival of the Irish language.

"Education and the language became inextricable threads in the fabric of Irish society," an historian has recently written. He noted that a presidential address to the annual congress of secondary teachers in 1947 complained that scarcely any minister of state or public figure ever mentioned education other than in connection with the revival of the Irish language.[24] The schools were used as a means to an extra-educational end, and schooling was directed not at developing the potentialities of the individual pupils for the pupils' sakes, but at developing certain cultural traits for the nation's sake. Rarely in the educational literature published in the first three decades of the Free State's existence — and equally rarely in Dail debates — does one find the Irish language presented as being good for the child; instead it is defended as being good for the nation and therefore necessary for the child.[25]

Obviously the regulations governing the use of the language in the primary schools which had been enforced by the former commissioners of national education in Ireland were unacceptable to the language revivalists. Only in 1879 had the commissioners allowed Irish to be taught and then as an "extra subject" after ordinary school hours. In 1900 school managers were permitted to teach Irish during ordinary school hours as an optional subject, provided the other instruction did not suffer. Then, in 1904, the commissioners introduced a bilingual programme for use during ordinary school hours in Irish-speaking areas. Thus, the teaching of the Irish language was permitted in all primary schools (but required in none) and the use of English for at least a substantial part of the school day was required in all.[26] The revivalists wanted something much different. The Sinn Fein constitution of 1917, a foundation stone of the revolutionary movement, declared that in an independent Ireland, education should be rendered truly national by the compulsory teaching of the Irish language and Irish history.[27] In 1920 the Gaelic league adopted a policy of demanding that in the Irish-speaking districts all subjects should be taught through Irish, that schools in the partially Irish-speaking areas should be bilingual, and that in the rest of the schools at least one hour a day was to be spent on Irish wherever a competent teacher could be found.[28]

In the pre-treaty Dail, it will be recalled, a minister for Irish was appointed even before a minister for education, and as a result early school planning was done within the linguistic rather than the educational rubric. In the financial estimates for the first half of 1921 the war-strapped Dail voted £5,000 out of its £185,900 budget to the ministry for Irish, a considerable sum when one realizes that agriculture received only £3,600 and labour £300.[29] As early as September 1920, the assistant secretary for Irish was talking confidentially of a scheme of education which was being put into operation, although precisely what that scheme was is not recorded.[30]

Soon after the provisional government took office, it issued a proclamation known as "public notice no. 4," dated 1 February 1922. "The Irish language shall be taught or used as a medium of instruction for not less than one full hour each day in all national schools where there is a teacher competent to teach it," was the central paragraph.[31] It came into force on St. Patrick's day, 1922, which is to say, almost at once. At the same time, the provisional government was drafting a constitution for the new state which, as finally approved in December 1922, provided (article four) :

The national language of the Irish Free State (Saorstat Eireann) is the Irish language, but the English language shall be equally recognised as an official language. Nothing in this article shall prevent special provision being made by the parliament of the Irish Free State . . . for districts or areas in which only one language is in general use.

(For future reference it should be noted that article 8 of the 1938 constitution drawn up for the deValera government changed things slightly by stating:

1. The Irish language as the national language is the first official language.
2. The English language is recognised as a second official language.
3. Provision may, however, be made by law for the exclusive use of either of the said languages for any one or more official purposes, either throughout the state or in any part thereof.)

But despite these official actions the pace in Irish language matters was being set by extra-governmental bodies and it was all the new government could do to keep up. At its Easter congress, 1920, the Irish National Teachers' Organization had called for a national conference to revise the primary school curriculum, with the intentions of, first, defining the proper position of the Irish language in the schools and, second, of adjusting the attention given to other subjects so as to reduce the overcrowding of the school curriculum. There is some evidence that in so acting the teachers were simultaneously affirming the value of the Irish language and attempting to limit the more fervid activities of Gaelic league enthusiasts.[32] In any case, the I.N.T.O. invited a large number of interested parties to send representatives: the Gaelic league, the central council of county councils, the national labour executive, the various schoolmasters and school managers' associations, the Christian brothers, the aireacht na Gaeilge (which represented Sinn Fein, that is to say the Dail), plus the professors of education in the national university colleges and Dublin and the Queen's University. When the conference assembled for the first time on 6 January 1921 it was found that the Catholic headmasters, the Catholic clerical managers, the Christian brothers, the Protestant schoolmasters association and the professors of education had declined membership. Nevertheless, the work was begun.[33]

Significantly, at that first meeting it was agreed that "in the case of schools where the majority of the parents of the children object to having either Irish or English taught as an obligatory subject, their wishes should be complied with." This recommendation was of such importance that it was the only one to be printed in bold face type in the final report.[34] The recommendation was surprising, and one can only speculate on the reasons for its inclusion: perhaps the teachers were entering this clause as a means of protecting themselves, through the parents, from the more fanatical language revivalists; perhaps the proviso was an attempt to calm the fears of the southern Protestant minority which believed it was about to face a cultural assault; perhaps because the educational apparatus of Ireland had not yet at that time been partitioned, the conference members were trying to impress northern Protestant sensibilities by showing flexibility on this issue. It is impossible to know.

In any case, this bold-type proviso was bracketed by two recommendations which were much more in keeping with the expected tenor of such a nationalist conference: (1) Irish was to be taught to all school children (subject to the above-mentioned proviso) at least one hour per day as an ordinary part of the curriculum; singing to be taught solely through the medium of Irish and all songs to be in the Irish language; history and geography, subjects taught in the third standard and upwards, to be given through the medium of Irish. (2) To make up for the time newly-given to the Irish language, drawing, elementary science, hygiene, nature study, and most domestic studies were eliminated as part of the obligatory curriculum.[35]

Then came the shocker. The conference recommended that in the two grades of the infant classes the work be conducted entirely in the Irish language.[36] This recommendation was tacked on to the preceding ones sometime during the fall of 1921 and was accepted by the teachers' representatives only with the most serious misgivings. It was accepted by the teachers because the representatives of both the Gaelic league and the aireacht an oideachais (formerly aireacht an Gaeilge) had been impressed greatly by the arguments of Professor Timothy Corcoran, S.J. who, although he had refused formally to join the conference, had become an influential consultant.[37]

In his gray, shadowy way Corcoran was one of the most influential men in forming the modern Irish school system. Even his admirers admitted that he was a solemn, silent, inflexible, basilisk-like man.[38] Intensely and parochially Irish, he was correspondingly anti-English. Corcoran's academic background was acceptable but not distinguished. After Clongowes Wood college, he had entered the Irish Jesuit novitiate and had taught classics and history at Clongowes from 1894 to 1901. Then he studied philosophy at Louvain from 1901–04 and theology at Milltown Park from 1906–09. He was appointed the first professor of education in the University College, Dublin branch of the new National University of Ireland, a post he held until the summer of 1942, shortly before his death.[39]

Unfortunately, in the two fields in which Corcoran propounded his strongest opinions, educational history and psychology, he was without obvious competence. In his historical writings he was one of the propagandists of the idea that the Irish language had been crippled intentionally and viciously by the national education system. Unfortunately, his love of indigenous Irish traditions, when combined with his detestation of the English government, not only blinded his critical judgement, but led him on occasion to distort the historical evidence to fit his own point of view.[40] With considerable charity, his obituary in *Irish Historical Studies* noted that "in his presentation of historical material Dr. Corcoran was frankly the apologist rather than the historian."[41]

His educational psychology was even more dogmatic and less scholarly. A typical example is an article "How the Irish language can be revived," published in June 1923, in which he propounded an entire psychology of linguistic acquisition without empirical data and without evidencing familiarity with the major breakthroughs in educational psychology which had occurred in the preceding decade.[42] But despite his lack of background, in firm, confident tones Corcoran told the Irish revivalists what they wanted to hear. He told the national programme conference of his visit to the United States where he had seen very young immigrant children from the eastern European countries taught by teachers who used no language other than English and who were, in most cases, entirely ignorant of the children's home language. This method, Corcoran said, was a great success, and he firmly stated that this was the best way for children to learn a new language. The Gaelic league and aireact an oideachais representatives leaped quickly at the opening this testimony provided. That Ireland and America were not educationally analogous was irrelevant; that the American scheme was designed to drive a cultural wedge between the immigrant child and his parents was ignored (in adopting a similar policy the Irish schools would be attempting much the same thing); that most educationists declared such practice educationally unsound and psychologically damaging to the children made no difference. The language enthusiasts had been given an excuse totally to exclude English from the infant schools and they did so.[43]

The representatives of the primary school teachers, frightened by the zealotry of the revivalists, obtained promises from the successive ministers of education of the revolutionary Dail and of the provisional government that haste would be made slowly and that teachers would not be victimised if they were not able at once to carry out the extensive demands of the new programme. The teachers' representatives understood the new programme to be an ideal which could be in operation, at the soonest, in five years' time.[44]

But *festina lente* was not, in fact, to be the government's policy. The provisional government accepted in its entirety the report which had been signed on 28 January 1922, and in April 1922, the new programme came into effect.[45] According to a subsequent national programme conference, "as time went on, it became more and more evident that in spite of the assurances given by the minister the teachers' apprehensions had not been unintelligent. . . . It was in connexion with Irish that the chief causes of trouble were found."[46] In particular, it appeared to the teachers that the principle originally agreed to by the education ministry, of using Irish as a medium of instruction only when the pupils were able to benefit from it and the teachers teach through it, was an "amiable fiction," which melted away under the influence of the school inspectors, many of whom were newly-competent in Irish, and who pressed for revival with the enthusiasm of the recently converted.[47]

For these reasons — and also because they were concerned that the government had not yet introduced the promised compulsory attendance bill — the Irish National Teachers' Organization, in March 1924, decided to reconvene the national programme conference, inviting all those who had been invited to the original conference. This frightened the higher officials and the minister for education, and they moved to convene the conference themselves, with I.N.T.O. cooperation. In particular, the department took over control of the invitation list, allowing the I.N.T.O. to choose its own representatives, but selecting for themselves the individuals who would be allowed to "represent" the other bodies. When asked why this was necessary, Eoin MacNeill explained that the Irish language policy was now governmental policy and if the findings of the conference or of even a significant minority of the conference were opposed to that policy, the government would find it very awkward.[48] The department's appointing its own nominees for most of the conference vacancies naturally cushioned it from harsh criticism. The report rebuked the department only in the most gentle terms for its excessive enthusiasm for the language revival, making the point that the language policy was a noble ideal, that the department's efforts had already met with gratifying success, but that certain conditions would make the complete and immediate attainment of its lofty goals impossible.[49]

The new recommendations regarding Irish in the infants schools slightly softened the original programme. Whenever the teacher was competent to teach through Irish the infants school classes were to be taught entirely in Irish, irrespective of what language the children spoke at home. When the teacher was marginally competent in Irish, but not able to use it as a medium for teaching, the infants were to be instructed in the language for at least an hour a day. The conference expected that the use of Irish would gradually spread until all infants in all national schools were taught solely through Irish during their regular school hours. As a special concession to those parents who might wish their children to learn English, that language was to be permitted, but only in classes conducted before or after the regular school hours.[50] As in the case of the first national programme conference, the second conference did not publish the evidence upon which it based these infant language conclusions (and later de Valera's government also refused to publish it).[51] But once again the crucial witness was the Reverend Professor Corcoran. He testified that even without parental support the schools could revive the Irish language, so long as the children were immersed in the language at the infant stage and schooled thereafter in a curriculum in which the Irish language was the dominant feature.[52]

As for the recommendations for the higher standards, they differed somewhat from those of the first programme, but the basic principle remained the same, namely that where a teacher was competent to teach through Irish and the children to learn, there Irish should be the medium of instruction. Teachers without a complete competency were, however, to teach those subjects which they could through Irish. The proximate goal was the gradual extension of Irish until it became the dominant teaching medium in all schools. In pursuit of this end the new programme specified that there would be two primary school courses, one being the "high Irish-low English" option, the other the "low Irish-high English" alternative. Those schools which offered the higher course in English and the lower one in Irish were expected to progress gradually to the point where they could offer the higher Irish course, and, correspondingly, reduce English to the lower course. This remarkable bit of curricular architecture was stated in pseudomathematical terms: "the sum of Irish plus English equals a constant quantity."[53]

In 1926, Professor John Marcus O'Sullivan, who had replaced Eoin MacNeill as minister for education early in 1926, stated that he had accepted the programme as recommended by the conference[54] and in July a departmental circular informed the school managers and teachers that the new programme was now officially adopted.[55] As was the case with the first primary programme, its success depended in large part on how sensible the departmental officials and inspectors were in adapting the programme to local situations. In large part it seems that a reasonable *festina lente* approach was followed, as had been recommended by the conference. The teachers were especially pleased with modifications in the inspectoral system introduced in 1928, which lessened the tensions between inspectors and teachers.[56] In 1928, 1,240 infant schools were taught completely in Irish, 3,570 in both Irish and English, and 373 solely in English.[57] Similarly, in the ordinary grades, the department did not push unreasonably hard: in 1931 the percentage of pupils who received instruction solely through the medium of Irish was for arithmetic $5\frac{1}{2}\%$; history $4\frac{1}{2}\%$; geography $5\frac{1}{4}\%$ and in all other subjects (excluding English), about 2%.[58]

Then, once again the government quickened the pace. A directive was issued in late 1931 instructing school inspectors, in rating teachers, to give close attention to their good will and capacity in relation to the Irish language. Only those teachers who were pressing forward with the introduction of Irish as a teaching medium could hope for efficient ratings. Specific instructions were given concerning which subjects, in the official view, could be most easily taught through Irish.[59]

Soon after the issuance of this circular the government changed, de Valera came to power, and Thomas Derrig became minister for education. Why de Valera did not appoint Frank Fahy, who had been shadow minister for education, is a mystery. Derrig, who had been a vocational teacher for a short time and the minister for lands in the shadow cabinet, was a prickly, defensive man, and during his long tenure relations between the department and the teachers often were strained.[60] He was an Irish language enthusiast and in June 1934 he summoned representatives of the I.N.T.O. to tell them that he was not satisfied with the progress the teachers were making with the Irish revival programme. After a long set of negotiations a bargain was struck between the department and the teachers, embodied in yet another language policy directive issued in late September 1934. Simply stated, the teachers agreed to place more emphasis upon the Irish language if the department would reduce correspondingly the standards of attainment previously demanded for other subjects. In the ordinary standards Irish language teaching was strengthened by reducing the English language course in all schools to the level of the "lower course" defined in the 1926 programme. (Also it now became only an optional subject in standard I.) Rural science (or nature study) disappeared as a required subject, a notable change in an agricultural country. The level of mathematics instruction was reduced: algebra and geometry became optional subjects in one-teacher and two-teacher schools, in three-teacher co-educational schools, and in all classes taught by women. In the infants classes, English, which previously had been permitted as a recognized subject before and after statutory school hours (as distinct from a frowned-on expedient for unqualified teachers), now was banished altogether.[61]

Implicit pressure, quite gentle at first, was added to various language policy directives by the instigation in the school year 1928–29 of a primary schools leaving certificate. The teachers were unenthusiastic about the certificate from its inception, and in 1935 went on record favouring its abolition, but this made no difference to the education department.[62] At first the test was not obligatory and it tested the pupil in a range of subjects at standard VI level: Irish, English, mathematics, history, geography, and (girls only), needlework.[63] The examination being voluntary, relatively few school managers presented their pupils. In 1937–38, for example, less than 19% of the pupils in the sixth standard or higher were presented for the test.[64] The department, therefore, decided to tighten the rules and in 1943 changed them in two ways. First, the primary school certificate examination became compulsory for all standard vi pupils. Second, the subject range of the examination was reduced, being limited to Irish, English, and arithmetic. To win the primary certificate a pupil had to pass each of these tests at a level of 40%, except for children from the predominantly Irish-speaking districts who only had to score 30% on the English section.[65]

The combination of the 1934 programme and the introduction of the compulsory primary certificate forced the schools to emphasize the Irish language above all subjects. A contemporary estimate, made in 1947, indicated that the average Irish primary school (excluding infant classes) spent half its total teaching time on the language.[66] Additionally, most schools taught some other subject (arithmetic, history, etc.) through the medium of Irish. In the year 1951–52, for example, all of the schools in the predominantly Irish-speaking districts (179 of a total of 4,876 national schools) employed Irish as the medium of instruction. Only twenty-five schools in the country used English as the sole medium of instruction, the remainder teaching through both languages, according to the ability of the teachers and pupils.[67]

Minor modifications in the school programme were recommended by a report of the newly appointed council of education in 1954, the most important of which was that outside the Irish-speaking districts, English should be taught in the infant classes for half an hour (except in those instances where the school manager, as representative of the parents, decided to have an all-Irish school).[68] In the main, however, the situation remained unchanged: the government continuing to insist that the primary schools should be the chief instrument for the revival of the Irish language and the critics charging that the Irish government in the twentieth century was making the same mistake that the United Kingdom administration made in the nineteenth, namely ignoring the linguistic background of Ireland's children.

A host of ancillary devices was designed to enforce the Irish language programme of the primary schools. For instance, de Valera's government introduced in the school year 1933–34 a grant of £2 per year to the parents of each child in the predominantly Irish-speaking and partially

Irish-speaking districts if the department of education was satisfied that Irish was the child's home language and that the child was able to speak Irish fluently. The child had to be between six and fourteen years of age and attending a national school.[69] This grant was raised to £5 per year for each child in the academic year 1945–46.[70] This was a useful source of income for Gaeltacht parents, the number of grant-earning children being, in 1938–39, 11,154[71] and in 1948–49, 9,654.[72]

Equally noteworthy was a programme of teacher preparation which not unfairly may be denominated the "missionary approach." For the government's Irish language policy to succeed a dedicated cadre of teachers, fluent in spoken Irish, was necessary. "Where are the vernacular teachers to be had? From the areas of Ireland that are as yet substantially Irish-speaking," was the answer of the Reverend Father Corcoran.[73] Young people from the Irish-speaking communities were to be recruited to carry the Word to the remainder of the country, to their fellow countrymen who had fallen from linguistic grace. The department embraced this idea (whether Father Corcoran was here the decisive advocate or merely one of a number of persons who had the same idea, is unclear) and in 1926 established the first of six "preparatory colleges" for Irish-speaking students. These were simply secondary boarding schools for Irish-speaking youths who intended to become primary school teachers. The Department of Education somewhat exceeded the boundaries of credibility when it publicized these new institutions as "fosterage schools," that is, a revival of the ancient Celtic tradition of sending children to be brought up in the house of a fellow clansman.[74] But at least this obscured the new colleges' rather embarrassing similarity in concept to English public schools.

From the beginning the colleges had their difficulties. Those higher civil servants in the Department of Education specially charged with the language revival opposed the founding of the colleges on the grounds that competent professors would be hard to procure and that there would not be an opportunity for the students and the natives to converse meaningfully, as the promoters of the scheme claimed.[75] Critics pointed out that the preparatory colleges could not be considered to be the equivalent of academic secondary schools, for no language except Irish and English was taught.[76] The Irish national school teachers organization objected to the strong discrimination against English speakers in admission to the schools. The teachers believed that such discrimination was to penalize a pupil for the geographic accident of his having been born and raised in the English speaking region.[77] Here the teachers had a point, for the discrimination was intense: in the mid-thirties the department raised to eighty percent the proportion of preparatory college vacancies reserved for fluent Irish speakers (previously it had been fifty percent); and for only one quarter of these reserved places was there open competition among Irish-speakers. Three-quarters of the reserved slots were awarded to candidates from the predominantly and partly Irish-speaking areas, even if candidates from other parts of the country had a superior knowledge of the Irish language.[78]

This degree of discrimination probably was necessary if the missionary principle was to operate. The trouble is that not even within the preparatory colleges themselves (let alone within the entire primary school network) did the missionary scheme prove effective: of the 142 ex-preparatory college pupils who graduated from the teacher training colleges in 1934, seventy-four failed to pass the bilingual certificate examination which would have certified them competent to teach through the medium of Irish.[79] The preparatory schools soldiered along and finally in 1959–60 the government decided to discontinue the five Catholic preparatory colleges, maintaining in the future only the one, co–educational Protestant college.[80]

Less gimmicky, and therefore more useful in facilitating the revival policy, were the teacher training colleges, two-year institutions which admitted candidates upon completion of their secondary school education. By 1927 four of the five training colleges then in operation taught the majority of their subjects through the medium of Irish.[81] From 1931 onwards, before a training college graduate received his final diploma, he had to first pass the bilingual certificate examination attesting to his competence to teach through Irish.[82]

A more pressing problem than training new teachers was giving those teachers already in service the necessary language skills. The first national programme conference had recommended that an intensive summer course in Irish be initiated[83] and from 1922 through 1925 such courses were obligatory for all non-Irish-speaking teachers who were under forty-five years of age in 1922. The teachers were paid a salary by the government and were eligible for a grant towards lodging and expenses. The four summer sessions cost the new government a total of more than £150,000.[84]

Inevitably, the inspectorate placed a good deal of pressure to become competent in Irish upon those teachers who had entered the profession under the United Kingdom regime. As mentioned earlier, before the reforms of 1928 the teachers' union complained bitterly about pressure placed upon their members. The inspectorial reforms of 1928 provided only a brief respite, for in April 1930, the department declared that effective 30 June 1932 all teachers in English-speaking districts who had been under thirty years of age as of July 1922 would have to obtain a certificate of competence to teach Irish (the "ordinary certificate") or face the loss of their salary increments; and as of 30 June 1935 those same teachers had to have the bilingual certificate, certifying their competency to teach through the medium, if they were not to lose their salary increments.[85]

In terms of the short-run goal of making the teaching force proficient in Irish, the various pressures and programmes were successful (whether the entire programme of reviving the language through the schools was a success is a question to be discussed later). Whereas it was found that in the spring of 1922 well under half the Irish national school teachers had a qualification in the Irish language (1,107 bilingual certificates, 2,845 ordinary certificates and 922 "temporary" certificates among about 12,000 lay teachers)[86] by mid–1937 the great majority of teachers were qualified (2,335 without any qualification, 3,989 ordinary certificates, 7,029 bilingual certificates, and 967 higher certificates, among a total of 14,320 national school teachers, including the religious).[87]

What about the academic secondary schools? There the approach was gentler, this being a corollary of the department's belief that the younger years were the most important ones for acquiring linguistic skills and that a firm base would be built before the pupil entered secondary school. Not that Irish was ignored, however. In early February 1922, soon after the provisional government was formed, the minister, Fionan Lynch, required that secondary school pupils would have the right to answer the intermediate examination questions in Irish if they wished,[88] but only about thirty of the more than 10,000 candidates who took the examinations answered either wholly or partly in Irish.[89] In 1924, when the old payment-by-results system was swept away and replaced by two examinations, the intermediate certificate (taken at about age sixteen) and the leaving certificate (usually taken two years later), the students in each course were required to take as an examination subject either English or Irish.[90] A year later the department decided that for a candidate to receive his intermediate certificate he had to pass in Irish.[91] Irish was made compulsory for obtaining the leaving certificate in 1934.[92]

As time went on it became clear that the certificate examination rules encouraged Irish in two ways: by penalizing those English-speaking children who did not learn sufficient Irish during their school course and by giving a positive advantage to fluent Irish speakers. The former occurred because, Irish being compulsory, a number of candidates failed the certificate solely because of their insufficiency in Irish. In 1959, for example, of the 1,068 unsuccessful candidates for the leaving certificate, 373 would have passed but for their failure in Irish.[93] This naturally engendered a good deal of resentment among the English-speaking community and in the view of some revivalists therefore was counterproductive. The commission on the restoration of the Irish language, reporting in 1963, attempted to mollify the critics by recommending that pupils who passed the entire leaving certificate examination in all subjects save Irish, should be given a second chance in the subject, a recommendation to which the government assented.[94] Further, although Irish and English were both official languages, the scoring system for the certificates discriminated for Irish and against English. For example the scoring system used in the late 'forties gave fifty percent more points on the intermediate examination to the Irish language than to the English and fifty percent more to literature in the Irish tongue than in the English. Similar differentials held at the leaving certificate level. Moreover, a further scoring bonus of five percent in the respective subjects was offered to students who answered the mathematics or modern languages papers in Irish. A student who answered the history and geography papers or the various science papers in Irish received a ten percent bonus on each examination.[95] With considerable exaggeration — but with a kernel of truth — a Dail deputy grumbled: "there are a whole lot of people who pass only because they have the Irish language, and but for that qualification, they could not pass anything."[96]

When the system of payment-by-examination-results was abolished in 1924 it was replaced by a scheme under which the department paid each school a certain amount for each pupil following an approved course of secondary schooling. At first a school did not have to offer Irish to be recognized as giving an approved course, but even so, in 1926–27, 281 out of the 287 secondary schools in the Free State taught the subject.[97] Nevertheless, for the academic year 1927–28 the department decided that in every grant-earning school "a reasonable proportion of the pupils must receive instruction in Irish," the "reasonable proportion" being undefined.[98] A few schools reacted to this decree by teaching Irish but giving it the same status as French or any other modern language. During his language offensive, Thomas Derrig, de Valera's minister for education, moved quickly to abolish this practice: his department decreed, in mid–

1932, that all pupils in secondary schools had to take Irish if they were to be recognized for grant purposes.[99]

To encourage secondary schools to teach through the medium of Irish a bonus scheme was articulated. Under it three classes of schools earned extra grants: class A schools which taught all subjects (except English and modern languages) through Irish; class B(1) schools which taught through the medium of Irish at least as much as through that of English; and class B(2) schools which taught at least one subject, other than Irish, through it. The precise amount of bonuses varied over the years, but those for the late 1950s are representative, being twenty-five percent of the capitation grant for class A, either ten percent or sixteen and two-thirds percent for class B(1), depending on how much Irish was used, and from two and one-half percent to ten percent for class B(2).[100] The three classes comprised, respectively in 1924–25, eleven, fifteen and twenty-four schools.[101] The corresponding figures for 1934–35 were sixty-seven, thirty-six and seventy-seven schools,[102] and for 1954–55, eighty-seven, sixty-seven and sixty-seven schools.[103]

Now it is time to draw up a balance sheet, to try to assess the benefits and liabilities of using the schools as a cultural lever to revive the Irish language. First, what about the language itself? On the benefit side of the ledger, it is clear that, at least as measured in census reports, the campaign stopped the decline of the Irish language. The percentage of Irish speakers expressed as a percentage of the entire population in the twenty-six counties was:

1911	17.6%
1926	18.3%

Expressed as a function of the number of persons three years of age and over, the percentages were:[104]

1926	19.3%
1936	23.7%
1946	21.2%
1961	27.2%

Admittedly, the areas classified as predominantly- and partially-Irish-speaking were shrinking,[105] with the result that the Irish which was learned was an academic tongue rather than as a living language,[106] but, undeniably, the language decline had been stopped.

Turning to the economic page of the balance sheet, we almost are stymied because the Irish government's accounting system was not designed to produce such information. But let us, as an approximation, work with some information provided by Ernest Blythe, minister for finance, in April 1929,[107] and try to determine what the *incremental direct cost* to the Irish taxpayer was as a result of the Department of Education's Irish language policy. In our estimate we will not include as a direct expense any item that comes from replacing one person or activity without another (for example, the replacement of an English language teacher with an Irish language speaker who drew the same salary) but only additional costs. Blythe stated that below the university level and excluding primary education, the exchequer spent an extra £40,408 in direct expenses on education in Irish. To this must be added £27,000 paid by the county and borough councils for the use of Irish in the technical schools. Additionally, one should add the full costs of the preparatory college, £70,520 a year (but not the cost of other systems of teacher education which had been operating in the English language era and were not incremental items). Further, let us add the £24,238 for courses in Irish for primary school teachers.[108] Note here that Blythe categorically stated that there were in the primary school section of the education department no persons exclusively concerned with Irish; and let us assume that those inspectors and officials who did their work in Irish represented no more of an economic cost than those who had previously done the same work in English. Thus, the total of direct incremental expenses for the school's effort in the language revival was £162,166 for the fiscal year 1928–29, this at a time when the Free State had a gross national product of £159,200,000.[109]

Undoubtedly there were hidden economic costs, but it is not useful to speculate about these in any detail. It has been clearly established (as will be discussed in a moment) that the heavy emphasis upon Irish at the primary school level meant that Irish children were less well educated in other subjects than they would have been had they not spent so much time on Irish, and there is every reason to believe that this conclusion holds for advanced levels of schooling as well. The reduced proficiency in the other academic subjects and in general critical skills undoubtedly cost something in terms of economic productivity, but how much is entirely problematical.

I would argue that the most important costs of the school-based revival programme were not those paid directly by the government or indirectly by the owners of production, but by the children. Similarly, the greatest benefits, namely the possession of a new set of linguistic skills, accrued to the children. Yet, although the most important page on the balance sheet concerns how the revival programme affected the children's education, the Irish government has provided little information on which to make a judgement. As mentioned earlier, the tradition of government secrecy had begun early, for the Free State government did not publish the evidence upon which the two national programme conferences made their recommendations and later resisted pressures to have that information made public. This was doubtless a necessary policy because the evidence upon which the high-pressure language policy was based had been presented by the Reverend Professor Corcoran in whose work dogmatism was matched only by lack of documentation; also, Corcoran's opponents apparently had made a very strong case for going slowly, which simply had been ignored.[110] When, in 1954, the first major inquiry into the primary education system conducted since 1926 was published, it operated in the almost total absence of empirical evidence. In response to the question, "Is the teaching of two languages detrimental?" it responded, "No scientific research to prove or disapprove this assertion has been carried out in this country," then made passing reference to a Welsh policy document, and left the subject.[111] Similarly, when an investigation of secondary education published in 1960 made its recommendations for the continuance with slight modification of the existing language programme these recommendations were backed by no data.[112] The commission on the restoration of Irish, whose report was published in 1963, based its report on no actual research conducted in Ireland and stated dogmatically — and incorrectly — that most work in other countries indicated that the acquisition of a second language had no detrimental effects upon the development of the first language.[113] Finally, in 1965, after more than four decades of accepting ex cathedra statements about the educational effects of the language revival, the Republic's minister for education stated that before anything else was done to further the Irish language in the schools, an investigation of the effects of teaching through a language other than the home language of the child should be made;[114] but there the matter rests and no such study has yet been published.

Fortunately, we do not have to rely upon the Department of Education for information. In 1930 the I.N.T.O. passed a resolution "that this congress considers that the time is now ripe for an educational assessment of the use of Irish as a teaching medium in schools in English-speaking districts." The idea was pressed upon the Department of Education, but to no avail. Therefore, in 1936, the I.N.T.O. decided to conduct its own investigation, the study eventually being published in 1941. The I.N.T.O. did not have the resources to conduct such an experimental study, but in their membership they had the majority of people who actually had taught through Irish. Thus, ingeniously, a questionnaire was designed which was to be answered only by those teachers who had used the language for their teaching. This was on the assumption that the next best thing to a massive empirical study would be a study of the judgements of those who had seen the results of the national programme in the classroom.

Within the obvious limits imposed by this method, the study was very revealing. For example, on the vexed matter of teaching infant school children solely through the medium of Irish, the I.N.T.O. garnered opinions from 422 infant school teachers who actually had done so, the average total teaching experience of this group being well over fifteen years. Among those experienced teachers, 345 of 390 who answered the question stated that their pupils did not derive as much benefit from having been instructed in Irish as they would had the medium been English. The I.N.T.O.'s interpretive report based on a series of related questions made it clear that most teachers believed the use of Irish to be intellectually inhibitive. The young child, already confused and frightened by entering the new, alien environment of the school, had his fear heightened by suddenly being at a loss linguistically. Instead of the infant school lesson growing out of the child's home experience, all the things he had learned to deal with at home in English were now rejected, and he was left to deal with this new world bereft of his hard-earned language skills. Inevitably, the infant school environment became repressive and unless the child was extremely quick in picking up the new language, school became a puzzle and a monotonous confusion. Some children, the teachers believed, were both mentally and physically damaged by the strain of the draconian linguistic code.[115]

In the ordinary grades most schools, as noted earlier, used both English and Irish as a medium of instruction, the precise mix depending on the subject involved. The I.N.T.O. tallied only the replies of those teachers who had experience in teaching each individual subject through Irish. The results can be conveniently summarized if we rephrase the individual questions to read: "Do children taught through Irish learn as much as if they were taught through English?"[116]

SUBJECT	YES	NO
Junior arithmetic	87	554
Senior arithmetic	58	271
Geometry	21	71
Algebra	27	75
History	55	382
Geography	51	403
Singing	308	86
Needlework	"80%"	"20%" of 206 replies

Of course, it was to be expected that the greatest retardation effect would occur in the acquisition of English language skills. This had been implicitly recognized in the second national programme conference's formula: English + Irish = Constant. Eamon de Valera, no enemy of the revival, had admitted as much in the Dail: "There is no doubt that the child who, today, is doing Irish as well as English, has to a certain extent double the work, so far as reading and writing are concerned, and if you want to get that language in the same time you must necessarily fall short of what was done when there was only one language involved. . . . We shall have to be satisfied with a less high standard in English. There is no other way for it."[117]

The precise degree to which the Irish primary school child was retarded in English language skills was not determined until 1966 when an extremely sophisticated empirical study was published: *Bilingualism and Primary Education: a Study of Irish Experience* (Edinburgh University Press) by the Reverend Dr. John MacNamara. MacNamara's conclusion, based on the testing of a large sample of Irish primary school children, was that at age twelve-plus Irish school children were about seventeen months behind British school children of the same age and background, a very significant loss.[118] Because he controlled for other variables, MacNamara was able to conclude, unambiguously, that the reasons for the Irish retardation in English language skills relative to the British children was the amount of time spent in teaching the Irish language: forty-two percent of the average school week was spent on Irish lessons, plus whatever other time was spent teaching through Irish.[119]

At the same time MacNamara's work confirmed the judgement made by the national teachers in the 1930s, that teaching through the medium of Irish inhibited children from the English-speaking community in learning the various school subjects. In arithmetic, the only skill in which an objective measurement was possible, MacNamara's work showed that at age twelve-plus Irish students were about eleven months behind their British counterparts.[120]

If the retardation in English language and arithmetical skills represent the debit side of the educational ledger, the positive side has its entries. First, the acquisition of a second language by all school children is an intellectual exercise which most educators would recognize as valuable. Second, the acquaintance with the ethnic language gives each child an introduction to his national cultural heritage which most Irishmen would recognize as valuable. But how valuable? More than the English and arithmetical skills lost? Would most Irishmen agree with the statement of a noted Jesuit educationalist, Father Martin Brennan: "If research were to show an undoubted drop in standards of English it would be regrettable; but it would have to be tolerated for the greater good: the production of integrated *Irish* personalities"?[121]

Unhappily we now have arrived at a cul de sac, for although we know the items on each side of the educational balance sheet we have been constructing, we cannot state the actual *value* of each item — and the Irish government has continuously shied from ascertaining what the Irish people actually think about the policy of reviving the language through the schools. The Irish language programme was given the people as a cultural prescription, a medicine that would cure the cultural ills of years of alien rule. None of the government's policy studies on the language, from the two national programme conferences and the Gaeltacht commission of the 1920s to the reports of the council of education in the 'fifties and early 'sixties, to the report and white paper on the restoration of the language published in 1963 and 1965, respectively, tried to determine if the Irish people really wanted the language revived at the educational price they were being asked to pay.[122] John Marcus O'Sullivan, second minister for education under the Free State office reflected in later years: "I did start this particular system in the hope that we might make Irish, and that we should make Irish, a living language. But I never deluded myself that I had the enthusiastic support of the great bulk of the people of this country. . . ."[123]

The I.N.T.O. report on the Irish language noted that:

There is . . . a constant theme running through all the replies which points to the fact that parents generally are opposed to a method for the Irish revival which would tend to lower the educational standard of their children according to their values. Infant teachers have stated that it is a common practice for parents to ask that infant children be provided with English primers so that they may be given in the home the instruction in English reading denied to them in the school. Many examples were cited of parents who endeavoured to teach their children at home through English, subjects that the same children were being taught in school through Irish, while it was repeatedly urged that complaints from the parents on the low standard of their children's general education were wide-spread. This attitude of the parents to the problem under review does not seem to have been adverted to by those directing the Irish revival.[124]

No one should have been surprised that the I.N.T.O. data were ignored, for in the year before the I.N.T.O. undertook its study, Thomas Derrig, minister for education, had replied to a question about widespread parental dissatisfaction with the compulsory school programme by declaring: that "I cannot see that parents as a body can decide this matter."[125]

When we ask why the successive Irish governments have been so prescriptive about the schools' language programme and so reluctant to consult the opinions of the populace, we have come full-circle, and are back where we began this chapter: There was a set of psycho-logic imperatives in the Irish nationalist mind which required the school-based language effort. To ask for the public's opinion would have been to admit that possibility of the Irish nation's being generally unconcerned about the revival of the ethnic tongue. And once that possibility was admitted, the complex webbing of the Irish nationalist belief-system would have begun to unravel.

Let us now return to the use of education as a cultural mirror. The most obvious point about the attempt of successive governments to revive Irish through the schools is that in so doing they defined the schools as instruments used towards a politico-nationalistic end. In defining the goals of the schools in extra-educational terms, the successive governments paid very little attention to the actual children. As long as the collective political purpose was being served by the school curriculum, the development of individual children bore scant notice. This apparent lack of concern for the development of individual children in the school *as children* — rather than as digits in the Irish revival statistics — is an aspect of Ireland's countenance not usually shown to the outside world.

An extension of this indifference to the children as individuals was the continued refusal of successive governments and ministers for education to consult the wishes of the children's parents as to the nature of the linguistic programme the children were following. Simultaneously, this refusal to consider parental wishes is reflective of the authoritarian stance assumed by the Irish state in many matters, a characteristic already discussed in considerable detail in the preceding chapter. Notice for a moment the words of Thomas Derrig about his own superior educational wisdom, certainly greater than that of mere parents, and the mixture of indifference and authoritarianism becomes obvious.[126]

But much of the politicians' and civil servants' rigidity about the school-based revival efforts stemmed not from indifference or from arrogance, but from fear. The language revival movement in some ways was a magical movement, one whereby the national culture and the nation-state were to be made secure through the collective invocation of the correct words. But to all but the most devout believers it is terrifying if one starts asking certain questions about a collective litany, questions such as "does everyone really believe in it?" and, "do these words really do what they are supposed to do?" Thus, decade after decade the various governments postponed evaluating the actual effects of the language programme and refused to find out whether or not the Irish people really favoured using the schools as the chief instrument in the language revival programme.

LEGACIES FROM THE
MANCHESTER SCHOOL

Compulsion, but Gently

Forcing children to attend school is an interference by the state in the lives of its citizens which evokes scant notice, much less opposition, in the present day. But in Ireland during the first half of the twentieth century compulsory school attendance laws were enacted and enforced only in the most tentative manner, with an ambivalence similar to that of a Victorian free trader forced by his social conscience to accept factory legislation. When in 1892 the United Kingdom parliament framed a compulsory school attendance bill for Ireland, the Catholic bishops denounced it as an infringement of parental rights. The bishops were willing to accept indirect compulsion, such as child labour laws, but not direct.[1] Although the bill passed, it was, as mentioned earlier, a woefully inadequate statute, applying only to the urban areas and even then the most important urban councils, such as Dublin and Cork, refused to cooperate on the grounds that the Christian brothers schools were not receiving government grants.

Nevertheless, influential leaders in the nationalist camp strongly felt the need for effective compulsory attendance laws and eventually the compulsory view prevailed. Most important in turning the tide was the report of the first national programme conference which made it clear that an absolute prerequisite for the nationalising of the primary school curriculum was the tightening of the compulsory attendance laws: "No matter how suitable the programme or how efficient or enthusiastic the teacher, the instruction cannot be effective unless the pupils attend regularly."[2] In a striking comparison, the conference noted that in the last year for which statistics were available (1918) only 68.9 percent of the average number of Irish children on the rolls were in daily attendance, but that "in the Orkney Islands the percentage of attendance is the lowest recorded for Scotland, yet in this remote and storm-swept district eighty-three percent of the children attend school every day."[3] The average school leaving age in Ireland was eleven years, much too low the educators said.

With the exception of a taxpayers' lobby (the Irish ratepayers' association demanded that the school leaving age be reduced from fourteen to twelve)[4] there was little explicit opposition to the national programme conference's recommendations. But still the government had to tread softly because of the pervasive, but ill-defined, suspicion of all state activities by many Irishmen and the more sharply focused opposition of the small farmers to any legislation which would lessen their control over those of their children who were old enough to be of help about the farm. Also, some concerned citizens, while favouring compulsory attendance laws, believed that, first, the ramshackle, unsanitary condition characterizing so many of the primary schools had to be improved. (This view was best stated by W. B. Yeats during the debates on the bill: "We should not force the children into schools unless we have such assurance from the government as will make us satisfied that these schools are fit to receive the children."[5] Oliver St. John Gogarty added that much of Ireland's health problem stemmed from the condition of the schools.)[6]

When the time came to move, the Department of Education under the direction of Professor Eoin MacNeill proved remarkably inept. In 1923 the department drafted a bill to improve the enforcement of attendance at elementary schools whereby the garda soichana (the civic police) were to be the enforcing agency. This idea had to be dropped, however, when it was realized that the police were not well enough trained or organized to take on this additional duty. Then the department tried to create an enforcement apparatus within the larger machinery of the local government system, but this too had to be abandoned when, in September 1924, the Department of Finance objected that the Education Department's plan was too cumbersome, too expensive, and that, in any case, local government was still in flux. Finally, the Education Department came to an agreement with the Department of Justice in early 1925, whereby, in most areas, the police would be the agency of enforcement.[7]

The actual statute, passed during the winter and spring of 1925–26, was gentle in tone and provision. School attendance committees were to be established in each of eight large urban areas and in the rest of the Free State a specified officer from the local garda soichana station was to enforce the law. Thus, in contrast to the 1892 act, the apparatus of compulsion covered the whole country, but in a manner which did not necessitate the establishment of myriad, cumbersome local attendance committees. Children were to attend school from the quarter day after their sixth birthday to the quarter day after their fourteenth. In most cases this attendance would be in a national school, but the minister for education could certify other, private, schools as suitable and could recognize home education as acceptable in certain cases. In recognition of Ireland's agricultural structure — the countryside was dominated by small farmers dependent upon family labour — the act provided that until 1936 (later extended) a child twelve years or older could be taken from school for light agricultural work on his parent's land for ten days a year during the spring sowing season and for another ten days annually at harvest.[8]

Notice here the unstated social and educational assumptions of the 1926 Act. First, it was assumed that a primary school education was sufficient for the bulk of the population. In his eight years in a national school the typical Irish child would reach Standard vi, which guaranteed functional literacy and certain computational skills. Second, the act was predicated upon changing the status quo as little as possible. By not necessitating the creation of new educational structures for early adolescents the act implicitly strengthened the existing primary school network and thereby minimized expenses, a major consideration for the struggling new government. Third, it was assumed that there was no benefit in separating young children and early adolescents. This contrasts sharply with the "Hadow doctrine" in England which postulated the need for a break at eleven-plus, and with the American movement for "junior high schools" for young adolescents. At the same time the act reinforced the essential tribalism of the primary schools, institutions arranged on a parish-by-parish basis, attended in the rural areas by children whose families had intermarried for generations.

Undeniably, the act was effective. Given below are the numbers of children in average daily attendance expressed as a percentage of the average number on the rolls:[9]

1920	(all Ireland)	69.6%
1921	(twenty-six counties)	73.3
1924		73.5
1925–26	(increase due to adhesion of Christian brothers schools to national system)	77.0
1926–27	(Attendance Act invoked)	79.7
1930–31		82.9
1940–41		82.4
1950–51		83.3

Attendance did not, however, reach the eighty-five percent level which was approximately the minimum acceptable even in remote areas elsewhere in the British Isles.

In apparent imitation of the 1918 English Education Act, the Irish Vocational Education Act of 1930 gave the minister of education the right to require that children in a given area undertake part-time continuation education from ages fourteen to sixteen,[10] but neither Messrs. O'Sullivan nor Derrig, successive ministers for education, exercised this prerogative.

Then, in response to pressure for the raising of the leaving age,[11] an inter-departmental committee was appointed in 1934 to examine the situation and recommend action. The report of this committee, written in 1936, was almost crystalline, so perfectly reflective was it of Irish attitudes on compulsory schooling. In the first place, the government's handling of the document was typical of the insularity of the Department of Education in many matters relating to children, for the department refused to publish the entire report, unanimous though it had been. The public had to be satisfied with extracts, compiled by the department.[12] Second, at the very beginning of their report the committee sounded a defensive, nationalistic note in regard to Irish child-rearing practices: it maintained that the existing requirements of the Saorstat in the matter of compulsory attendance were as comprehensive as those of other European nations. That this statement was untrue — Irish school attendance in the early 1930s was only up to the level reached by the Orkney Islands in the World War I era! — makes it all the more valuable, for it tells us what Irish educationists wanted to believe about their country; just as the distance between a man's fantasies and his real life situation tells us about his emotional life so social fantasies of this sort are revealing about a country's cultural life. Third, the committee affirmed the necessity of fitting Irish educational practices to the agrarian nature of the society. Large numbers of children between the ages of fourteen and sixteen were employed on their parents' farms, and the withdrawal of their labour from the farms through the raising of the leaving age would cause considerable hardships to their parents.

Finally, the report discussed the relationship of the state to the employment of children in terms that could have been used by Jeremy Bentham or Edwin Chadwick. Young people, the report contended, were mature enough to enter employment at age fourteen. Granted, a large proportion of juveniles employed in the towns and cities were in blind-alley jobs, such as messenger boys, etc., but, the report reasoned, keeping these young people in school for two more years would only raise the age of entrance into such blind-alley employment. (That the same line of argument would lead one to push children out of school at age twelve, ten, or even younger, was a point lost on the committee.) Further, increasing the leaving age would raise the question of providing maintenance allowances to the parents of juveniles who otherwise would be employed, and "it would," said the report, "be entirely wrong in principle to start young people in life with the conception that the state is responsible for their support. . . . If young people can obtain suitable employment on attaining the age of fourteen, the state should not interfere, except perhaps to require them to attend part-time continuation classes."[13]

The committee's only suggestion for action was that compulsory continuation education under the terms of the 1930 Vocational Education Act be introduced experimentally in selected areas. Such experiments were later begun in Cork (1938), Limerick (1942), and Waterford (1947), and although they were successful,[14] the national impact was slight and the nation's pattern of school attendance in the early 1950s was little different from the early 1930s.

In the fall of 1951 a report of an almost forgotten commission appeared, recommending the raising of the leaving age. The reporting body was the commission on youth employment which had been set up in May 1943 under the chairmanship of the Catholic archbishop of Dublin, John Charles McQuaid. In an interim report published in June 1944, the commission had suggested that the leaving age ultimately be raised to sixteen years and that this goal be attacked piecemeal, with varying degrees of speed in urban and rural areas.[15] The final report of 1951 reiterated the need to raise the leaving age, first to fifteen and then to sixteen, area by area, with special consideration for the problems of the Dublin area.[16]

At first it seemed as if the McQuaid report would have some impact, for in the spring after its appearance the secretary of the Department of

Education told the secondary school teachers convention that the raising of the leaving age was now accepted in principle, although there were practical difficulties.[17] But then, in 1954, appeared the report of that extraordinary body, the newly-appointed "Council of Education." One says extraordinary because the council soon earned a reputation as an opponent of all but the most minor educational changes (recall here its refusal to inquire into the effect of the Irish language programme and its insistence on maintaining the government's language programme despite the lack of supporting evidence). And extraordinarily because of thirty members of the council only three were primary school teachers, the great majority of members being managers and officials with an investment in maintaining the status quo. And also extraordinary because in spite of most witnesses before the council having declared in favour of raising the school leaving age, the council said no, not for full time attendance and not for part time. Why not? The answer echoed the century-old speeches of the Manchester school. The state, the council said, had the right to require a minimum education, but what that should be was unclear. Merely from the fact that the state required education to a certain age did not mean that it would be proper to add on another compulsory year, for adding on one year could lead to adding another and then another, and so on indefinitely. If this happened there would be an inevitable trend towards the determination by authorities other than the parents of the aptitude of a child for the various types of education. All this, the report said, would interfere with parental rights.[18]

In true free-trade tradition, the Council of Education noted that "parents in a position to do so" were eager to provide for their children's further education at their own expense and that this voluntary approach was preferable to forcing every child to attend school longer than he or his parents might desire.[19] In point of fact the council report was correct in claiming that Irish parents were anxious to have their children schooled beyond the compulsory age of fourteen, as the figures given below for the early 1960s clearly indicate:[20]

COUNTRY	PERCENTAGE OF CHILDREN IN FULL TIME EDUCATION		
	14	15	16
Irish Republic	66.4%	51.5%	36.8%
Northern Ireland	92.4	39.3	22.7
Scotland	99.3	35.3	20.4
England and Wales	100.0	42.2	22.4

Nevertheless, one must emphasize that such a situation was economically discriminatory since primary education was free and post-primary was not. A study of relative rates of participation by children of leaving age in full time education in 1961 revealed a sharp correlation between socio-economic status and chances for post-primary schooling. In the extremes of the range, the children of unskilled workers had only a 29.1% chance of receiving any full time schooling after leaving primary school, while the children of professionals had a 70.2% chance.[21] This degree of social class discrimination is acceptable if one assumes (a) that the existing socio-economic system which determines social class is just and (b) that the economic position of the father should be a major determinate of the educational opportunities of the son. Apparently the council accepted both of these premises.

A Polite and Private Secondary Schooling

"Our attitude to education is still Victorian and is based on a conception of class which is no longer valid but which the systems themselves perpetuate," was the judgement of an independent study group which evaluated Irish education in the early 1960s.[1] Children were sorted into slots by the various systems, primary training being for labourers, secondary schooling for clerks and clerics, and university education for professionals and aspiring gentlefolk. Within the academic secondary school system, the sorting process ground exceedingly fine. The intermediate school certificate, usually taken at age sixteen, was a means of qualifying for business posts, and the leaving certificate, taken at eighteen, acted as a screening device for entry into professional careers.[2]

As a private possession, Irish secondary schooling was a polished and venerable antique. The curriculum harked back to an era before the upstart sciences had shouldered aside linguistic studies, and to the mid-nineteenth century, before strong rules and sturdy regulations were bent by twentieth century permissiveness. Granted, the Irish secondary school system was emancipated from some of its restrictive shackles when, in 1924, the Free State government made two signal changes in the intermediate school arrangements. The first of these was the abolition of the mercenary mechanism, payment-by-examination-results, whereby the marks earned by individual school children determined the state grant given to each school. The Free State government replaced this scheme with capitation grants, a set amount being awarded for each child following an approved course. The second change was the redefinition of the basic academic unit. Previously, this had been one year's work in a given subject, tested at the end of that year by an external examination. The Free State substituted two certificate courses, the junior course covering three to four years and concluding with the intermediate certificate examination at about age sixteen, the senior course covering an additional two years and leading to the leaving certificate taken at about age eighteen.[3]

These changes, however, were more apparent than real. The monetary mechanism had been modified, not abolished. In order to earn capitation grants each school had to provide a course of study that was keyed to the certificate examinations. Further, individual children could still win for themselves monetary awards by doing well on the examinations, notably advanced secondary school scholarships given by the state according to intermediate examination results and university scholarships offered by county councils on the basis of the leaving certificate examination results.

Most important, the subjects to be studied for the two certificate examinations were tightly regulated by the Department of Education. For example, in the late 1940s, a representative time, the department demanded that in the junior course an approved syllabus be followed in at least six subjects, four of them — Irish, a foreign language, history and geography, and mathematics — were specified by the state. At the senior level the pupil had to take five subjects, only one of which, Irish, was specified. But even here there were implicit restrictions, since it was almost inevitable that the schools would try to channel the student into studying further the subjects he had learned at the intermediate level, and these subjects had been determined for the most part by the Department of Education.[4] Inevitably, the combination of state-determined syllabus and examinations with the social and economic advantages acruing to the student from acquiring one of the secondary school certificates, meant that the new system which had been intended to emancipate the Irish secondary schools from slavish cramming, did no such thing. The Reverend Peter Birch, an experienced Catholic educationist, wrote in 1944 concerning the English course that: "The new programme is not satisfactory: it has all the faults and none of the virtues of the old. 'Cramming,' which it was intended to banish, can be as prevalent as ever; pupils will be asked to memorize more and more miscellaneous uninteresting details which 'might be asked.' Apart from Shakespeare the textbooks consist of anthologies. . . ."[5]

Much the same note was sounded by the Tuairim report of the early 'sixties which said: "Languages are taught as grammatical exercises; history and geography are sets of facts and figures learned by rote; literature consists of a few simple poems, extracts from an anthology of essays and one or two plays of Shakespeare. . . . It is possible to complete the whole secondary school course and matriculate without ever having read a complete book."[6]

Indeed, among many Irish educators there seems to have been a flight from educational freedom. In 1924 the Free State Department of Education issued a new secondary school programme which abolished set texts in all subjects. The department's syllabus indicated in a general way the extent and character of the course to be pursued in each subject, but in theory it was up to each teacher to develop his own syllabus, submit it to his local inspector for approval, and then proceed on his own.[7] The trouble with this plan was that it was impractical. In the first place, the Irish secondary school teachers, long used to cramming their pupils for annual examinations, were uncomfortable with this new freedom. Many were unsympathetic to the plan and others, one may speculate, were unable to face the responsibility such freedom entailed. Equally important, the department's system of external examinations inevitably made a mockery of the idea of freedom — for how could one encourage each teacher to design his own syllabus, and then test all the nation's secondary school children by a single, inflexible examination? Each year the Department of Education published the examination results of each school, thus placing the teachers under heavy public pressure to coach pupils for examination success.[8] It was no surprise, then, when the department reintroduced prescribed texts in 1940 for English, Latin, Greek, and for the modern continental languages. The next year prescribed texts were extended to Irish.[9] This flight from freedom stands in sharp ironic contrast to the ideals of that visionary secondary schoolmaster, Patrick Pearse, who in 1912 wrote in his famous indictment of the United Kingdom system of schooling, *The Murder Machine:*

In particular I would urge that the Irish school system of the future should give freedom — freedom to the individual school, freedom to the individual teacher, freedom as far as may be to the individual pupil. Without freedom there can be no growth.[10]

. . . .

The idea of a compulsory programme imposed by an external authority upon every child in every school in a country is the direct contrary of the root idea involved in education.[11]

Underlying this preternatural uniformity of the secondary school curriculum was an underlying assumption about human nature, namely that all bright children were the same and that individual abilities and tastes should be bent to fit the prescribed curriculum. Because the possession of the two secondary school certificates was economically and socially advantageous, to evaluate Irish secondary school pupils according to the single national template of the certificate examinations was also to assign them to social and economic levels according to that same, unbending standard. In 1912 Pearse had condemned the old intermediate system as it operated under British rule:

In each of our great colleges there is a department known as the "scrap heap," though officially called the fourth preparatory — the limbo to which the *debris* ejected by the machine is relegated. The stuff there is either too hard or too soft to be moulded to the pattern required by the civil service commissioners or the incorporated law society.[12]

Fifty years later, long after Ireland had become a self-governing nation, the Tuairim report indicated that little had changed:

The Department of Education in laying down rigid curricula and examination syllabuses for primary and secondary schools assumes that all children are capable of following an identical course of studies regardless of their individual talents or abilities. . . . Those who obstinantly refuse to fit are discarded as "failures."[13]

The curricular pattern into which the secondary school pupils were pressed was remarkable chiefly as an indication of modern Ireland's rejection of the twentieth century's dominant intellectual trends. The curriculum was almost entirely linguistic, resembling that of the English public schools of the mid-Victorian period. Significantly, candidates for the two examinations, while required to take mathematics, were not required to offer a science paper. Moreover, a secondary school could be approved as offering a full curriculum even though it taught no science whatsoever as long as it offered either a language other than Irish and English or a course in commerce.[14] Thus, as late as the academic year 1962–63, only about thirty percent of the boys and about fourteen percent of the girls taking the leaving certificate examination wrote papers in the sciences. Equally striking, among the languages offered, Latin far outstripped the others. In 1962–63 eighty-eight percent of the boys taking the leaving certificate examination presented themselves in Latin, but only twenty-one percent chose French.[15]

Because the secondary schools were not free, the system was economically and socially discriminatory and tended to reinforce existing class differences. Unless he were extremely bright a working-class child had little chance of receiving a secondary education and therefore was condemned to spend the remainder of his days in the class to which he was born. By the same token, a middle-class child of even moderate abilities was almost certain of finding a place in some secondary school as long as his parents could pay the fees and thus he was able to retain his ascriptive status throughout life.

The key to understanding this situation is to underscore the point that almost all secondary schools in Ireland were *private* institutions. The schools were built and improved with private funds, in most cases those of the Catholic church, with no aid from the state. This held both under the United Kingdom government and under the independent Irish state.[16] State grants were limited after 1924 to capitation grants which were intended to pay the day-to-day running expenses of the schools and incremental salary grants to teachers to top-up the basic lay teacher's salary provided by each school.[17] Since both the capitation grants and teachers' salary increments were tied to ongoing expenditure, it is obvious that the Irish secondary schools could only provide for physical renovations and capital expansion by charging fees.

Income from tuition fees (not including boarding fees) accounted for twenty-one percent of the income flow of the Irish secondary schools in 1961–62, the first years for which there is comprehensive data. (In all probability the percentage had been even higher in the past, when salary grants were proportionately much smaller.) The average tuition fee at that time was the reasonably low amount of £16 for a day pupil and £93 for a boarder, but in addition the students' parents had to pay for school books, transport, and incidentals.[18]

Given the ideological position that secondary schools should be private property, it was still possible, in theory, to prevent entry into them from being highly discriminatory as between social classes: conceivably a sufficiently generous system of scholarships could have been established to enable children of the working class to enter the secondary schools on the same terms as those of the middle class. But in reality the Irish scholarship system was conspicuous not for its generosity but for its austerity. There were two forms of scholarships given by governmental authorities: one by county and county boroughs, and the second by the state. In 1921 the Dail issued a decree authorising each county and county borough council to strike a rate of a penny in the pound to provide scholarships to allow primary school pupils to proceed to secondary or technical schools. This decree was confirmed by section seventeen of the Local Government (temporary provisions) Act of 1923, and in 1924 a programme of examinations, set by the Department of Education, was instituted to facilitate the local government bodies in granting these awards.[19] An amending act of 1944 left the conditions of awards unchanged, but under it every county borough council established a scholarship scheme, the previous provision having been very irregular.[20] The other scholarship scheme was administered by the central government, awards being known as "intermediate scholarships." As implied by the name, they were awarded on the basis of a student's results on the intermediate examination. The scheme came into effect when the new secondary programme was introduced in 1924–25, and provided pupils with a subvention for their leaving certificate course.[21]

The chief problem with this dual scholarship system was simple: as indicated by the figures given on the next page the total number of scholarships was tiny.[22]

Obviously not all working class children of ability received a secondary scholarship. For example, in 1944, even according to the very high standard set on the county and county borough scholarship examination, fifty-five percent of the 2,217 pupils who sat the examination passed it, thus indicating their ability to perform at a high level in secondary school: yet only 428 new scholarships were awarded.[23]

The stipend ranged from £15 to £50 a year in the case of the county and county borough scholarships and from £15 to £40 annually for the state intermediate scholarships.[24] When set in the 1920s these amounts were generous enough, but they remained at the same level through the 1950s,[25] and their actual value was considerably eroded by the inflation of the 'forties and 'fifties. Although there were rules to guarantee that most of the awards went to children from less-than-privileged homes (most of the scholarships were set aside for children of families with less than a specified income, and there were special scholarships for students from the Gaeltacht, who in the usual case were economically disadvantaged), the scholarships seemed chiefly to have benefited what could be called the upper-working class. These were families who could afford to put aside some money or at least forego the income the child would have earned.

	AVERAGE NUMBER OF PUPILS ON ROLLS OF PRIMARY SCHOOLS	NUMBER IN ATTENDANCE AT SECONDARY SCHOOLS	NUMBER OF SECONDARY SCHOOLS	COUNTY OR COUNTY BOROUGH SCHOLARSHIPS HELD	INTERMEDIATE SCHOLARSHIPS HELD	TOTAL SCHOLARSHIPS HELD	AVERAGE SIZE OF SECONDARY SCHOOLS	MAXIMUM AVERAGE NUMBER OF GOVERNMENT SCHOLARSHIPS AVAILABLE FOR EACH SECONDARY SCHOOL
1925/26	493,382	25,488	283	694	124	818	90	2.9
1930/31	502,393	28,994	300	958	203	1,161	96	3.9
1940/41	462,245	38,713	352	1,615	208	1,823	110	5.2
1950/51	452,114	48,559	424	2,036	217	2,253	115	5.3
1960/61	490,016	76,843	526	2,609	224	2,833	146	5.4

But children of very low income families seem to have benefited very little.[26]

The inequities of the secondary school system were seriously compounded by its geographic irregularities. Opportunities for academic secondary education varied greatly, being much less in relation to the population in the poorer remote areas — most notably Donegal, Monaghan, and Cavan, — than in the rest of the country.[27] Thus, children from these areas were more apt to have to attend school a considerable distance from home, thereby incurring boarding fees which a working class family could ill afford.

The acceptance of social inequities resulting from economic inequities was a characteristic of the laissez-faire era — for in the Manchester school's marketplace a man earned what he was worth, and inequity was in the very nature of civilized life. For bright children, the high Victorians were willing to erect a scholarship ladder whereby the very talented poor child could raise himself through exertion above the station of his father. This approach satisfied most Irish educational officials and key politicians until the 1960s. The idea that the secondary schools should be open equally to children of all classes, provided they had the requisite ability, was rarely broached and the radical idea that admission arrangements should redress social discrimination by favouring children of the poor was even more rarely murmured.

An accurate reflection of Irish attitudes on this topic is found in the report on the secondary schools by the Council of Education, based on an investigation conducted in the late 1950s and published in 1960. In reading the excerpt below one should remember that on the question of secondary school scholarships the council was a progressive body, not a reactionary one, but even so it questioned neither the continuation of the secondary schools as private property nor the necessity of parents buying secondary education for their children as a marketplace commodity:

> The unqualified scheme of "secondary education for all" is utopian: if only for financial reasons. . . . There are also objections on educational grounds. One of these is that only a minority of pupils would be capable of profiting by secondary (grammar school) education, as is attested by the experience of many countries. Furthermore if secondary education were universally available free for all, the incentives to profit by it would diminish and standards would inevitably fall.
>
> . . . We believe that better provision could be made to ensure more extensive facilities for secondary education. The most obvious means to be employed is, firstly, to maintain grants at such a level that the schools can continue to give

secondary education at a moderate cost and, secondly, to provide more numerous and liberal scholarships from primary schools. Such measures would go far towards ensuring secondary education for all suitable for it and yet would preserve the principle of contribution on the part of the parents in proportion to their means, a principle desirable on general social grounds and also because it preserves in both parents and children a sense of the value of education.[28]

Investing in Children

The idea that spending money on education is a form of economic investment is relatively new in Ireland, not having been broadcast until the 1960s. Before then Irish educational investment was similar to capital investment in the England of the Manchester School: there was no national investment policy and the national situation was the result of the interaction of myriad individual decisions with idiosyncratic governmental regulations. No one who has read the preceding chapters should be surprised to find that the level of educational investment per child in Ireland during the four decades after independence was low relative to Ireland's counterparts in the British Isles and Europe. As explained earlier, the decision on whether or not to initiate a primary or secondary school building programme in a given area was in private (usually religious) hands, and the private individual had to cover up to one third of the costs of building a primary school and all of the costs of a secondary school. Paradoxically, although the Irish educational structure placed great reliance on local initiative, there were only rudimentary mechanisms for involving local government institutions in the investment process. Local taxation could only be struck in aid of vocational education and in support of secondary schools and university scholarships. Direct aid to the primary and secondary schools, either in the form of building grants or subventions in aid of day-to-day educational expenses, was impossible. Thus, in 1962–63 for example, educational costs were only 5.4% of local authorities' expenses.[1] Perforce, localism meant voluntarism. Nonetheless, a vigorous, coherent policy by the central government could have produced a focused and efficient plan of educational investment. But, it must be recalled, the great majority of Dail politicians viewed education within the rubric of the Irish language revival and not as something deserving attention on its own merits. Thus, the Irish polity lacked mechanisms for encouraging local civic investment in education, while simultaneously, they held attitudes which made large-scale state investment unlikely.

How much did the Irish nation actually invest in education? Given below for representative years is the total public expenditure on public education (including university education) and the proportion that amount bore to the Irish Gross National Product, at factor cost:[2]

YEAR	TOTAL PUBLIC EXPENDITURE IN £'000s	G.N.P. IN £'000s	PERCENTAGE
1926/27	4,798	154.1	3.1%
1931	5,151	156.2	3.3
1936	5,513	151.5	3.6
1941	5,929	184.0	3.2
1946	6,781	283.6	2.4
1951	10,999	357.9	3.1
1956	15,674	485.1	3.2
1961	20,385	585.3	3.5

When one compares the proportion of national resources spent on education by the Irish with that spent by other European nations, the results are not, at first glance, unfavourable to the Irish. Expressing public educational expenditures in the early 'sixties as a function of National Income (a slightly different procedure than relating education to the Gross National Product as done above), one obtains the following figures for other countries in the British Isles:

England and Wales	3.9%
Northern Ireland	5.4
Scotland	6.5

Continental European countries
Denmark	3.0%
France	3.0
Italy	3.0
West Germany	3.5

Other industrial countries allocated resources to education in the following manner:

Japan   4.3%

United States   5.5

The percentage of Ireland's national income given over to public educational expenditure was 3.4%, seemingly a reasonable amount.[3]

Unhappily, one must hasten to add that the percentages mask the low level of actual expenditure in Ireland, for Ireland was poor, relative to most other developed nations. Thus, although Denmark and France reserved a smaller proportion of their national income for public educational expenditure than did Ireland, their income per capita was nearly twice as great as Ireland, with the result that these nations were actually spending a great deal more money per inhabitant than were the Irish. In fact, only the Italians spent less than did the Irish.[4] Thus, Ireland was afflicted by one of the painful paradoxes of modern education: for a poor country to keep pace educationally with its richer neighbours it is necessary for it to spend a greater proportion of its national income on education than do its neighbours, something the Irish were either unwilling or unable to do. It well may be that Irishmen through private philanthropy made up some of this gap between their nation and its neighbours, but undeniably a gap remained.[5]

To a considerable extent the low actual level of Irish public educational expenditure has to be ascribed to the attitudes of those who determined the allocation of the nation's public resources, which is to say the members of Dail Eireann. A clear indication of the low priority assigned to educational endeavours by these politicians is the fact that the proportion of public expenditure given over to public education decreased from 1931 through the mid-fifties.[6]

YEAR	TOTAL PUBLIC SECTOR BUDGET IN £ MILLION	PUBLIC EDUCATIONAL EXPENDITURE AS PERCENTAGE OF PUBLIC SECTOR
1926/27	34.0	14.1%
1931	32.0	16.1
1936	42.0	13.0
1941	49.0	12.1
1946	65.5	10.4
1951	118.6	9.3
1956	175.4	9.0
1961	214.7	9.5

Yet, the managers of the Department of Education did not always expend the Dail vote they actually received: from 1941–42 through 1950–52, the unexpended balance on the vote for primary education totalled slightly more than £410,000.[7] Thus, imprecise budgeting practices within the department reinforced the effects of the politicians' parsimony.

At this point a critic might point out that in noting unexpended educational votes, in comparing public educational expenditure to total public expenditure, and in contrasting to other countries the amount the Irish spent per inhabitant on education, we are running the danger of becoming lost in excessive relativism — and that the real question is whether or not enough money was budgeted to keep Ireland's school system running efficiently. Of course this "real question" is pseudo-absolute, for it really asks if enough money was allocated relative to Ireland's educational needs, educational needs being a concept almost impossible to define. But, if we interpret the question to mean, simply, "was there enough money budgeted to keep the schools clean, warm, and up-to-date?" and "was enough money voted to allow a reasonable teacher/pupil ratio?" then we are dealing with questions which can be answered with considerable accuracy. In practice, such questions are best focused on the primary school system, for that system received the great bulk of Ireland's educational resources:[8]

Distribution of Public Expenditure on Education:

YEAR	PRIMARY	SECONDARY	VOCATIONAL	UNIVERSITY	OTHER
1926/27	80.3%	5.4%	6.0%	4.4%	3.9%
1936/37	73.9	9.1	8.9	3.5	4.6
1946/47	68.0	11.3	11.2	3.7	5.8
1951/52	67.6	11.1	11.7	4.1	5.5
1961/62	46.3	14.7	15.2	10.4	13.4

Let us look first at the primary school buildings. Here, certainly, the educational authorities faced problems precluding complete rationality in educational investment even if they had possessed adequate resources. First, the dual system of capital financing meant that each new primary school had to be the product of an arrangement between local interests, usually represented by the parish priest, and the Department of Education. In theory the priest, as representative of local interests, was to provide one third of the cost of the primary school and the Department of Education two-thirds. In actual fact, the local, private, religious sources often lagged, and the state had to invest more than the customary two-thirds: in the early 1950s, for example, the state proportion averaged eighty-three percent,[9] but even then, this was not always enough to overcome local inertia. Second, the actual construction procedures involved not only the local parish priest and the Department of Education, but the Commissioners of Public Works as well. Usually there was a long time lag between the decision to replace an old building and the completion of a new one. For replacement schools completed in the late 'fifties and early 'sixties the lag was almost twelve and one-half years.[10] Third, Ireland's unique demographic character — its population was continually falling until the 1960s — meant that in many rural areas it was impractical to replace an obsolete school building because there would be only a diminishing handful of local children to use the new facility. Hence, the small one- and two-teacher schools were very old: in 1963–64 the modal date of construction of one- and two-teacher schools was between 1850 and 1899. In contrast, schools with three or more teachers had modal construction dates in the years 1935–1964.[11]

Irrationalities affecting capital educational investment cannot, however, explain entirely the inadequate nature of so many Irish primary schools; the flaws were too great. In 1960 twenty-two percent of the national schoolhouses in operation (1,078 of 4,882 schools) had been inspected and declared "obsolete" by the Office of Public Works.[12] Even this figure underestimated the number of schools which were inappropriate as educational environments, because the Office of Public Works was not able to examine all the Irish national schools. If one defines as "non-effective" all schools formally declared obsolete by the Office of Public Works, plus all schools more than eighty years of age, one finds that in 1960, 40.5% of Irish primary schools (1,978 of 4,882)[13] were unsuitable for use. Such a situation cannot be blamed entirely upon the irrationalities of the educational investment process, but must be ascribed in large degree to the state's insufficient allocation of resources to public education.

Other dimensions of the situation are equally striking. Take, for instance, the matters of heating and toilet facilities, simple things to be sure. But note that the parliamentary secretary to the taoiseach admitted in 1952 that there were 460 national schools below modern health standards for which new replacements had not been authorized, much less effected.[14] And note that in 1963–64 a sample of Irish primary schools revealed 52.6% did not even have drinking water in the school or on the school site.

Only 47.5% had either a chemical or a flush toilet.[15] Further, the government grants toward heating and cleaning the buildings were pathetically small. Even as late as the early 'sixties individual schools could claim no more than £100 annually for cleaning and heating, a sum insufficient to pay a caretaker. In fact, the average actual grant for school cleaning was nearer to £50.[16] Even in 1963–64, 63.0% of the primary schools were heated by open fires, and 17.2% by stoves of various sorts. Only 12.4% had central heating and 7.4% electric heating.[17]

As for educational equipment, 42.0% of the primary schools had, in 1963–64, a school library, 1.3% a radio, 6.1% a record player, 5.6% a film strip projector and 2.7% a soundfilm projector. Facilities for teaching cookery were found in 13.3% of the schools and manual instruction facilities in 5.1%.[18]

Moreover, although the Irish constitution made primary education free for all, this did not mean that schoolbooks or requisities were free. In 1939–40 a scheme for the state subvention of books for necessitous primary school children was introduced, the maximum grant for each school being set at one shilling per child on pupils in the second and higher standards and up to two shillings per child in certain necessitous Gaeltacht areas.[19] Generous? In 1958–59 the total amount of state aid for national school requisites for poor children was £2,019, representing less than ten shillings per school, and the grants for books £4,845, less than one pound per school.[20] The amount spent on free requisites for disadvantaged children in 1961–62 was £3,477, or 0.03% of state educational expenditure, and the cost of free books for necessitous children was £4,452, equal to 0.040% of state educational expenditures.[21]

Significantly, although the Irish children clearly suffered through the nation's under-investment in school buildings, equipment, and educational supplies, they did not suffer from a grossly disadvantageous teacher-pupil ratio. In 1962–63, the nation's ratio was one primary teacher for each thirty-three students, a figure identical to that of the Netherlands and Yugoslavia. That for the United Kingdom was twenty-six, for France twenty-eight, and for West Germany, thirty-four.[22] Granted, there were inconsistencies, especially in Dublin where, in 1956–57 for example, there were thirty-nine pupils for each primary teacher, while the national ratio was thirty to one.[23] But, overall, the Department of Education's policy was successful: by concentrating its very limited resources on the teaching personnel — who accounted for seventy-three percent of all public expenditures on primary education in 1961–62[24] — the department was able to overcome some of the worst effects of the nation's parsimony in educational affairs.

The manner in which a nation allocates its national income tells one a great deal about that nation, in the same way knowledge of how a man spends his money reveals much about his character. Educational investment patterns, therefore, are part of the cultural mirror we are holding to Kathleen's face. If one assumes that a people spend their money on things they care about, then notes the chronic pattern of under-investment in education, one is led to the conclusion that Ireland as a nation placed a surprisingly low priority on the educational welfare of its children.

This conclusion clashes so strongly with the stereotyped image of the warm, supportive Irish family, that it is tempting to reject it, despite its being based on four decades of data on the nation's economic priorities. But wait: the clash is apparent, not real. The classic anthropological studies of the Irish conducted by Conrad M. Arensberg and Solon T. Kimball in the early 1930s revealed that the Irish family was warm and close-knit indeed, but that it was also a gerontocracy. Social position and economic power within each family correlated very closely with age. Offspring were kept in a dependent, often subservient condition for a very long time: an adult male whose parents were still managing their own farm was a "boy" whatever his actual age, and it was not at all uncommon for "boys" upwards of fifty years of age to be prohibited from marrying by strong-willed parents.[25] Obviously the result of the fact that age and social position were positively correlated within the Irish family was that children were the lowest rung on the social ladder. Implicitly this social ordering affected economic priorities. Within the family when the time came to choose between father's tobacco and son's school fees, the scales were loaded against the fees. Nationally, when the choice had to be made between rebuilding outdated primary school buildings and macadamizing a network of boreens, the scales were loaded against the schools.

THE MEDIEVAL HERITAGE

The Catholic Church Triumphant

Modern Irish history could easily be viewed by a Catholic apologist as a morality play, with the unfolding of events leading to a virtuous and meaningful conclusion, in this case the enthronement of the Catholic authorities as the conscience of the nation. Undoubtedly the church, like any other organization, has tried to maximize its own power in Irish society, but one must continually emphasize that the laity has accepted the church's great influence with considerable (if not always complete) enthusiasm. The laity itself is notably devoted to the church. The church in Ireland has exercised more power than in any other advanced country in the twentieth century. Its power has been based both on practical realities, such as its great financial resources and social influence, and upon the church's control of various esoteric mysteries relating to the other-world with which the Celt always has been preoccupied.[1]

To look first at the pragmatic aspect of the church's power in education, it is clear that the hierarchy was the key to the church's power. According to a French ecclesiastical authority, writing in 1960, "The bishops of Ireland appear to have more power, in practice, than those of any other country in the world."[2] The bishops were not bashful in defining their powers, as is indicated by the following statement made in 1935 during a local education controversy by the Reverend Dr. Kinane, bishop of Waterford and Lismore:

Bishops are successors of the apostles and as such are divinely constituted authoritative teachers in faith and morals. Each residential bishop is, subject to the supreme magisterial power of the Holy See, the authoritative teacher of faith and morals in his own diocese and his authority includes the right to determine when faith and morals are involved, so that one cannot evade his authority by the pretext that he has gone outside his own proper sphere.

From the fact that a bishop is the authoritative teacher of faith and morals in his diocese, it follows that his teaching is binding and that his subjects must obey it, even under pain of mortal sin, whenever the matter involved is notable.

Accordingly, among other consequences of this position, subjects should not oppose their bishop's teaching in any way, whether by word, by writing, or by another external act, and they should positively carry out whatever is demanded by it.[3]

Although the bishops never engaged directly in electoral politics, in defining what constituted the sphere of faith and morals, they drew a very large circle indeed. Few Irishmen would have said that it was beyond the competence of the Reverend Dr. Collier, bishop of Ossory, to declare in a New Year's pastoral, 1933, that "no Catholic can be a communist; no communist can be a Catholic."[4] Cardinal D'Alton, addressing the Catholic Truth Society in Dublin in the autumn of 1951, felt it was within his archepiscopal sphere to denounce the tendency of Irish legislators to copy welfare-state legislation which had "evolved in the materialistic atmosphere of Great Britain where state paternalism is gradually destroying personal independence and initiative."[5] The following spring, the Reverend Dr. Lucey, co-adjutor bishop of Cork, condemned the theory that farmers did not own their land but held it in trust for the community.[6] And although there were some lay objections, the bishops were successful in vetoing in 1951, on allegedly moral grounds, a mother and child health scheme.[7]

Undoubtedly much of the church's influence in social matters resulted from the high level of religious devotion of many Irish politicians (John A. Costello's statement in the Dail, regarding his government's acceptance of the hierarchy's veto of the 1951 health scheme, was quintessential: "I, as a catholic, obey my church authorities and will continue to do so. . . .")[8] but one should also remember that the politicians and the bishops long had honoured a pragmatic constitutional alliance. In the early 1920s the bishops had supported the new state and condemned those who continued in violent opposition to it, a position which doubtless was assumed for reasons of conscience but which inevitably yielded important political benefits once the new government was firmly established.[9] Significantly, the implicit church-state alliance was strengthened during the 1930s. Eamon de Valera who, despite his once having opposed the Free State, became its head and introduced a new constitution embodying Catholic teachings on social questions and dignifying the position of the church. Whereas in the 1922 constitution it had been necessary to follow the contours of the British liberal state (article 8, the only article dealing directly with religion was a guarantee of religious freedom and of the religious neutrality of the state), the 1937 constitution was redolent with doctrinal overtones. The preamble invoked the holy trinity in phraseology characteristic of the Catholic church and acknowledged the people of Eire's obligation to Jesus Christ who "sustained our fathers through centuries of trial," a reference to the persecution of the Catholics in the penal days — and an implication that to be Irish one must be Catholic. Article 44 declared that "the state recognises the special position of the Holy Catholic Apostolic and Roman church as the guardian of the faith professed by the great majority of the citizens." Precisely what this meant never has been adequately explained, because under other sections of the same article it was added that "the state also recognises" the various Protestant denominations, and Jewish congregations and "other religious denominations." It then added guarantees of freedom of conscience and prohibited the state's endowing any religion. Precise exegesis of article 44 being impossible, it is most useful to view the article as the public affirmation of the pre-existing constitutional alliance whereby the church would support the state, if the heads of government would pay attention to the church's wishes.

Directly relevant to educational questions was the 1937 constitution's definition (in article 41) of the family in terms derived almost directly from the Catholic theory of natural law. "The state recognises the family as the natural primary and fundamental unit group of society, and as a moral institution possessing inalienable and imprescriptible rights, antecedent and superior to all positive law," was the beginning of the article, and the detailed prohibition of the dissolution of marriage was its conclusion. Next, article 42 placed the primary and natural duty for education of the child on the family, the state being obliged to help parents provide this education. The powers of the state did not supersede parental powers, but the state was to provide an opportunity for free primary education and to require that each child receive a certain minimum education, consonant with the religious and moral scruples of the parents. Finally, article 44 (4) provided that legislation providing state aid for schools should not discriminate between denominations.

If, at the national level, the bishops were able to wield great influence, at the local level the parish priest's influence was equally pervasive. The power of the parish priest in rural areas is too well known to need discussion here, but one point should be made: priestly influence was not limited to rural areas. In sharp contrast to patterns in the rest of the English-speaking world, when an Irishman moved from the farm to the city, he brought his religion with him. During the period here under study, 1920–60, urbanization did not, therefore, become a synonym for secularization.[10]

Certain theological precepts concentrated much of the church's great power on the school system and at the same time legitimated the exercise of that power. According to the Irish bishops, the purpose of education was chiefly to prepare man for the world to come. Education, the bishops stated in 1927, "means the training and development of the whole man ... for the purpose not merely of fitting him for a career of usefulness and honour in this life, but also and still more for the purpose of guiding him to attain the high and happy destiny designed for him in the life to come."[11] Who was to determine the proper education for service in this world and salvation in the next? Under natural law theory the responsibility for the child's welfare lay in the first instance with the parent, but, as the following statement by John Charles McQuaid, archbishop of Dublin, indicates, parental powers in education were effectively subsumed by the church:

Parents have a most serious duty to secure a fully Catholic upbringing for their children in all that concerns the instruction of their minds, the training of their wills to virtue, their bodily welfare and the preparation for their life as citizens.

Only the church is competent to declare what is a fully Catholic upbringing; for, to the church alone, which He established, our divine Lord, Jesus Christ, has given the mission to teach mankind to observe all things whatsoever He has commanded. ... Accordingly, in the education of Catholics every branch of human training is subject to the guidance of the church, and those schools alone which the church approves are capable of providing a fully Catholic education.[12]

And the state? The encyclical of Pius xi, promulgated in 1929, emphasized that the role of the state in education was only to serve as an auxiliary to the family and to the church. The duty of the state was "to protect the prior right which the parents possess to give their children a Christian education, and therefore also to respect the supernatural right of the church over such Christian education."[13] So consonant with Irish cultural values was this papal formulation that the same sonorities were written into the 1937 constitution.

The church's metaphysics of education served to focus much of its general power into a single confined social area, in the same way a lens concentrates the energy of sunlight on a single physical area. Such intense energy could not be resisted and, as Edward Byrne, archbishop of Dublin, contentedly observed in 1933, "the past history of education in this country was a sad one, but it is ending very well."[14] Actually, the state system of academic secondary education, founded in 1878, never had been a threat to the church, for it had been avowedly denominational from the beginning. The Catholic schools were firmly under religious control and most of the teaching personnel was religious. On the primary school level, the course of history had been a bit more difficult — the system when founded in 1831 was supposed to be nondenominational and religiously integrated — but well before independence, the schools had become denominational in practice if not in theory. Schools for Catholic children were managed by local parish priests under the supervision of the diocesan bishops. The priests appointed the school teachers and, within the framework of state curricular regulations, determined the timetable of each school. According to the 1938 statement of the Reverend Michael Brenan, professor of education at St. Patrick's College, Maynooth, "the situation really is that the Catholic people or parents of Ireland, for whom the bishops and parish priests are trustees, submit their schools to a system of national education, as a result of which the state pays the teachers and gives other financial assistance."[15] The bishops echoed this conclusion when, at their plenary council of 1956 they took the unusual step of declaring specifically their approbation of the national system of education.[16]

Lest the arrangement of Irish educational institutions to suit the church be misinterpreted as a clerical dictatorship, one must hasten to add that the overwhelming majority of the laity seem to have been satisfied with the situation. The laity concurred in the clergy's emphasis upon the prepotence of other-worldly matters in determining the school's management and curriculum. This point is illustrated by the attitudes of leading laymen concerning formal religious instruction. For example, the report of the second national programme conference of 1926 stated that "of all parts of a school curriculum, religious instruction is by far the most important, as its subject matter, God's honour and service, includes the proper use of all man's faculties, and affords the most powerful inducements to their proper use.[17] Significantly, the conference did not presume to define what religious instruction actually should be, this being left to the clergy; thus, the conference affirmed both the primacy of other-worldy considerations in education and the hegemony of the professionally religious in dealing with these matters. These words were repeated in the Department of Education's rules and regulations, 1932 which sounded, the professor of education at Maynooth noted, almost as if they had been taken from the encyclical on the *Christian Education of Youth,* so closely did lay opinion conform to the ecclesiastical ideals.[18] Certainly the religious authorities must have been pleased when the Council of Education's major report on the primary school, published in 1954, affirmed that in Ireland there was no disagreement as to the place religion should occupy in the school. The first purpose of the primary school was to train children in the fear and love of God.[19] Nor could the clergy have been displeased to hear the minister for education, General Richard Mulcahy, say in the following year that Ireland's precious heritage of faith, handed down from the forefathers, was being carried faithfully onward by the primary schools.[20] Later, the 1960 report on secondary education published by the Council of Education declared that Irish secondary schools, however diverse their origin, had in common the following: "The dominant purpose of their existence is the inculcation of religious ideals and values. This central influence, which gives unity and harmony to all the subjects of the curriculum, is outside the purview of the state which supervises the secular subjects only."[21]

The pervasive religious tone of the schools, heightened by formal doctrinal instruction, had two important effects.[22] The first of these was to complete two circles of religious devotion, and thus to guarantee the stability of the religious milieu in which the schools operated and thereby preclude any significant deviation from clerically-articulated norms by educational reformers. One says "circles of devotion" because both among laymen and clergy the process turned in on itself. The loyal adhesion of the adult laity to the church allowed the primary schools to be orientated towards the other-world and to be administratively dominated by the professionally religious. The primary school system produced successive generations of laymen imbued with a loyalty to the church, a respect of the supernatural and a deferential attitude towards the clergy. In their turn these new generations of national school-educated adults approved the education of their own children in the same religious atmosphere in which they had themselves been educated.

For the professionally religious, a circle of devotion was completed at the secondary school level. Most Irish secondary schools were operated by diocesan authorities, by religious orders, or by religious brotherhoods, and most teachers in these religiously-run schools were themselves in holy orders. As a result of their pervasive influence, the clergy as a profession reproduced themselves through the secondary schools at a remarkable rate. For example, in the years 1956–60, of 5,428 final-year students in diocesan colleges and secondary schools surveyed, 1,346 professed religious vocations. When one considers that there were 288 priests teaching in the diocesan schools, the remarkable degree of professional reproduction becomes clear, being .93 vocation per priest per year. Among the 559 students who passed through the final year of juniorates or schools run by missionary societies, 364 had vocations, a ratio, for the seventy-three priests involved in teaching, of 1.0 vocation per priest per annum. The vocations in schools run by religious orders were lower, but notable nonetheless. Six hundred eighteen students leaving school in the years 1956–60 professed vocations of a total number of 4,395 students enrolled in final year classes. The professional reproduction rate was .35 vocation per year per priest teaching in such schools.[23] Obviously, since the secondary schools were the life-line of the priesthood, the church could brook nothing which would have reduced the supernatural emphasis of the curriculum or the clerical control of the institutions. One generation of clergy controlled the schools and the schools produced the next generation of clergy who in turn controlled the schools, on and on, generation by generation.

At points the two circles of devotion, the lay and the clerical, touched. So successful were the secondary schools in stimulating religious vocations that the number of priests in Ireland continually grew, even though the total Catholic population was dropping:[24]

YEAR	TOTAL PRIESTS	PEOPLE PER PRIEST
1911	3,689	879
1926	3,836	827
1937	3,823	838
1946	5,004	642
1951	5,135	634
1961	5,723	558

The increasing ratio of clergy to population meant that the formal religious apparatus could continually be improved at the parish level, thus reinforcing with ever greater efficiency the laity's adherence to the church. Certainly in these years it would have been a remarkably insensitive educational reformer who introduced any educational change that would have weakened the bands of devotion which bound the church and the schools.

Writing in 1958 John J. O'Meara, professor of Latin at University College, Dublin, aptly summarized the impact of these attitudes: "I must remark that as long as the vast majority of the people of this country continues in such loyalty to the church, and while the church holds, as she will continue to hold, a very special viewpoint in connection with the end of education within any community, the influence of the church here in education will be not only paramount, but decisive."[25]

If the first effect of the pervasive other-worldly orientation of the Irish schools was to complete the two circles of devotion, the second was to reinforce certain Irish attitudes regarding child-rearing. Recall here the point made at the close of the preceding chapter, namely that the Irish nation's investment in the education of its children was surprisingly low. In part this was the result of the dominance in twentieth century Ireland of nineteenth century English economic orthodoxy and in part it was the product of a gerontocratic social structure. Significantly, the other-worldly orientation of the Irish schools also tended to shunt the child in his present, imperfect state, aside. The fundamental premise of the Irish education system was forcefully articulated by the bishops in 1927: "The ultimate end of his existence, namely the salvation of his immortal soul, is what really matters most for every man, and education, which is not systematically directed to help him towards this end, is fundamentally defective in its aim."[26] Given this premise and the doctrine of Original Sin, it followed that the aim of education was not, as in the "progressive" theories of Dewey and Montessori, chiefly to bring out the latent perfections in the child, but primarily to help him overcome his imperfections of behaviour and belief and so to preserve his immortal soul unto eternal life. The Irish distrust of theories of human nature which presented the child in a rosy light is well represented in the authoritative statement made in 1942 by John Charles McQuaid, archbishop of Dublin:

In violent contrast to our system and with the sane [scholastic] philosophy, stand those types of the so-called New or Active School (such as the materialist system of the authentic Madame Montessori and the experiments of Decroly, Ferriere and Laparde) wherein, because the child is supposed to be his own end or to be physiologically predetermined or to make his own truth, the task of the educator is practically reduced to observing the spontaneous activities of the general and individual needs of the children.[27]

Distrust of theories of human nature which presented the child as an end in himself and which defined the educator's job as enhancing, rather than suppressing the child's natural inclinations, was reinforced by Irish distrust of foreign cultures. One clerical contributor to the *Irish Ecclesiastical Record* wrote in 1923 that he had come into contact with the men and books which were the typical products of the educational systems of England, France, Germany, and other countries and the experience had convinced him that if Ireland were to "avoid the mistakes which have led to the deformation of the intelligence, and through the intelligence the literature and institutions of these countries, especially in relation to the supernatural order, we must aim at a return to the saner education ideal of the Middle Ages. . . . "[28] A quarter century later, the bishop of Ardagh and Clonmacnois, James Joseph MacNamee, opened a new school by telling his auditors that, "they all knew the result of mere secular education in various parts of the world; it was well known that in modern times youth had got out of hand. . . . "[29]

By this point in the book a constellation of interlocking Irish educational characteristics has emerged. Think back to the discussion of the position of the Irish language in the schools: the academic subject that was most emphasized in the curriculum was Irish, taught not for its inherent cultural content, but for extra-educational, politico-nationalistic reasons. Recall that the adherence to Manchester School economic attitudes limited severely the amount of money the Irish invested in the education of their children. Remember that the Irish social structure was an age-graded pyramid and that the child was at the bottom. And from this present chapter note that the clergy, the single most important citizen in most rural communities, and the authorities of the church, representing the most influential voluntary organization in Irish society, defined the purpose of the schools in other-worldly terms: the schools were to teach the child to overcome his human frailities and thereby to save his immortal soul. Thus, medieval theology, nineteenth century economic orthodoxy, linguistic nationalism, and social conventions all led to the same result: nearly universal agreement that education was not an end in itself, and that the educational process should shape the child to the measurements of his masters.

Irish Catholic theology and practice were related to secular economic orthodoxy in another way: the bishops and clergy were opposed to an increase in the power of the state in most fields and especially leery of any augmentation of the state's power in education. The fact that the state in independent Ireland was administered by successive cohorts of politicians who were loyal to the church and solicitous of its needs makes the church's fears all the more striking. Although the Irish church's anxieties about the state were out of touch with the political realities of independent Ireland, their existence is perfectly understandable. The church had gone through centuries of unpleasant relations with the Irish government before independence. Further, the Irish Catholic church, as part of the international church, was aware of the pressures which the modern state had brought to bear on the church in certain continental countries. Hence, the Irish Catholic church responded to the new Irish state in ways derived from its own history and from the experience of the contemporary continental church.[30] That these attitudes and patterns of response were unrealistic is irrelevant. Such were the powers of the bishops and clergy that their fears and actions were in themselves political and educational realities.

The leading authority of Irish church-state relations, John Whyte, has established that, despite the serious social evils in Ireland, the Catholic social movement during the late 1940s and '50s was almost exclusively concerned with the question of state power.[31] Typical of this concern was Bishop Lucey's answer to the question, "What then should we expect from the state?" His answer was:

Help to enable us to help ourselves. Thus, instead of providing directly through its own agencies free housing for all, free health services for all, free school meals for all etc., it should rather see to it that these are available and that people can afford to avail of them. Thus, the real answer to the problem of the man who cannot afford medical care for his wife and children is not a free mother and child service for all, but a rise in wages — or cut in taxes — sufficient to enable him to pay.[32]

Similar statements were issued by other members of the hierarchy.[33]

Actually, in the field of education the preoccupation with the problem of state power went back to the 1920s. In 1926 the Irish National Teachers' Organization began to agitate for the government to increase the state proportion of capital construction costs for primary schools and for local government agencies to bear the entire cost of heating and cleaning the schools. A stranger to the Irish scene might have expected the Catholic clergy and bishops to favour such proposals, for the government's taking over the cleaning and heating costs and a larger share of capital costs would have given the church more money to use on other activities; but such an expectation would miss the church's obsessive fear of the state. Viewed through the lens of fear, an increase in grants was seen not as a case of largesse, but as a danger, since the state conceivably could now demand greater control over the primary schools. Hence, no one should be surprised to learn that the annual meeting of the central council of the association of Catholic clerical managers in May 1926 opposed the new ideas and recommended that expenses should be borne as hitherto by the government and the managers.[34] The I.N.T.O. agitation was neither focussed nor continuous, but it was a nagging worry to clerical authorities. Hence, one finds Michael Browne, bishop of Galway, speaking at the 1945 I.N.T.O. conference in strong opposition to the idea of handing over to the state or to local health authorities the responsibility for building and maintaining the primary schools. "The managerial system," he said, "has been the legal safeguard of the freedom of Catholic education in this land for a century."[35] Obviously, he believed that such a safeguard was necessary, even in a society whose constitution specifically recognized the special position of the Catholic church.

Eventually, in the early 1950s, the I.N.T.O. agitation came to a head.[36] For a time, early in 1952, it appeared that the minister for education, Sean Moylan, would agree to the I.N.T.O. proposals,[37] but that was before the attitude of the Catholic bishops became clear. No Irish politician could ignore the angered tone of Eugene O'Callaghan, bishop of Clogher, certainly not if his words typified the attitude of the entire hierarchy, for the bishop believed that the teachers wished to take the schools out of the hands of the church and give them over to the state. He said early in June 1952 that the I.N.T.O. plan would lead to an intolerable state of affairs whereby civil servants from Dublin might come down and attempt to take control of the primary schools. It was time, the bishop thought, for the clerical managers to assert themselves to show that the schools belonged to them and to the church.[38] Was Bishop O'Callaghan representative of the hierarchy? Yes. In June 1952, the I.N.T.O. addressed a letter to Cardinal D'Alton who brought the whole question before the hierarchy at their October 1952 meeting. The bishops' decision was that present arrangements were desirable and that the school teachers should now stop their campaign to have the expense of building, cleaning, and heating schools taken over by the government. The teachers tried to rebut /

the hierarchy's argument, but in October 1954 the bishops reaffirmed their own judgement, making it clear that in their view the continuance of a system of denominational primary education was possible only if the managerial system continued unchanged, which in turn meant that the legal ownership and control of school buildings had to be in church hands.[39] There, effectively, the matter ended. Concern with clerical prerogatives amongst the bishops reinforced preference for economic individualism among the laity, and produced the situation detailed in chapter six: too little money was spent on the schools and Irish school children were educated in antiquated, ill-equipped and often unsanitary buildings.

On another problem, namely the predominance of too small primary schools, the church's interests clashed with the educational interests of the children as defined by the educational professionals. As discussed in Chapter One, an amalgamation campaign originated before independence and was continued by the new Irish government. Some results were achieved, for whereas in 1904 more than three-fifths of the Irish national schools had an average daily attendance of less than fifty pupils,[40] fewer than half were below the fifty-student line in 1925–26.[41] As noted earlier, the Catholic bishops had opposed the amalgamation campaign even before it was publicly announced and continued to fight it even after the Free State government came to power.

But despite this opposition there were pressing reasons, in addition to educational considerations, for the Free State's Department of Education to pursue the school amalgamation policy. The most important of these was demographic: the population of southern Ireland was dropping continually and in some rural areas this drop was so sharp as to leave only a handful of pupils in the local primary school. Second, and in almost paradoxical counterpoint to the first reason, the 1926 Compulsory School Attendance Act increased school attendance in many areas to the point where an additional teacher was needed. Across the nation it was estimated that an additional 500 teachers would have to be appointed if no changes were made in school organization.[42] But in many cases this additional expense could be avoided if the newly-overcrowded school was merged with a neighbouring school which still was under-subscribed. For these reasons the Department of Education pressed forward, increasing in 1928 the minimum size for schools operating under normal conditions from thirty to thirty-five.[43] Each year thereafter the department's annual report mentioned a significant number of amalgamations, usually in the neighbourhood of half a hundred, as having been effected that year. This achievement must have been won by great tact and controlled effort. The comments in the Dail of Thomas Derrig, minister for education, gave as much public indication of the religious impediments the department faced as any politician could safely express: "It is obvious that if [an] amalgamation is to be brought about it must be brought about in the same parish. There would be difficulty, as the deputies realize, if schools in certain parishes were abolished and the pupils transferred to adjoining parishes."[44] But for all the department's efforts, it could not overcome the combined effect of demographic decline and clerical opposition. In 1925–26, 48.4% of the Irish primary schools had fewer than fifty pupils. The corresponding statistic for 1953–54 was 48.0%.[45]

In another sector, namely the vocational schools, church authorities showed an ability to bend a state educational programme to fit their own purposes. It will be recalled that the vocational school network (or technical schools system as it was called prior to 1930) was the only part of the Irish educational structure, below university level, which was administered by laymen and in which local government authorities provided rate aid and appointed governors of local institutions. The hierarchy, therefore, was highly suspicious of the system and when, following the report of the Technical Education Commission in 1927, it became clear that the government would draft a new vocational education bill, the bishops moved to protect their own interests. Precisely what provisions were included in the 1930 Vocational Education Act by the government to placate the bishops is unknown, but one subsequent investigator has found strong evidence that the minister for education, Professor O'Sullivan, gave the bishops a written promise that the vocational system would be limited to the technical field and would not impinge upon the academic territory of the church-run secondary schools.[46] Still, the 1930 act did not contain precise provisions regarding the place of religious instruction in these lay-controlled schools, and a decade later the department found it necessary to direct a memorandum to the committees which stated: "Committees should provide facilities for religious instruction and incorporate it in the general class time-table. The local ecclesiastical authorities should be approached with regard to the provision of the actual teaching. In any particular course the time set apart for religious instruction should have a reasonable relation to the time given to the course as a whole, being more in whole time than in part-time courses."[47]

Even then, influential Catholic educationists, such as the Reverend Professor Brenan, had misgivings.[48] In practice, however, the church's disquiet was allayed by the simple realities of Irish social life: although a clergyman did not control the local vocational education committee *ex officio*, as he did the primary school, he was eligible for appointment to the local vocational technical education committees. And so engrained was the Irish habit of deferring to the clergy in educational affairs that a priest usually was elected committee chairman: In the mid-'fifties, for example, twenty-two of the twenty-seven vocational education committees were headed by priests.[49]

For a time the church's jealousy of its educational privileges made it an ally of the politicians against the teachers and laity. This occurred in response to demands for the establishment of an independent educational advisory council. These demands, as discussed in Chapter Two, originated in the early 1920s and were especially strong among the members of the I.N.T.O. Successive governments resisted them, however. President Cosgrave's opposition ostensibly was on constitutional grounds, but it is hard to resist the conclusion that the opposition of both Cosgrave and, later, de Valera, was based on *realpolitik*. The last thing either wanted was an independent body of citizens criticizing the government's educational policies. What held true for the politicians held true for many bishops, because they too wished to minimize interference in their own educational activities. Archbishop Gilmartin of Tuam probably was speaking for many of his fellow bishops when, in late 1938, he pointed out that any educational advisory council necessarily would have to be undenominational in membership and that in his opinion it would be "a highly dangerous and objectionable experiment" to establish an undenominational body which might "prescribe tests and courses to which the church as representing Catholic parents and Christ Himself could not agree."[50]

But the church's opposition gradually was eroded, chiefly as a result of the influence of Pope Pius XI's encyclical of 1931, *Quadragesimo anno*, which proposed the development of vocational groups, corporations, or guilds, in which workers and employers would collaborate for their mutual benefit. The corporatist, or vocationalist, theory gradually spread in Ireland and led to a number of notable social experiments by members of the lower clergy.[51] Some outstanding younger clergymen, notably Cornelius Lucey (later bishop of Cork) interpreted vocationalist principles in the field of education to imply the necessity for a guild, or council for education, which would represent all aspects of the profession and would have considerable powers in defining teacher qualifications and alternate school curricula.[52] The idea was endorsed in 1944 by the commission on vocational organization which was chaired by Bishop Browne of Galway.[53] In all probability its acceptability was increased because the vocationalists presented their scheme as an alternative to bureaucracy and to unnecessary state control, precisely the kind of vocabulary which would appeal to the Catholic prelates. Although the vocational organization report received a cool reception from the de Valera government, the Fine Gael party promised the I.N.T.O. on the eve of the election of 1948 that if they attained office they would establish a council of education, and they kept their word.[54] In actual fact the Council of Education, appointed in 1950, need not have worried anyone, church or state. As discussed in earlier chapters, it was extremely timid about criticizing either church or state and reluctant to suggest any significant educational reforms.

John Whyte, in the concluding chapter of his pioneering work *Church and State in Modern Ireland 1923–1970* emphasizes that the interrelations of the church and state have been extremely complex and that any simple formula representing these relations would distort and mislead. Certainly this is true when the whole gamut of social and political interaction of church and state are surveyed, but in the limited area of primary and post-primary education, three clear, simple conclusions emerge. The first of these is that education was one of the chief concerns of the church; indeed, next to his liturgical and confessional duties it was the parish priest's most pressing responsibility. Education was crucial because it related directly to this- and to the other-world. Through the appropriate schooling children were shown the way to eternal life. And in this world the schools were a social aorta, feeding the heart of the church with young adherents. Some of these youths gave their lives to the church as religious professionals, and most of the remainder became lifelong lay adherents. Second, given that it was imperative from the church's viewpoint for the schools to be run along religious-directed lines, it is undeniable that at the local level the church's representatives maintained a tight control over the individual schools. Even the technical schools, in theory lay-controlled institutions, in the usual case were supervised by a priest as chairman of the local vocational education committee. The state determined in large degree the secular curriculum, but the interpretation of that curriculum was almost entirely under clerical control. Thus, our second point leads us to suggest that in modern Ireland if the Catholic authorities *really* cared about a given issue or set of institutions, they had sufficient influence and power to have their own way.

Before one concludes that the church's triumphs in education were won at the expense of the rights of others, a third point should be emphasized: the Irish laity, as citizens, granted the churchmen a license for their activities. There is no evidence that except for those laymen involved professionally in education there was anything but general approval for the church's activities. This is understandable, for most Irishmen were the product of the church's educational system and therefore had been indoctrinated during childhood years with the very ideas and assumptions upon which the clergy's actions were based. Further, most of the bishops' ideas concerning the secular world followed the same intellectual contours as did Irish public opinion: the Catholic bishops' distrust of state activities in all fields was parallel to the lines of distrust etched upon the minds of so many Irishmen, even though the sources were different. Similarly, the theological assumptions which led the clergy to reject the ideas of the "progressive educators," that the child was inherently good and that education should be concerned primarily with encouraging the child to express this natural goodness, paralleled the unspoken assumptions of the Irish social structure: socially the young occupied the lowest rung and the outgrowing of childhood was the first step towards acquiring social status.

The true triumph of the Catholic church in the field of education was not that it gained such extensive control over the schooling process; rather the triumph was that its hegemony was won not by the repression of popular sentiment but by articulating ideas and attitudes compatible with the popular will.

Protestantism Abashed

If the consonance of social patterns and religious practices was the glory of the Catholic church in the twenty-six counties, it was the nemesis of the Protestant churches. The dominant Protestant denominations were, in order of numerical strength, the Church of Ireland (Anglican), the Presbyterians, and the Methodists. Each had its own corporate structure, but for the sake of convenience hereafter Protestants usually are referred to as if they comprised a single group. In any case, members of all Protestant denominations were affected by the simple fact that the Catholic church was a dominant element in Irish society. Therefore, the Protestants' position was often uneasy and sometimes extremely uncomfortable. It hardly could have been otherwise. Yet, one of the cherished myths of Irish society has been that since independence southern Ireland has been a virtual sanctuary for the Protestants, who have not only been tolerated but, on some matters, such as education, treated more favourably than their Catholic counterparts. Like all viable myths, this one contains a kernel of truth, enhulled in fiction. Distinguishing fact from fiction, however, is very difficult in this situation for the myth is one in which both Protestants and Catholics have wanted to believe (in itself a virtue, I think), and in any given statement it is hard to sift fantasy from reality.

Moreover, the frames of reference within which various groups have viewed the toleration issue is skewed (albeit in differing ways), so as to minimize the apparent difficulties of the Protestant position. The first misleading frame is the all-Ireland perspective. Within the framework of the entire island's experience, it is clear that since 1920 the Protestants in the south have fared better than the Catholics in the north. This is a fair comparison and, quite rightly, reflects creditably on the southern Catholic population. But among many Irish Catholics this accurate observation has led to an illogical conclusion: that the Protestants in the south have been treated perfectly fairly. Being less given to any vice than one's neighbour does not necessarily make one virtuous, so it is best to forego comparisons with Northern Ireland and deal solely with the situation in the south.

A second misleading perspective is common to both Catholic and Protestant, and is assumed by many outside observers as well. This frame of reference equates toleration of Protestants with religious toleration. Undeniably, the southern Protestants have been allowed to practice their religion freely. The state has scrupulously protected religious rights and the Catholic population has affirmed the Protestants' right to practice their own religion. But to define toleration of Protestants in solely religious terms misses the point that Protestantism (like Catholicism) in Ireland has been an interlocking set of religious, cultural, social, and (formerly) political characteristics. On the eve of independence, the typical southern Protestant was a substantial, well-off broker or land owner, who wanted the union with England to be preserved. Unlike his Ulster counterpart, he was not willing to take up arms in forwarding his political views. Culturally he identified with the tradition of Shakespeare, Milton, and Swift, not that of Celtic mythology and the Irish language revival. After independence he quietly became what was known as an "ex-unionist" and proved no threat to the new state. The new state guaranteed his religious freedom, but refused to countenance many of his social patterns and was hostile to his cultural convictions. Although the Protestants were tolerated as a religious group they were under constant attack as a cultural group.[1]

Yet another set of distortions occurs if one adopts the perspective of the Protestants who went through the Irish revolution and stayed on in the new Ireland. Many of these people were so pathetically grateful not to have been totally decimated that they fell over themselves in the 'twenties and 'thirties expressing their gratitude to the new government. Did they really have that much to fear? Definitely. They were, for the most part, on the losing side. Most of them had opposed home rule, much more the dominion status which was won through violent revolution.

Further, there was only a handful of Protestants among the revolutionary leaders. Whereas Protestants had acted in leadership roles in almost all of the unsuccessful risings from 1798 onwards, and whereas the unsuccessful home rule movement had been founded by Isaac Butt and led by Charles Stewart Parnell, both Protestants, the successful revolution of 1918–21 was nearly devoid of Protestants at the top. Second, the Protestants were threatened by the racialist tones implicit in Irish nationalism. To be Irish in nationalist rhetoric was to be Celtic, and this was in direct antithesis to everything foreign and especially to everything British, the very culture from which the Protestants drew their nourishment and to which most traced their ancestry. Thus the notorious "ban" by the Gaelic athletic association, a premier nationalist organization, on those who played "foreign games" such as rugby, soccer football, and cricket effectively excluded almost all Protestants from membership.[2] Similarly, most Protestants found it impossible to affirm the Celtic cultural values of the language revival movement, another central nationalist body. (That Douglas Hyde, founder of the Gaelic league, was Protestant tells us a great deal about Hyde, but almost nothing about Protestants in general.) Such affirmations were especially difficult for Protestants because the assertion of the value of Celtic culture implied a denigration of their own, British culture. The Gaelic league's policy, "the de-anglicization of Ireland," may not originally have been meant to derogate British culture, but from it grew the defamatory epithets of "shoneen" and "west Briton" for those who were not Gaelophiles.[3] Third, the nationalist equation which so frightened Protestants went further than merely to equate political acceptability with Gaelic culture and Celtic racial stock; it also associated being Irish with being Catholic. Before the revolution this equation was made mostly by negation: a common rhetorical device was to refer to the centuries of English domination and to the horrors of the penal code of the eighteenth century when both the true Irish people and Holy Mother Church were trod upon by Ireland's enemies. The invisible word was "Protestant" enemies and two equations were formulated: "British = Protestant = foe and Irish = Catholic = friend." As discussed in the preceding chapter, after the revolution this equation was enshrined in the preamble to the 1937 constitution.[4]

Many of the reasons for Protestant fears were to a great extent abstract, but the outrages perpetrated upon the Protestant population in the years 1920–23 were concrete events. Most of the outrages consisted of burnings of Protestant homes, but murders also occurred. One tally found that between 6 December 1921 and 22 March 1923 there were 192 houses and residences burned as part of widespread violence directed chiefly at the Protestant minority. Nearly all the counties were affected; only Queen's (Leix) and Carlow escaped. Protestants in Tipperary were especially savaged, and the county Leitrim saw an efficient and regular crusade against Protestant farmers which in mid-1922 sent them pouring into Enniskillen in Northern Ireland.[5] For reasons that are obvious, these ugly activities have been almost totally ignored by Irish nationalist historians who have preferred to concentrate their attention on the attacks of Belfast Protestants upon Catholics. Actually, the actions in both north and south are of a piece in two ways. First, and most important, they were the product of the same viciously sectarian spirit. The chief difference was that sectarian persecution in the north of Ireland occurred within a concentrated geographic area and with more evenly balanced opposition forces, and therefore was more visible and spectacular, whereas the southern violence was sporadic and geographically scattered and perpetrated against a weaker minority, with the result that the southern outrages drew scant attention. But hate is hate. Second, some of the outrages perpetrated against the southern Protestants were legitimated on the grounds that they allegedly approved the Belfast sectarian riots.[6] Of course it is possible to claim that the southern outrages were not directed at the Protestants as a religious group, but as loyalists, but that is to make a distinction without a difference; Protestantism, as discussed earlier, was a matrix of religious, social, and political characteristics and to attack Protestants on any level was perforce to attack the entire constellation.[7]

Faced with threats to their continued existence as a social and religious group, in May 1922, the members of the general synod of the Church of Ireland resident in the twenty-six counties delegated the archbishop of Dublin, John A. F. Gregg, and Sir William Goulding to interview the provisional government of Ireland "in order to lay before them the dangers to which Protestants in the twenty-six counties are daily exposed."[8] These two deputies cringed before the head of the new provisional government, Michael Collins. So sad was their position that they seriously asked "to be informed if they were permitted to live in Ireland or if it was desired that they should leave the country."[9] Collins promised to employ all the energies of the provisional government to prevent the further persecution of Protestants,[10] but the Protestants hardly can have been convinced that success would greet these efforts. Only slightly later a Protestant deputation waited on Winston Churchill, who as secretary of state for the colonies was assigned responsibility for the provisional government of Ireland, with a memorial stating that "it seems miraculous that up to this [sic] all the Protestants and loyalists have not been massacred. It is a moral certainty that they will be in the future."[11]

Actually, the provisional government made a reasonable effort to keep faith with the Protestant minority. On the military level the government was able to limit the violence against Protestants directly as it was able to overcome the militant republican forces in the civil war. On the political level, the provisional government honoured the spirit of undertakings which had been given the Protestants previous to the signing of the Anglo-Irish Treaty in late 1921. Arthur Griffith had promised them that the Free State would have a bicameral legislature with a restricted upper house in which they would be well represented, and that the upper house would have sufficient legislative powers to protect minority rights.

Although the Protestant leaders were disquieted to find that the Senate as actually established had only 270 days' legislative delaying power, they were gratified by the government's choice of senators. In appointing the thirty members to the first senate (thirty of the sixty members of the first senate were to be nominated by the government, the other thirty chosen by the Dail), the government nominated sixteen persons who previously had been unionist in their sympathies.[12] As the *Church of Ireland Gazette* reported, the "southern Protestants have every reason to be satisfied with the nominations which President Cosgrave has made to the first Free State senate."[13] Implicitly a bargain was sealed with the new government: the government did its best to protect Protestant lives and political rights and in return the Protestants became clients of the new regime.

But the Protestants as a group were now as broken reeds. The Irish situation in 1922–23 was so debilitating that they lost their ability to operate as an effective political bloc. The campaign of intimidation, murder, and arson speeded the pace of Protestant emigration and weakened the determination of those who previously had been engaged in political activities. Hence, the pre-revolutionary unionist organization failed to become the nucleus of a conservative party in the new state.[14]

As indicated in the following tables, the Protestant portion of southern Ireland's population continually declined:[15]

Southern Irish Population 1911–1961

YEAR	TOTAL POPULATION	ROMAN CATHOLIC	CHURCH OF IRELAND	PRESBYTERIAN	METHODIST	JEWISH	BAPTIST	OTHER AND NO INFORMATION
1911 (26 counties)	3,139,688	2,812,509	249,535	45,486	16,440	3,805	1,588	10,325
1926	2,971,992	2,751,269	164,215	32,429	10,663	3,686	717	9,013
1936	2,968,420	2,773,920	145,030	28,067	9,649	3,749	715	7,290
1946	2,955,107	2,786,033	124,829	23,870	8,355	3,907	462	7,651
1961	2,818,341	2,673,473	104,016	18,953	6,676	3,255	481	11,487

Southern Irish Population Percentages 1911–1961

YEAR	% ROMAN CATHOLIC	% NON-ROMAN CATHOLIC
1911	89.6	10.4
1926	92.6	7.4
1936	93.4	6.6
1946	94.3	5.7
1961	94.9	5.1

The reasons for this decline appear to have been threefold. First, the withdrawal of the British garrison and its associated personnel produced unusually heavy emigration in the 1920s. Second, Protestant marriages had unusually low marital fertility, doubtless due to the practice of birth control. Indeed, the Protestant birth rate was so low in the years 1946–61 (the only inter-census period for which comprehensive data are available) that it did not equal the death rate, let alone offset mortality and emigration combined. Third, the contracting of mixed marriages, especially by Protestant men, had a serious impact because of the Catholic church's insistence that the off-spring of such marriage be raised Catholic. An estimate based on 1961 census data indicated that approximately thirty percent of all Protestant grooms and twenty percent of Protestant brides married Catholics.[16]

Not surprisingly, the ever-shrinking Protestant minority lapsed into a passive clientship to the new state. "Now on the defensive, the minority became intensely aware of their isolation and withdrew into a kind of ghetto. A ghetto can be just as much a state of mind as a physical locality and . . . the most striking characteristic of the minority in the twenties and thirties, is the persistence of precisely this ghetto mentality."[17]

Here let us leave generalities and turn to the specifics of the educational system. Obviously a shrinkage in the overall Protestant population implied a significant shrinkage in the number of Protestant children of school age:[18]

YEAR	TOTAL NUMBER OF NON-CATHOLIC PUPILS ON PRIMARY SCHOOL ROLLS
1926	27,213
1936	19,478
1946	14,237
1961	13,030

Considered denominationally, in terms of percentages on the school rolls, the contraction was as follows (1929 is the first year for which these statistics are conveniently available):[19]

YEAR	CHURCH OF IRELAND	PRESBY- TERIAN	METH- ODIST	OTHER	ROMAN CATHOLIC
1929	3.54%	0.78%	0.16%	0.17%	95.34%
1936	3.01	0.67	0.14	0.16	96.02
1946	2.33	0.53	0.13	0.12	96.89
1961	1.98	0.39	0.11	0.10	97.42

These demographic losses must be juxtaposed with the fact that the Irish Protestants, no less than the Irish Catholics, desired segregated schools. In 1930, the *Church of Ireland Gazette* noted that many changes in education had been wrought by the Free State government, "but in all essentials it remains as it was, . . . denominational education with a conscience clause. . . . On the whole our people of all religious bodies are fairly satisfied with it."[20] Clearly, the continuing affirmation of the need to maintain separate schools for Protestant children, when combined with the continual shrinkage of the Protestant youth population, could produce only one result: a predominance of small and uneconomic Protestant schools, especially in the rural areas.

The Irish government responded to the Protestants' problems by reaffirming the principles of denominational education but in a very generous manner. Special rules were framed allowing the minority to operate schools with fewer children on the rolls than was permitted for the Catholic majority. In the 'fifties, for example, the Department of Education normally required a minimum average daily attendance of twenty pupils for a primary school to be "recognized" and thus eligible for a state grant. In cases where children of the minority could not find a religiously acceptable national school within a convenient distance from their home if the rule were applied, the average daily attendance requirement was lowered to ten pupils. And once recognized, a school's average attendance actually had to fall below seven pupils for two successive calendar years before the state grant was withdrawn.[21]

This governmental generosity reinforced the tendency for Protestant schools to be small, inadequate, one-teacher institutions, even while it simultaneously relieved some of the dangers to the religious identity of the Protestant children. In 1942–43, for instance, there were 573 Protestant-managed primary schools; 400 of which were one-teacher schools with seven to thirty pupils in average attendance.[22] Or, to take a later date, 1962–63, one finds that although Protestant children represented less than three percent of the children on the rolls, nine percent of all elementary schools were Protestant. Further, Protestant schools accounted for almost half of those schools with less than twenty-five pupils, but for less than one percent of schools with one hundred or more pupils on the rolls. Whereas the average pupil/teacher ratio for Catholic primary schools was one to thirty-five, there were only twenty pupils on the roll for each teacher in the Protestant primary schools.[23] Admittedly, as discussed in Chapter Six, small one-teacher schools tended to be old, poorly equipped, and educationally obsolete, but the favourable teacher/pupil ratio in the Protestant schools must have gone some way to overcoming these physical disadvantages.

Further evidence of the liberality to the Protestants as a religious minority by the Irish government — and indirectly by the Catholic population which composed the bulk of the government's constituency — was the special programme for transporting Protestant children to primary schools which otherwise would have been too far from their homes for them to attend. In order to preclude the possibility of Protestant or Jewish children being forced to attend a Catholic school, the Compulsory Attendance Act of 1926 had excused from its provisions children to whom a national school of appropriate religious persuasion was not accessible.[24] This exclusion, however, was only a stop-gap and it obviously was desirable that all Irish children attend a school compatible with their parents' religious convictions. Estimates varied, but in the early 'thirties somewhere between 1,000 and 1,500 Protestant children lived too far from the nearest Protestant primary school for them to be able to attend unless special transportation arrangements were made.[25] Transporting these children to a school some distance from their home would be expensive: an informed estimate in 1932 was that it would cost £10,000 a year, and the church at that time was allocating only £1,500 to the task.[26] Accordingly, in the late 'twenties the Anglican general synod through its Board of Education began pressing the government for aid.[27] Meetings between Anglican representatives and the minister for education took place in 1929[28] and continued thereafter at intervals, but it was not until May 1934 that progress was made towards a solution of the difficulties.[29] Under a plan initiated 1 July 1934 the Department of Education, which was already operating van and boat services for children on islands or in extremely isolated rural areas, expanded the programme to cover Protestant children who lived far from a Protestant school. The department paid £5 a head each year to the representative body of the Church of Ireland. Thirty-six Protestant transport schemes were introduced the first year, the minimum contribution guaranteed by the government being set at £1,500 a year.[30] In subsequent years it became the practice to state that "grants were allowed to an extent of fifty percent of the total cost of the scheme," but this annually-repeated phrase was misleading, for although the state contributions increased, the total contribution usually was limited to a specific maximum amount and in practice this was well under the fifty percent line. For example, the Church of Ireland's Board of Education reported that for the year 1938–39 the total cost of transporting their children was somewhat over £8,000. Of this amount nearly £7,000 was engaged in transport schemes operated jointly with the Department of Education, but the state's contribution was £2,825, closer to one-third than one-half of the costs.[31] Undeniably the state's grants kept alive many small Protestant schools which otherwise would have been extinguished. Quite properly, the Protestants were grateful. A striking expression of gratitude came from Thomas Harvey, bishop of Cashel, who said at the annual synod of his diocese in 1939, that "I would like to pay the warmest possible tribute to our government for the more than generous way in which they have treated us and met our desire to keep our schools open. No British government treated us with like consideration."[32]

But stop. While recognizing that the preceding piece of educational history reflects genuine toleration in the Irish social character, this quality should be recognized for what it was, no more, no less. It was toleration of the Protestants as a *religious* minority. It was toleration which involved no risk for the Catholic majority. Aiding the Protestants in supporting their own denominational schools followed from the theological and social assumptions of Catholic educational orthodoxy, namely that all education was essentially religious education and that children should be religiously segregated in their schooling. As a key to the great complexity of the Protestant position in Irish society, we can turn to a segment of Irish educational history wherein the Catholics generally and the state specifically, are shown to have been cruelly insensitive to the minority viewpoint. This will lead us to the apparently paradoxical conclusion that the Protestants were tolerated and well treated as a religious minority but were penalized and ill-treated as a *cultural* minority.

Of all the governmental changes of the period, "the measure which aroused most resentment among members of the Church of Ireland during the 1920s was the introduction of compulsory Irish in schools."[33] Despite the highly publicized enthusiasm of a few Protestant language revivalists, most notably Douglas Hyde and Ernest Blythe, the overwhelming majority of Irish Protestants found the compulsory revival of the language incompatible with their own cultural and educational principles. It is almost a truism to say that the Protestant resistance to the compulsory Irish programme in the schools was an inevitable corollary of their strong affirmation of English language culture, but that is indeed the heart of the matter. Three aspects of their commitment bear note. In the first place the Protestants were committed to resisting incursions on their culture because their basic religious documents and formularies long had been associated with the English tongue. A special report to the representative body of the Church of Ireland stated that "representations should be made that as English is the language of the Bible and Prayer Book and church services for the vast majority of our children, any deterioration in the standard of English hurts us from the religious point of view."[34] This was not to say that there was an absolute doctrinal incompatibility between the use of the Irish language and Protestant religious formularies (there were after all Irish language editions of the Prayer Book and Bible), but that there were strong cultural associations between Protestantism and the English language and an attack on the latter was viewed perforce as an attack on the former.

Second, and more important, the Protestant community believed in the supremacy of English language culture, especially literature, and in the value of English as an international linguistic currency. The Reverend Dudley Fletcher, an Anglican clergyman, voiced the general conviction when, in a reply to the harangues of a language enthusiast, he said that, "to deprive our children of their priceless inheritance of the English language as their vernacular — the most effective means of communication in the world — and to substitute for it a language which is useless for all practical purposes, is a policy which we will resist by every means in our power."[35] If we recall here F. S. L. Lyons' point that the Irish Protestants felt themselves surrounded by a hostile culture and that they therefore tended to shrink into ghettos of the mind, then the intensity of their concern for keeping in close contact with the international linguistic and literary network formed by the English language becomes understandable. English was their cultural lifeline and the bulwark of their collective identity.

The third point about the Protestants' affirmations of the primacy of English cultural patterns is that in so doing they were affirming the integrity of their families. As established in Chapter Three, the programme of compulsory Irish was based on American precedents and was an attempt to drive a linguistic wedge between parents and children (whether for worthy and sufficient reasons or not is irrelevant at this point). Such a policy of linguistic divisiveness was no threat to the Catholic majority, which was as secure socially in the new Ireland as Gibraltar is geologically secure in the Mediterranean. But it was easy for the Protestant community, locked into a ghetto mentality, to view this policy as a danger to the Protestant family and thus to their community. Hence, there was considerable Protestant concern when the second national programme conference of 1926 removed the safeguard proposed by the first conference which had promised that if the majority of the parents of the children in a school objected to having either Irish or English taught as an obligatory subject, their wishes would be honoured.[36]

Admittedly, some Protestant opposition to the Irish language revival was based on prejudice against the Catholic majority, an attitude all the more reprehensible in the eyes of the language revivalists because it often was elegantly expressed. That quintessential Protestant snob John Pentland Mahaffy, provost of Trinity College, Dublin, from 1914–19, set a tone sometimes imitated and often remembered in the leaner days of the Free State. As an investigator for the Endowed Schools Commission of 1879 Mahaffy reported that under the rules of the Irish Intermediate Education Commission, "boys spend every leisure moment and even part of their proper school time, in learning little text-books on natural science, music, and even Irish, to the detriment of their solid progress," words circulated widely when quoted in the *Irish Essays of* Matthew Arnold.[37] The Gaelic league made great play with Mahaffy's testimony on intermediate education wherein a central bit of dialogue ran:

Chairman: Now, Celtic is of course a very interesting study from a philological point of view:

Mahaffy: Yes.

Chairman: In your opinion, viewing it as a living language, has it any educational value?

Mahaffy: None.

Mahaffy   [later qualifying his previous answer]: It is sometimes useful to a
man fishing for salmon or shooting grouse in the west. I have
often found a few words very serviceable.[38]

The same condescending tones characterized the contentious statement
made by an Anglican clergyman in 1923 that the goal of substituting Irish
for English as the vernacular of the Free State was comparable to substituting "bows and arrows for rifles in the army, for the sentimental reason
that these were the weapons of the Irish nation in days gone by."[39] The
same implication, that the Irish language was primitive and contemptible,
was found in the well publicized 1938 speech of the headmaster of Bishop
Foy School, Waterford, in which he claimed that the present overemphasis on Irish in education was rapidly driving the country into illiteracy; that no increase in natural Irish had been noticeable in the last
fifteen years; and that, in what he apparently believed was an apt analogy,
the Australian aboriginal tongue had done little for the culture or nationality of the bushmen.[40]

But for each bit of snobbery indulged in by Protestants, one could quote
a nasty bit of barracking from the language revivalists. While the echoes
of Mahaffy had the ring of fantasy, harking back to the days of Protestant
supremacy, the tough words of Frank Fahy, former revolutionary Dail
official and now secretary of a major Gaelic organization, had the harsh
ring of reality when found in the letter page of the *Church of Ireland
Gazette.* "Do you desire that your church should stand in opposition to
the national will, that it should deny Ireland's nationhood?" he asked.
Then do not stand in the way of the language revival.[41] The threat
implicit in this sort of message was too obvious to be ignored, and instead
of escaping in snobbish fantasy, most Protestant authorities showed themselves willing to follow a realistic policy of cooperating in the language
revival, but attempting to modify its more extreme tendencies. Even the
Reverend Dudley Fletcher, who was constantly writing and speaking
against the government programme, admitted that Irish should have a
place in the school programmes, two or three hours a week being his
suggestion.[42] Protestants generally came to accept the necessity for studying Irish, but continued to oppose what they felt was compulsory overemphasis on the subject. An editorial in the *Church of Ireland Gazette*
(30 May 1941) reflected the general position: "That Irish children should
be encouraged to study the language which was once spoken throughout
the country is only wise, but that a knowledge of a nearly dead tongue
should be made a *sine qua non* of education seems strange. Surely those

who urge such a policy should be compelled to produce overwhelming reasons in its favour."

On some specific points the government responded sympathetically to Protestant grievances. For example, the Protestants found it extremely difficult to meet the requirements of the second national programme that Irish be taught in all primary schools for an hour daily to each pupil, that is for an hour daily to every class or combination of classes. This related to the preponderance of one-teacher schools. In such a school, under the regulation, two to three hours of the teacher's time would be given to teaching Irish and a reasonable standard could not be achieved in other subjects. When a Protestant delegation called this point to the attention of the minister for education, Professor O'Sullivan, he modified the regulation to require only one-half hour of oral instruction and the second half hour to be spent in the silent study of Irish at the pupils' desks, thus leaving the teacher free to teach other subjects.[43]

The government also was sympathetic but not entirely successful in dealing with Protestant fears about the content of Irish language texts. The fears of some Protestants concerning the textbooks stemmed from the conviction that the Irish language was conducive to Catholicism and inimical to Protestantism. This idea was not quite as strange as it might at first seem to an outsider. As a native tongue the Irish language never had been the language of a significant number of Protestants, which is to say that as a tongue, in so far as it was influenced by any religion, it was moulded by the Catholic faith. Several basic phrases encapsulated Catholic doctrines: the customary Gaelic greeting invoked not only God but the Blessed Virgin as well, and numerous phrases reflected Catholic dogma concerning saints and the after-life. It is within this context that one should read statements such as the following: "The recent craze for Irish, which many Roman Catholic laymen deprecate as much as we, is looked upon as a hopeful expedient, chiefly because thereby unwary Protestants are familiarized with Roman ways of thought."[44] The most clearly argued statement of this position was penned by the Reverend A. A. Luce, a fellow of Trinity College, Dublin. Luce was a man of considerable standing in the Anglican community, who eventually became a full professor at Trinity and Chancellor of St. Patrick's Cathedral, Dublin. He wrote:

Reluctantly, I have come to the conclusion that [compulsory Irish] . . . is a measure of state proselytism and Protestants must fight it on religious grounds; the language movement once it gets beyond the *a chara* stage, becomes a cultural movement. . . . I venture to predict that in a hundred years time half the Protestant population of the Free State will be converted to Roman Catholicism if the policy of compulsory Irish goes through.

The minister of education the other day spoke of his policy as controlled by a "one-nation theory." We have every reason to take that as equivalent to a "one-religion" theory.[45]

That most Protestants did not accept the idea that the Irish language policy was by intent a covert to Romanize them[46] does not obviate the fact that many of the Irish language textbooks did contain material which on religious grounds was offensive to Protestant sensibilities. In 1922, the Anglican Board of Education reported that numerous expressions had been found in the Irish language textbooks which contained Catholic doctrines; the board also reported, however, that when a delegate had called this to the attention of Professor MacNeill, the minister for education, he agreed to the omission from the lessons of anything which did not accord with Protestant teaching.[47] The southern Ireland subcommittee of the Presbyterian Board of Education had much the same report to make to its parent body two years later: "In many of the reading books in Irish expressions occur which imply acceptance of distinctive Roman Catholic doctrine," but the Department of Education was willing to make arrangements to meet the difficulty.[48] Despite the apparent willingness of the state officials to respond to Protestant difficulties, as late as 1951 a sub-committee of the Anglican Board of Education reported that no series of readers, either in Irish or English, as specified on the Department of Education list, was wholly acceptable to Church of Ireland authorities.[49]

But in noting that the state authorities often were flexible in dealing with Protestant complaints about the details of the language revival movement, one should not obscure the overriding fact that on the basic issue of whether or not massive amounts of school time should be devoted to the compulsory revival of the tongue, an unbridgeable gap existed between the state officials and most Protestants. One evidence of how great the cultural chasm was is indicated by the fact that an increasing proportion of Protestant parents preferred to send their children to be educated outside the Free State rather than have them lose ground in English language and classical subjects, a loss which the new emphasis upon Irish necessarily implied. The Protestant school heads recognized this situation and one of the pragmatic reasons for their opposing compulsory Irish was that they stood to lose pupils to the English schools.[50] The Church of Ireland's Board of Education found that also there was a tendency for parents of older children to transfer them to secondary schools in Northern Ireland if they lived near enough to the border to be able to do so conveniently.[51]

Another dimension of the cultural gap between the Protestant minority and the government concerned not the substance of the revival, but the style of its inauguration. The political style of the minority, grounded as it was in British parliamentary democracy, dictated that major governmental decisions should be reached only after deliberation and only by democratic means. But, as discussed in Chapter Two, the political reflexes of the new Irish government were markedly authoritarian. Further, in the matter of the Irish language revival the operant mythology of the nationalist movement precluded consideration of the possibility that Irishmen might not favour language revival by radical compulsion. Thus, when the editors of the *Church of Ireland Gazette* expressed their objection to the imposition of the language programme in 1922 by administrative fiat and without any mandate from the country[52] they were acting from assumptions about the nature of the governing process which were inapplicable in the new Ireland. When the warden of St. Columba's, the Reverend C. B. Armstrong, challenged the government to subject the question of compulsory Irish in the secondary schools to a public referendum[53] (a feasible procedure under the Free State constitution), he was equally out of touch with the authoritarian nature of the dominant political culture. So too was James MacManaway, bishop of Clogher, when he complained that it wasn't "fair" to force Irish on those who did not want it and "who will only submit to it as part of their curriculum because they are powerless to shake it off."[54]

Official bodies representing the Protestant churches were not at all reticent in stating their disenchantment. In 1925, awaiting the appearance of the second national programme, the Presbyterian church's Free State education subcommittee reported, dryly, that "it is hoped that this programme will bring within proper educational limits the time and energy now given to the teaching of Irish,"[55] a statement which stands either as an example of ironic wit or of naive optimism. But there was neither irony nor optimism in the formal resolution of the general synod of the Church of Ireland in 1936 endorsing the view that for children from English-speaking homes the regulations enforcing the use of Irish in the infant schools "are harmful to the education of the infant and tend to stunt rather than foster infant mental development."[56]

To the Protestant minority, schooled in the British political tradition that major state policies should be based on the foundation of investigatory commissions, empirical evidence, and thick blue-books, it long had been a scandal that there was no evidence about the educational effect of the Irish language programme, and that the Department of Education seemed determined to avoid generating any. In the general synod of 1938 some members pressed for a resolution asking for a governmental investigation,[57] but instead the churchmen followed the more productive approach of commissioning their own board of education to garner information from teachers in Protestant primary schools (the similarity to the I.N.T.O. investigatory technique is obvious). The preliminary analysis of the data, presented in 1939, was brutal. First, it was found that the primary school curriculum had been restricted in an undesirable fashion by the exclusion of some subjects of a practical or cultural value, such as domestic economy and drawing. Why the exclusion? The answer was implied in point number two, that except in schools where the teacher and pupils all were of super-normal capacity the development of the pupils has been retarded by intensive teaching of Irish, and more particularly by teaching through Irish. Third, if teachers desired to maintain the intellectual standard of their work, an increased strain was placed upon them by the Irish language programme and that strain produced an undesirable tension in educational relationships. Fourth, it was found that in many cases teachers' salaries, especially those of experienced teachers, were seriously affected by their not having certain qualifications in Irish. (This problem affected all national teachers but was especially painful to the Protestants since there was no significant indigenous Irish language tradition in their community.) The report's fifth point noted that despite all the language revival efforts no progress was being made in making the tongue a living language used outside of school hours. Sixth, despite their having taken up Irish, the Protestant children had not benefited by any increase in scholarships or employment as distinct from the normal opening which always had been available. Finally, the report affirmed, as a result of the language policy, that there was a definite tendency for parents to remove their children from the state-connected primary schools and to send them either to independent primary schools or to schools in Northern Ireland.[58]

These findings concerning the effect of the revival upon Protestant children were remarkably similar to those of the I.N.T.O. study which was conducted at about the same time and which surveyed the entire primary school system, Protestant and Catholic. (On the I.N.T.O. report see Chapter Three.) However, although the effects of the compulsory language revival were essentially identical in educational terms for Protestants and Catholics, they were radically different in cultural terms. Whereas it was possible for many Catholic parents to feel that the educational loss in most school subjects was in part or whole compensated for by the induction of their children into linguistic patterns which once had been part of their ancestral culture, this compensatory belief was barred to most Protestants because they looked to Great Britain for their cultural antecedents.[59] That Protestants and Catholics were operating within totally different cultural frameworks in evaluating the value of the language programme becomes clear when one considers three facts: that during the period under discussion (1920–60) no body of Catholic parents of any significance came out against the language revival programme; that the only group comprised chiefly of Catholics which lodged a protest was the I.N.T.O., and its objections were those of professional educators opposing the educational retardation caused by the revival programme; that, in marked contrast, the Church of Ireland, as representative of the bulk of southern Irish Protestants, continued to articulate and document its disenchantment with the entire range of effects of the language revival programme, educational, social, and cultural.[60]

The final report of the Protestant language study, published in 1942, indicated that in addition to the influences on the primary schools, the rather milder revival programme in the secondary schools also had had seriously deleterious educational effects.[61] Increasingly, government secondary school regulations placed the Protestants in a bind on the Irish issue. Protestant parents always had the alternative of sending their children to Great Britain or to Northern Ireland if there was too much time "wasted" on the subject. Yet, government regulations became ever more strict, forcing more and more attention to the language. From mid-1932 onwards it was required that all pupils in secondary schools had to take Irish if they were to be recognized for grant purposes, a decree which forced the Protestant headmasters to choose between the cruel knife of decreased grants or the hard steel of decreased enrollments because of parental disapproval. In 1925 a pass in Irish was required if a student were to receive his intermediate school certificate and in 1934 it became compulsory for obtaining the leaving certificate. The decree that a failure in Irish meant failure in the entire examination was especially hard on the Protestant schools which as a group were weak in the subject. In the 1950s the Anglican church's Board of Education tried to convince the Council of Education that the policy was educationally dysfunctional but to no avail.[62] In response to the council's report, which recommended no change in this matter, the church's Board of Education charged that it was contrary to the spirit of the constitution "that English should be put in a position of inferiority in that it is neither a compulsory subject nor a prerequisite for passing the certificate examination [s]."[63]

Even for those pupils who were well above the pass-line in secondary school Irish the scoring system seemed biased, for as noted in Chapter Three, much more credit was given to the Irish language than to English and more to Irish literature than to English literature. In addition there were bonus points for writing answers in various papers in Irish. This discrimination hurt those Protestant pupils who came from families of slender means and who needed to win a scholarship based on one of the certificate examinations in order to continue their schooling. There is no evidence that this discrimination against Protestants was conscious, but one can see how members of the minority could have interpreted it as such. In this regard, the words of John Pentland Mahaffy, expressed in 1916, served as a prophetic key to Protestant perceptions:

Mahaffy frankly admitted that when the Protestants were in the ascendancy they treated the Catholics unfairly, and that what they now dreaded was the "tit for tat policy," this "so-called redressing of the balance which generally means to make good one injustice by doing another." As an example of what the Protestants were afraid of he referred to "the making of the dying and impracticable Irish language or rather a smattering of it, of no value to anyone, a condition of county council scholarships. Do you imagine it was done really from patriotism? Not a bit of it. It was done to exclude the Protestant schools of the country from competition."[64]

Implicitly, the scheme introduced in 1924 of bonus grants for secondary school teaching through Irish discriminated further against Protestant schools. Probably some Protestant schools could earn the minimum two and one-half percent grant for teaching one subject other than Irish through the medium, but it was inconceivable that very many ever would reach the ten percent bonus grant for teaching as much through Irish as through English, and, as the *Church of Ireland Gazette* noted (20 June 1924), they never could get the twenty-five percent grant for teaching all subjects through the medium.

Whether from conscious prejudice or merely from unintended cultural blindness, the officials of the Irish state were unable to perceive what the Protestants had at stake in the language issue and that the survival of the minority depended not merely upon religious toleration but upon cultural toleration as well. Far from being sympathetic to the idea of cultural pluralism, many Irish politicians and state officials tried to tread the anglophone serpent under their heel. One of the foremost of these attackers was Thomas Derrig whom Eamon de Valera appointed minister for education in 1932. Derrig, it will be recalled, felt that the language revival had been carried on too gently and he therefore invoked strict new regulations to accelerate the campaign (see Chapter three). He was especially irritated by any hint of Protestant obstinancy on the language issue and tried to prosecute recusants in the Free State's courts. Under the terms of the 1926 Compulsory Attendance Act, a child had to attend a "national or other suitable school."[65] What was a suitable school? It was a school certified as suitable by the minister for education: "The minister may if and when he so thinks fit by a certificate in the prescribed form certify any particular school to be a suitable school within the meaning of this act for the attendance of children to whom this act applies for the purpose of receiving elementary education, and the minister may at any time as and when he thinks fit revoke any such certificate."[66] And how was the minister to decide if a school deserved a certificate of suitability? He was, the next sub-clause said, to make whatever reasonable inquiries, investigations, and inspections he thinks proper. But what should he investigate? The act did not say. In other words, it lay down no criteria of suitability whatsoever!

Derrig saw this legal vacuum as an opportunity to move against those parents who preferred to send their children to English-language private schools rather than to the national schools. In 1934 Derrig had his department bring a test prosecution against the parents of certain children who attended a private preparatory school in Enniscorthy, Co. Wexford. He charged them with being in violation of the compulsory school attendance law since the minister for education adjudged the school their children attended as unsuitable because the Irish language was not taught. The purpose of the prosecution was to obtain a judicial ruling that educational suitability automatically implied the necessity for Irish language study.[67] The district judge who had primary jurisdiction in the case ruled against the defendants. He admitted that the School Attendance Act did not expressly state that the teaching of Irish was obligatory, but added that since Irish was the national language he could not see how a school could be regarded as suitable if it did not teach the tongue. He fined the defendents a shilling but gave them liberty to appeal.[68] This they promptly did and at the circuit court level were heard and the appeal allowed. The appeal decision by Judge Devitt stated that nowhere in the

Attendance Act was Irish made compulsory and that the constitution of the Free State expressly recognized English as an official language equally with Irish.[69]

Thomas Derrig was not a man to forget a failure. Since the courts interpreted the law as defending minority linguistic rights, the law would have to be changed. Eventually, in 1942 he brought forward in the Dail a school attendance bill which would end the practices of those members of the minority who sent their children to private schools, or, worse yet, sent them abroad to be educated. The operative clauses were:

A child shall not be deemed for the purposes of this act to be receiving suitable education in a manner other than by attending a national school, a suitable school, or a recognised school unless such education and the manner in which such child is receiving it have been certified under this section by the minister as suitable.

The minister may, before giving such certificate in respect of a child, require such child to be submitted by his parent to such educational test at such time and place as the minster shall direct, and the minister may refuse to give such cerificate if such parent fails or refuses to submit such child.[70]

Thus, all children of Irish parents, whether educated inside or outside of the twenty-six counties, whether in private or state-aided schools, could be held to the same curriculum. During the debates on the bill Derrig disclaimed that the Irish language was the operative link in his mind in moving the bill, but that fooled no one, least of all the opposition.[71] In any case the taoiseach, Eamon de Valera, made it abundantly clear that promoting the Irish language was the point of the whole exercise: "If the state, regarding the matter from the point of view of the common good and of the interests of the citizens as a whole, says Irish ought to be, and is, a compulsory subject, and ought to form part of the minimum education that is given to the children, then I think that is perfectly good reason for doing this."[72] He continued with a passage which to an outsider seems shocking, equating as it does the adherence to minority cultural norms with uselessness within the Irish polity: "Supposing there are parents who, through prejudice or some other reason, are not going to give their children an opportunity of learning Irish and of fitting themselves to be useful members of the community; and if we take it that Irish is part of the state policy, and if we regard it as part of the equipment necessary for a good citizen—and if there are people who are likely to do that—then I think the minister would be entitled to say that we are going to close that gap."[73] The bill, which passed both houses of oireachtas without great difficulty, was a marked incursion upon civil rights. It was potentially repugnant to the clauses of the 1937 Irish constitution which defined the supreme rights of parents in educational matters and was also potentially in violation of basic civil rights, for as General Mulcahy (himself a language enthisiast) noted, "We are making it a crime for persons to send their children across the border to school without telling the police."[74] As a result of the constitutional issues, in late February 1943, Douglas Hyde, President of Ireland, referred the bill to the Supreme Court.[75] After deliberation the bill was found to be repugnant to the constitution. Consequently Hyde refused to sign it, and the whole matter dropped.[76]

It would be easy to shrug off this entire episode because, after all, the bill was voided and the Protestants were not hurt. But consider what had happened. The legislative representatives of the Irish people had indicated their approval of a measure which would have impaired the Protestants in exercise of what was to them a cherished civil right, namely the right to remain Irish citizens and still send their children to schools outside of the twenty-six counties. The taoiseach had made it clear verbally, and the legislature affirmed by its voting, that Irish nationality and cultural pluralism were incompatible concepts. The legislature and its leaders had attempted to limit the constitutional definition of parental rights in education to read, effectively, "Parental rights in educaton to be protected—except when exercised by Protestant parents who are not enthusiastic about the language revival."

An additional cause of Protestant discomfiture from the 'twenties through the 'forties was the absence of any representative governmental institution in the field of education. As discussed in Chapter Two the early Free State government was highly distrustful of any such agency and abolished both the commissioners of national and of intermediate education. Not until the early 1950s was an educational advisory council appointed and then only a tame one. Actually, the authoritarian style of educational administration did not affect the Protestants any more than it did the Catholics, but it was especially disquieting to the minority to have the independent primary and secondary school commissioners replaced by powerful bureaucrats who were not directly accountable to the citizens. To many Protestants this appeared "to be exchanging the safeguards of an oligarchy for the dangers of an autocracy . . . . We are familiar with the slaughter of the innocents, but this is the slaughter of the wise men."[77] Further, it was public knowledge that in dismissing the commissioners of national education, Patrick Bradley, chief civil servant for primary education, had implied that one of their failings was that their board had been too much under Protestant influence.[78]

Simultaneously the new government abandoned the former imperial policy of taking religious affiliation into account when appointing members of the educational civil service. Under this policy Protestants had been over-represented relative to their numbers in the population because many of the highest appointments were arranged in dual fashion, co-equal posts being held by members of the two faiths. Protestants began to fear they were being locked out of the educational branches of the civil service. "In the control of education," the bishop of Cashel complained in 1923, "we have not been given any representation whatsoever . . . . Inspectors, heads of departments have been appointed, and in no case that I am aware of has the minority received any recognition."[79] Because the Department of Education does not provide any public access to its records it is difficult to tell how justified this complaint was, but a reasonable evaluation would be as follows: that there probably was very little discrimination against Protestants *qua* Protestants in the appointment policy of the new educational service, but that there were very few Protestants appointed anyway. Why? Because even to this day the education service is the one department of the Irish civil service, aside from the Gaeltacht services, wherein the Irish language is used regularly in departmental communication and in which a high degree of Irish language facility is a functional, not merely a formal requirement. And this facility was something few Protestants were apt to have by the very nature of their cultural background. The operative point is that whatever the reality, many Protestants perceived their minority as being excluded from the corridors of educational power.

Given the handicaps, real and imagined, under which the Protestant educational establishment operated, it is not at all surprising that the minority had great difficulties in recruiting sufficient numbers of its young people to enter the teaching profession. This problem was a function of three specific factors and one general one. In the first place the requirement that students entering the teacher training colleges have a high level of Irish acted against children of Protestant background, making it difficult for them to do well on the qualifying examination for admission. In the early days of the Free State, the Department of Education's requirements were so high in the Irish language that a period of as much as five years' preparatory study probably was necessary for entrance, something clearly impossible for most Protestants, since Irish had been in most of their schools only a year or two before the new examination was introduced.[80] This threatened the existence of the only Protestant training college in the south, the Church of Ireland college, Kildare Place. Wisely, the Department of Education recognized the difficulty and allowed the admission of students with only one year of Irish language background.[81] But the problem was not a passing one. In 1931, the Reverend Canon Hodges, the Church of Ireland's chief spokesman on primary education, noted that in order to provide teachers for Protestant schools it still was necessary to admit to training students who did not meet the requisite standards of knowledge and intelligence. This was necessary, he said, partially because of the nature of the entrance examination and partly because of the generally deleterious effect of the intensive teaching of Irish in the schools.[82] The great educational panacea of the late 1920s and 'thirties, the recruiting of large numbers of teacher candidates from the Gaeltacht, did the Protestants little good since the population of the Gaeltacht was almost exclusively Catholic. Despite all the special programmes and even despite the shortage of regular employment opportunities during the depression of the 'thirties, the Protestant schools had great difficulty in finding efficient teachers of Irish.[83] It is not an accident that in the early 1960s, when all save one of the preparatory schools founded specially to produce fluent Irish speakers were closed, the one which the government kept was Colaiste Mobhi, the Protestant school.

A second cause of the shortage of Protestant teachers was related to the first. During the 1930s, new regulations were introduced withholding salary increments from teachers already in service who did not obtain certain levels of competence in Irish. Eventually, no teacher was recognized who was not minimally fluent in Irish. Such a rule encouraged wastage among existing teachers, although how much it is impossible to say.

Third, other Department of Education regulations were almost perfectly designed to cause a shortage of Protestant teachers. The departmental regulations virtually precluded the recognition of a teacher trained outside of Ireland or of one not fluent in oral Irish. Further, no recognition was given for teaching service in other countries, except in certain underdeveloped areas in Africa and South America, and in Northern Ireland.[84] But regarding Northern Ireland, the Board of Education of the Presbyterian church noted that secondary teachers "could not even come from Northern Ireland without heavy loss."[85] Thus, a perfect one-way conduit was established. Since many other countries in the English-speaking world recognized Irish qualifications and gave credit for teaching service in Ireland, the door was always open for Irish teachers to go elsewhere. But there was no reciprocal arrangement either for encouraging foreigners from other English-speaking countries to come to Ireland to be trained (the Irish language prerequisite was prohibitive) or for luring experienced teachers, either of Irish or foreign origin, to Ireland (the financial loss would be too great since all credit for seniority gained elsewhere would be lost). For the Protestants this situation was crippling, since it simultaneously cut them off from the Protestant English-speaking countries which might well have been a source of recruits, while the basically British cultural background of the minority meant that its young people would be particularly tempted to try their hand elsewhere in the British Isles or dominions—and once they had left to teach elsewhere the rules prevented their return save at considerable financial sacrifice.

The fourth and general reason for difficulty in recruiting teachers is impossible to quantify, but real nonetheless: many Protestant youths were convinced that there was no future for people of their outlook in the new Ireland. As can be inferred from the demographic figures cited earlier in this chapter, the Protestant emigration rate was much higher than that of the population as a whole. That the trend worried many of the older generation of Protestants is well indicated by a pamphlet which in the late 1950s the Church of Ireland directed at its young people. Entitled *Careers in Ireland,* it had one purpose: to convince the young Protestants that they could indeed live successfully in the land in which they were born, a point which was both true in the telling and illuminating in its urgency.[86]

Thus, from the 'thirties onward one finds evidence of serious shortages of Protestant teachers.[87] A survey published in 1965 revealed that in thirty-four Protestant secondary schools (of all Protestant denominations) on which full information was available, a total of 465 teachers were employed. One hundred and sixteen of these were Catholics.[88] In 1970 the Presbyterian Board of Education noted, almost plaintively, that "no Presbyterian male student has been trained as a national teacher in the last ten years."[89]

In charting the history of the Protestant minority in Ireland there is a great danger of propagating what aptly has been termed an "agreed lie."[90]

It is easy to overestimate the importance within the Protestant community of those atypical Protestants who, before independence, sided with the nationalist movement and those who after independence held positions of civic importance and cultural leadership. Actually most Protestants were at sea in a culture to which they were historically alien, and governed by a state which was in increasingly close alliance with their religious rivals.

The Protestants as a group in post-independence Ireland merit further study. If, as I would contend, we have in the Protestant educational experience a synecdoche of the Protestant experience throughout southern Irish society, then a full study of southern Protestantism will reveal that on all levels their relations with the dominant majority and its political representatives were extremely complex. As in the field of education one can expect to find that on some matters the Protestants were treated with great generosity, but that on others they were hectored, bullied, or ignored.

Undeniably, using education as a cultural mirror reveals some ugly scars on Kathleen's face, particularly the insensitivity to the Protestants' problems as a cultural minority. But, if I may here anticipate material in the concluding chapter, I am optimistic about the future. During the 'sixties there were unmistakable signs that the Protestants as a group had finally become confident of their position as Irish citizens. They began escaping from their self-imposed ghetto and asserting themselves. As they became more confident of themselves as Irish nationals, their objections to assimilating many components of the Irish cultural identity diminished greatly and their ability to reject those aspects of the general culture which they still would not assimilate was clearly established. Simultaneously, the culture of the dominant majority was becoming less parochial. Therefore the majority was less and less given to prescriptive formulas which defined anything associated with a foreign culture as a national danger. Accommodation, and toleration, was becoming the new tone. Blessedly, with time, Kathleen's scars seem to fade.

The Pauline Code

One afternoon, in idle curiosity, I tried to find how many primary schools in the Irish Free State and its successor, Eire, were co-educational, and how many single-sex. A simple question, seemingly, but one which I still could not answer after three months searching, two of that in Dublin. Something was decidedly odd here. This point became especially obvious when I juxtaposed the Department of Education's energetic willingness to broadcast the sex-breakdown of the academic secondary schools with its steadfast refusal to publish the same information for the elementary schools. It became clear that once again a simple direct question concerning the Irish school system had called to notice an easily-ignored aspect of the national countenance, in this case an uneasy nervous tick which had something to do with the relationship of the sexes.

But what? Obviously if the secondary school statistics could be spread abroad they presented a picture which at least was acceptable (if not necessarily desirable) to Irish society. Given below are the figures on academic secondary schools for representative years:[1]

YEAR	BOYS SCHOOLS	GIRLS SCHOOLS	CO-EDUCATIONAL SCHOOLS	TOTAL
1924-25	133	119	26	278
1930-31	137	132	31	300
1940-41	160	160	32	352
1950-51	186	192	46	424
1960-61	216	244	66	526

Now, assuming that during the years encompassed by this table, approximately one third of the co-educational schools were Protestant institutions,[2] it is clear that well under ten percent of the Catholic secondary schools were mixed, which is to say that the educational norm of the religious majority implied sexual segregation. And from this inference any alert social observer would guess that the reason the primary school statistics were never published is that they diverged signally from the national ideal.

Using extremely indirect means we can arrive at a reasonable speculation about the variance between the ideal of sexual segregation and the actual situation in the primary schools. Take the academic year 1962-63 as an example. There were in that year 1,440 Catholic schools whose average numbers of pupils on the rolls were below fifty; this of a total of 4,375 Catholic schools.[3] Departmental regulations required that a single-sex school had to become co-educational if the average number of pupils on the roll fell below forty. In the case of an existing co-educational school, it could be replaced by separate boys and girls schools only if the number of pupils in each was likely to be sixty or more.[4] Hence, one can justifiably take the number of schools with under fifty pupils on the rolls as the approximate *minimum* number of co-educational Catholic primary schools. The actual number, I would speculate, is probably twice this minimum figure, but even using the minimum figure one finds that almost one third of the Catholic-managed elementary schools failed to conform to the ideal of single-sex education. What held true in 1962-63 held true earlier. Indeed, the closer in time one goes towards the origins of the Free State, the greater the proportion which small, and presumably co-educational, schools bore to the total number of schools.[5]

The existence of a large number of co-educational primary schools was especially embarrassing because it produced geographic cleavages within the church. The overwhelming majority of small, presumably co-educational schools were in rural areas.[6] Purely on a demographic basis, then, one was most apt to find co-educational elementary schools in the far west and southwest and least likely to find them on the eastern seaboard. Demographic divergences were exacerbated by pastoral differences among the bishops. Whereas the bishops with rural dioceses for the most part found it possible to accept the pragmatic need for co-educational schools in sparse parishes, the Archbishop of Dublin, John Charles McQuaid, forbade co-education even in small primary schools throughout the Dublin archdiocese. Co-education was thus the only regional sin in Ireland.[7]

But can a norm from which there was so much deviation accurately be described as a norm? In this case, yes, for despite the necessity of individual bishops sanctioning co-educational schools in rural areas, the collective voice of the church was clear. Even before the new state was founded, the hierarchy had fought against amalgamation of primary schools, partially on the grounds, as stated in 1910, that "apart altogether from moral considerations, we believe that the mixing of boys and girls in the same school is injurious to the delicacy of feeling, reserve, and modesty of demeanour which should characterize young girls."[8] The bishops repeated this opinion at a special meeting in May 1926 resolving that: "mixed education [that is, co-education] in public schools is very undesirable, especially among the older children. We would suggest to the Government to endeavour to restrict the project of further amalgamation to cases where efficiency demands the change."[9]

The church's fear of co-education stemmed from its general concern with the sexual mores of the Irish people. During the 'twenties and 'thirties the bishops and clergy engaged in a long and nervous campaign against certain social practices which led, they believed, to sexual immorality. At a time when violence, social disorder, and poverty were common, the bishops' published statements dwelt chiefly on the alleged decline in sexual morality.[10] "Company keeping" was a fine old practice, but, said Archbishop Gilmartin of Tuam, "if company-keeping is an occasion of mortal sin there is no use in people going to confession if they do not mean to give it up."[11] If the old customs could lead to sin, the new ones were much worse. "The people who were engaged in the production of the cinema pictures were people without morality or religion for a very large part," entoned Thomas O'Doherty, Bishop of Galway. "The people of this town," he continued, "should show their indignation and should take measures that these people would not be allowed to make money at the price of the souls of the good boys and girls. . . ."[12] But most worrisome to the bishops were the new dances which spread after the Great War and which had the twin vices of being "foreign" and licentious. The equation of alien with immoral is well illustrated by a lenten pastoral of Edward Byrne, archbishop of Dublin, who stated: "suggestive dances imported from countries whose outlook is largely pagan, dances which give offence to the eyes of the onlookers, and . . . must often be a source of temptation to the performers, should be strictly banned by our Catholic people and discouraged at gatherings of clean-minded boys and girls."[13] Having obtained no satisfaction from his earlier efforts, in his 1925 lenten pastoral Bishop O'Doherty of Galway formally forbade Catholics in his charge to take part in Saturday night dances. Should this formal prohibition be ignored, he warned, he would make the offence a reserved sin, and if that was not sufficient he would "use the further powers which Christ and His Church have placed in my hands."[14] Finally the hierarchy as a group felt compelled to speak and issued a statement in the fall of 1925 which was read in all Irish Catholic churches. The bishops noted that "dancing halls, more especially, in the general uncontrol of recent years, have deplorably aggravated the ruin of virtue due to ordinary human weakness. They have brought many a good, innocent girl into sin, shame and scandal, and set her unwary feet on the road that leads to perdition."[15] The bishops further noted: "It is no small commendation of Irish dances that they cannot be danced for long hours . . . Irish dances are not to be put out of the place, that is their due, in any educational establishment under our care. They may not be the fashion in London or Paris. They should be the fashion in Ireland. Irish dances do not make degenerates."[16] (Belief in the natural relationship between Irish folk custom and sexual morality could be carried to strange extremes, as in the case of an Irish priest of long experience who gave as a reason for extending and preserving the use of Irish in church, that it was so much easier to speak plainly about the sixth commandment without shocking people if one used Irish!")[17]

While the bishops made pronouncements from the bench, local priests and curates energetically moved against anything which smacked of sensuality in their own parishes, a campaign which increased in intensity throughout the 'thirties and 'forties. John Whyte in *Church and State in Modern Ireland 1923-1970*, gives examples of these priestly activities, ranging from destruction of roadside dance platforms, to the smashing of concertinas, to the extraordinary effort of the county Monaghan priest who forced the local cinema manager to seat male and female patrons on opposite sides of the aisle.[18] Often moral vigilance societies were organized by the local clergy, such as that among the Catholic women of Limerick, the "Modest Dress and Deportment Crusade." Members were distinguished by the wearing of badges stamped with a cluster of silver lilies and the initials of their organization. The campaign spread in the west of Ireland and was so successful that Archbishop Gilmartin described it as a "national crusade."[19] Examples of this sort could be multiplied by the score.

The key point in understanding the popularity of the priestly crusades is to realize that they were not imposed upon a restive populace by an autocratic clergy, but that the morality campaigns fitted almost perfectly with the existing social framework and sexual code of the average Irishman. Irish society already was among the most sexually limited in the world. This characteristic would have held true even without the church's activities, for the economic customs and social practices which severely restricted sexual activity had little to do with theology. After the Great Famine of the 1840s the Irish adopted a pattern of agriculture whereby small holdings were passed on intact to one son, rather than subdivided among the entire family as in pre-Famine days. Obviously such a custom limited the opportunity for family-formation since only one son could count on acquiring the agricultural resources necessary to support a family. Other members of the family were extruded, often emigrating, or, in the case of unmarried sisters, spending an unpleasantly dependant spinsterhood. Even the son destined to inherit the farm was precluded from marrying until his parents finally decided to retire from active management of the holding, this often not occurring until the son was in his forties or fifties.[20] Thus, a high degree of voluntary celibacy and late marriage characterized Irish society. Throughout the period under study, 1922-60, southern Ireland had the lowest marriage rate in the western world. In 1951, for example, the census breakdown of people aged fifty-five to sixty-four showed that one of every three men and one of every four women had never been married, which is to say had spent their life in bachelor or spinsterhood. Among those who did marry, the average age of marriage was the highest in the western world: in 1946 it was somewhat over age thirty-three for men and twenty-eight for women.[21]

The Irish Catholic church's emphasis upon sexual purity dovetailed perfectly with the people's social and economic patterns. In his sermons the local curate articulated as moral virtues a code of sexual mores to which the people were committed through social usage. Simultaneously, he legitimated the restrictive sexual practices by fitting them into divine law, and by so doing he reinforced the people's belief in the necessity of severe sexual limitation.[22] The one area in which the church not only reinforced existing sexual patterns but introduced constraints of its own was in its banning of contraception. By morally proscribing contraception and making it virtually impossible to obtain birth control devices in all but the largest cities (and then only illegally) the church guaranteed that the limits Irish society set on marriage would be, mutatis mutandis, the effective limits on sexual activity. In a society wherein birth control techniques were widely disseminated it would be possible to have restrictions on marriage, but widespread sexual activity; not so if sexual activity inevitably meant a high risk of unwed pregnancy with all the economic and social penalties that implied.

Significantly, in the light of the preceding chapters' discussions of the intolerance of the cultural patterns of the Protestant minority, it is clear that the minority did not adhere to the same familial-sexual patterns as did the members of the dominant Catholic culture. The Protestant minority, having been economically privileged, did not undergo the same economic pressures which were fundamental to the formation of the Catholic familial-sexual code. Further, Protestant moral theology, although, far from libertarian, did not dwell upon sexual repression to anything near the same degree as Catholic theology. In addition, the pastoral tools of the Protestant cleric did not allow as close control over his flock as did those of the Catholic priest: in particular the absence of oral confession limited the ability of the Protestant rector to monitor the family and sexual life of his parishioners.

An analysis of the 1946 and 1961 censuses reveals that within each social class "non-Catholics" (the awkward census category which included Protestants and a sprinkling of Jews and atheists) tended to have fewer children per family than did Catholics.[23] In all probability this was because Protestants used birth control devices, a practice to which the last vestiges of theological opposition were removed by the 1930 Lambeth conference's approval of scientific birth control. Freedom from the tight economic constraints which had been crucial in determining the Catholic familial-sexual sructure, combined with an acceptance of birth control techniques, meant that the Protestants were freed from many of the sexual restrictions operant among the Catholic majority, although in the absence of an Irish Kinsey report, how much freer cannot be known.[24]

Protestants aside, the Pauline code was embraced both by laity and clergy of the majority and it is not surprising that after independence they used the new state to bulwark the accepted mores. For example, in 1929, a Censorship of Publications Act was passed, creating a government board which could prohibit the sale and distribution of any book considered obscene. In practice the board was nothing if not rigorous, banning from

Ireland hundreds and hundreds of books, including scores which have come to be recognized as modern classics. The same act made it a criminal offense to publish, sell, or distribute literature which advocated birth control. This 1929 Literary Censorship Act paralleled the intention, if not the precise structure, of a 1923 Dail measure that had established a national film censor who had the power to cut or ban films subversive of public morality. But controlling what the Irish people read in books or saw in the cinema was not enough for there were always misguided citizens, especially non-Catholics, who might not accept the culture's preference for strict monogamy. Although it had been extremely difficult to obtain a divorce in pre-independence Ireland (a private parliamentary bill was required), even this was too liberal and the new Cosgrave government soon made divorce impossible. De Valera's constitution of 1937 went so far as to prohibit the dissolution of marriage, a proviso much more strict, even, than Catholic canon law which at least offered grounds for annulment in certain circumstances.[25]

This brings us back to the schools, for if both laity and clergy were disposed to use social and legal agencies to reinforce the sexual code they naturally looked to the schools as one of the best weapons in their arsenal. The schools were especially appropriate for inculcating sexual attitudes because as institutions they were joint clerical-secular agencies in the same way the Irish sexual code was a conjoint product of moral theology and secular customs. (Notice here that the inculcation of sexual attitudes is not the same thing as sex education; education in sex was one of the things which Irish sexual attitudes prevented.) The schools can be seen, in simplest terms, as forming the sexual attitudes of the young in three ways. Initially, of course, the curricula included a thorough education in Catholic moral precepts including the virtues of chastity and purity. Second, by segregating the sexes into separate institutions wherever possible, the school system taught by example, implicitly suggesting that the sexes properly are separated and that contact between them should be limited. Third, besides teaching by direct example, the process of segregating the sexes became in itself something of a community ritual. When day after day the young boys of a small town walked together to a small one teacher school whilst the girls went in bands by themselves to another, which was equally small and which by any educational standard should have been merged with the boys school, they were ritually affirming for the entire village a fundamental social attitude. Taken together, these three aspects of the schools' influence on sexual attitudes were a marvelously efficient means of reinforcing the Irish social fabric.

Given these functions of the single-sex school arrangements, the Department of Education's refusal to let the Irish people know how many elementary schools were co-educational was sensible; to admit that economic necessity had forced co-education in large numbers of rural schools would be to admit publicly that in many cases church and state tacitly had agreed that it was more important to save money than to safeguard sexual morality. The eyes of the religious and state authorities flickered embarrassingly away from squarely viewing this fact and so produced a nervous tick upon Kathleen's face.

Or was there more? Future students of Irish social life may wish to note two facts: first, southern Ireland has the highest proportion of persons in psychiatric hospitals of any nation in the world. There were, in 1961, 7.3 psychiatric beds per 1,000 citizens, compared with 4.6 in England and Wales and 4.3 in Scotland. High as the comparative statistics are they probably underestimate the relative gravity of the Irish problem, for the southern Irish health services are considerably less efficient than those of the United Kingdom. Nevertheless, at any given time, a government report noted in 1966, about one of every seventy southern Irishmen above the age of twenty-four was in a mental hospital.[26] Second, juxtapose the extraordinarily high incidence of serious mental disorders with the report released in August 1972 by the Republic's medico-social research board: most of the unusually high number of schizophrenic patients in Eire are single. Unmarried farm workers have the highest rate of hospital treatment for schizophrenia, widows much less, and married persons the least.[27]

St. Paul, that most strict sexual disciplinarian, endorsed celibacy: "I say therefore to the unmarried and widows: It is good for them if they so continue even as I." "But," he added realistically, "if they do not contain, let them marry: for it is better to marry than to burn" (I Corinthians 7:8-9). So perhaps the nervous tick on Kathleen's face ran deeper than mere embarrassment about educational arrangements, to an uneasy recognition that the Irish sexual code acted as a crucible, purifying some, but leaving others charred in mind and spirit.

Looking Ahead

Southern Ireland in the 1960s and early 'seventies underwent great social and economic change; educational institutions, acting as always as a cultural lodestone, swung about. Frustratingly, the degree of that swing cannot be determined with the precision historical scholarship demands, if for no other reason than that the Department of Education has been remarkably reticent in providing the public with records of its activities during the past decade. At the time of writing the most recent annual report of the Department is for the year 1963–64 and there is serious speculation among educational observers that the Department may have quietly abandoned altogether this vehicle of public accountability. In discussing the last decade and a half one is forced to rely heavily on journalists' reports and on private interviews and thus to be aware that all judgements must be tentative. Undeniably, early in the 1960s the Republic's politicians discovered education. Almost overnight the schools were changed from legislative orphans to a topic of continual public interest and debate. The most important innovations came in the financing of schools, the introduction of free post-primary education and the creation of new forms of post-primary institutions.

Fundamental to all these changes was the Republic's abandonment in the later 1950s of its laissez faire stance on governmental activities and its adoption of large-scale economic planning. State planning was intended to turn the nation into an industrial society and was specifically tailored to facilitate Eire's entry into the European Economic Community.[1] Both a symbol and an instrument of the new approach to schooling was the appearance in 1965 of a monumental study *Investment in Education*.[2] This was the first governmental document to treat education as a social and economic activity and not chiefly as a theological abstraction or a linguistic exercise. Prepared by a special survey team, the report abjured the deductive, scholastic approach which characterized the Council of Education reports; instead it was based almost entirely upon empirical data. Behind the myriad tables and detailed recommendations was one simple conclusion: that if the Republic wished to enter Europe it would have to spend more money on its school children and would have to spend it more effectively.

The Investment team had been appointed in 1962 by the Minister for Education, Patrick Hillery, who was personally committed to spending more money on the schools even before the report appeared and was able to bring the cabinet to share his conviction. The new approach is clearly revealed by the following table which indicates the investment in primary school facilities made by the central government from 1958 through 1967.[3]

YEAR	NUMBER OF NEW SCHOOL BUILDINGS SANCTIONED	ENLARGEMENTS SANCTIONED	AMOUNT SANCTIONED
1958	55	18	£1,096,486
1959	81	21	1,249,998
1960	73	14	1,499,999
1961	74	28	1,600,000
1962	104	33	3,146,320
1963	87	28	2,135,823
1964	112	39	3,098,031
1965	154	65	4,086,352
1966	70	70	2,518,239
1967	58	171	2,518,076

Equally important, early in 1964, a radical change was made concerning the secondary schools. During a major policy speech on investment in education the Taoiseach, Sean Lemass, announced that, in the future, the building of academic secondary schools was to be subsidized directly by state grants.[4] Previously, all capital investment in secondary schools had been made by the individual school management, who in most cases were religious. Now sixty percent grants were to be available to build new schools with a prospective population of 150 pupils or more, and for the extension of old schools which intended to add an incremental seventy-five or more pupils.[5] This new secondary school investment policy long had been recommended by the teachers, but in the past had been resisted by clerical authorities as a danger to their own control of the schools. Yet, now the bishops not only did not oppose the new grants, but actively sought the new policy.[6]

The result of increasing investment in the schools was to increase the education of the people and presumably, therefore, to increase the nation's economic productivity. Hence, as an integral part of its discussion of economic planning, the second programme for national expansion (the national economic plan, 1964) stated that the school leaving age would be raised to fifteen by 1970.[7] In the actual event this extension of compulsory education had to be postponed until the academic year 1972-73,[8] but the commitment, not the postponement, is the crucial point for understanding the educational temper of the 1960s.

Obviously if children were to stay in school until fifteen—which is to say, if they all were to receive some form of post-primary education—new financial arrangements would have to be made, for almost all post-primary schools charged fees and not all parents could afford them. A preliminary step in this direction had been made in 1961 when the Local Education Scholarship Amendment Bill was passed, enabling the state to augment county and county borough scholarship funds by a grant of at least fifty percent of the entire cost. Hitherto about £150,000 had been spent each year by local authorities on scholarships; the framers of the new bill envisaged that within four years from the start of the scheme the total amount spent would be about £600,000 a year.[9] In terms of actual scholarships awarded by county and county borough councils, the numbers increased from 2,609 in 1960–61 to 9,614 in 1966–67, most of these being awarded to students in academic secondary schools.[10]

The 1961 Scholarship Act helped those children of high ability who excelled on rigorous examinations, but something more radical was needed if all Irish children were to attend post-primary schools. Dramatically, on 10 September 1966, Donogh O'Malley, Minister for Education, diagnosed the problem and propounded a solution.

The problem:

Every year, some 17,000 of our children finishing their primary school course do not receive any further education. This means that almost one in three of our future citizens are cut off at this stage from the opportunities of learning a skill, and denied the benefits of cultural development that go with further education.

This is a dark stain on the national conscience.[11]

The answer:

I propose, therefore, from the coming school year, beginning in September of next year [1967] to introduce a scheme whereby, up to the completion of the intermediate certificate course, the opportunity for free post-primary education will be available to all families.

This free education will be available in the comprehensive and vocational schools, and in the general run of secondary schools.[12]

Specifically, a four-fold plan was activated, involving first, the payment of a £25 grant to each academic secondary school which agreed to stop charging school fees and second, the abolition of school fees in vocational schools, "secondary tops," attached to primary schools, and the new comprehensve schools (of which more in a minute). Third, transport was provided for children living more than three miles from the nearest post-primary school. Fourth, free books were given to children whose parents could not afford to buy them.[13] This scheme did not make post-primary education completely costless (most parents still paid for books and requisites) and did not apply to all schools (in 1969–70 there were thirty academic secondary day schools outside the scheme, charging fees ranging from £40 to £85 a year),[14] but it did ameliorate the harshest forms of social discrimination while simultaneously increasing the nation's investment in its children. Undeniably the attempt to reduce the most obvious forms of social class discrimination in education marked a change in the way Irish people thought about the social inequalities in their entire society, just as the large incremental investments in education marked a shift in the position of the child in Irish culture.

Paradoxically, yet another shift in southern Irish society, this one involving the position of the Protestant minority, was indicated by their opposition to the form (but not the substance) of the government's post–primary reform scheme. To its considerable surprise, the Department of Education found the secondary education committee for Protestant schools (formed in 1965 by the Anglicans, Presbyterians, Methodists, and Quakers to protect Protestant interests)[15] sharply critical of its proposals. The Protestant committee charged that the O'Malley scheme provided for free post-primary schooling for Catholics, but, as one spokesman said, "the phrase is, however, a misnomer when applied to Protestant schools."[16] Why? because in the first place the average fee in a Protestant day school was somewhere between £50 and £55 per year[17] a sum far exceeding the government's £25 per child grant. Most Catholic schools could afford to accept the government's £25 per child as sufficient compensation for abolishing fees because those teachers in Catholic holy orders implicitly subsidized the schools; in contrast the Protestant schools were staffed entirely by salaried lay teachers. Further, about two fifths of the Protestant children lived outside the range of a Protestant-managed day school. In these cases either special transport arrangements would have to be provided or some special grant made for boarding pupils whose fees in the usual case ran about £200 a year.[18]

Recognizing finally that few, if any, Protestant schools would be able to abolish fees and thus that almost all Protestant children would be excluded from his grand scheme, Donogh O'Mally announced that the Protestant schools would be given £70,000 a year for day pupils. This was calculated by determining the proportion of Catholic pupils who would be receiving free education (not all Catholic schools joined) and deflating the £25 basic grant by this proportion. The result, £14 per child, was then multiplied by the number of children in Protestant day schools.[19] This was both generous (the total amount far exceeded the Protestant entitlement under the strict terms of the scheme) and inequitable (Protestant children on the average had a lower percentage of their total fees paid by the state than did Catholic children). Reluctantly, the Protestant board agreed to administer the funds but it was far from happy. The unhappiness was especially sharp because there not being enough money for all Protestant children, the grant had to be administered on the basis of a means test,[20] always an unpalatable administrative procedure and the more so because none applied to Catholics.

But in Protestant minds the central isue lay unresolved. *If* one accepts the basic premise of the O'Malley plan, that no child should be prevented from obtaining post-primary education through lack of money, and *if* one accepts the existing denominational segregation in Irish education ("the Protestants suffer from the fact that there is no such thing as Irish education; there is Catholic education and Protestant education . . . .")[21] *then,* according to the Protestant syllogism, should fees in Protestant schools be higher than those in Catholic schools, the obvious conclusion is that Protestant pupils will need greater help than Catholic.[22] But that is politically impossible,[23] so one is at an impasse: the government remains reasonably generous to Protestant schools as a group (£86,000 for day pupils and £90,000 for boarding pupils in 1969–70)[24] and the Protestant authorities remain dissatisfied.[25]

From the viewpoint of the social historian the notable thing about the entire episode is that it took place at all. For the first time in the history of education in independent Ireland the Protestant minority had the courage to spurn the politicians' largesse. Whether or not the Protestants were right is irrelevant. What is relevant is the self-confidence behind their actions and especially their obvious sense of security within the Irish Republic. The timidity and ghetto-mentality of the "ex-unionist" generation had disappeared and in its place a new generation had arisen which was proud of its Protestantism and sufficiently secure in its Irish nationality to allow it to actively assert that Protestantism.

Although the changing patterns of educational investment and the altered educational attitudes of the Protestant minority indicated important shifts in southern Irish society relating to the status of children and the position of religious minorities, one should not overemphasize the changes in Irish society. The 'sixties were not the years of a second Irish revolution. This is well illustrated in the areas of education wherein the pivotal arrangements determining the control of the school systems remained unchanged and, apparently, unchangeable. Recall at this point that early in the twentieth century, long before independence, it had been well-argued by professional educationists that parental involvement in the schools was lacking but that it was educationally necessary. Nothing happened during the administration of successive Irish governments to change this situation. As Seamus O'Buachalla of the Department of Education stated in mid-1971: "In the realities of our educational system the voice of the parent has been all but eliminated. Church and state are effectively collaborating in excluding from democratic participation in the education system those to whom they both hypocritically accord the primary right."[26]

Granted, in 1969 the Irish bishops announced their willingness to accept parental association with local primary schools,[27] but this acceptance scarcely percolated below the episcopal level. "In general," the *Irish Times* education editor noted, "clerical managers, teachers and department officials, divided in so many other ways are united in their apprehension about the activities of the organised parent." He added: "To put it at its simplest, organised parents can be a dreadful nuisance."[28] Only in the early 1970s were parents given a slight voice in educational affairs, this being a minority role on the management committees of the newly-founded "community schools" (see below pp. 151-154).

One can accept John Whyte's authoritative statement that the 'sixties saw a great improvement in church-state relations and yet still question his notion that "a revolution by consent occurred."[29] Granted, in the mid-sixties the church was pleased to accept capital grants for secondary schools, something it never would have done even ten years previously and, granted, most Catholic secondary schools chose to join the government's free post-primary education scheme, an adhesion that would have been unlikely in the 'fifties. And certainly in an earlier day the authorities would not have sat still as they did in 1968 when the Jesuit periodical *Studies* printed an article by an assistant secretary of the Department of Education stating that, "no one wants to push the religious out of education; that would be disasterous in my opinion. But I want them in it as partners, not always as masters."[30] Yet this apparent docility hides a crucial fact: in return for massive dollops of money the church had surrendered no powers of any significance. It still controlled directly all the Catholic primary and academic secondary schools, and priestly chairmen still dominated the vocational education committees. Far from being revolutionary the new financial arrangements reinforced the existing division of power between church and state.

The continuing power of the church in the field of education is illustrated by the confused history of a potentially far-reaching governmental reform idea, the "comprehensive schools." The original plan for comprehensive schools was announced in May 1963 by Patrick Hillery, Minister for Education and radical the plan seemed. Hillery proposed that the state construct a number of post-primary schools to provide schooling for children from about the age of twelve-thirteen to about fifteen-sixteen. At the end of a three years' course the children would take the intermediate certificate examinations. Those who excelled would have the opportunity to go on to an academic secondary school, those who did reasonably well could continue in a technical school and the rest presumably would leave school, having obtained a sound basic education. Not only would the state depart from established precedent and pay for almost the entire cost of building the schools, but it would also pay the teachers' salaries directly and entirely.[31]

The key to understanding the Hillery scheme is to realize what the word "comprehensive" meant, for it was used in a very narrow, Irish, sense. It meant that the curriculum in the new schools would be comprehensive in that it would meet both academic secondary and vocational needs. It did not mean comprehensive in the sense of comprehensively covering the country with these new schools. Hillery strongly implied in his original proposal[32] that the scheme would operate only in areas inadequately served by existing secondary and technical institutions, and the location of the first comprehensives, confirmed this implication.[33] Nor did the word "comprehensive" mean that the new schools would come under some new form of comprehensive national control. Before publicly promoting the plan Hillery consulted with the Catholic hierarchy and came to an agreement with the bishops that each school would have a management committee constituted to suit all interested parties,[34] which is to say that the church's powers would be preserved. In practice, the comprehensive schools framed under the Hillery plan were managed by a three man committee representative of the local vocational educational committee, the Department of Education, and the local Catholic religious authorities. The first three schools were opened in 1966.

Such were the original comprehensive schools, or, more accurately, the Catholic comprehensive schools. For the sake of clarity we may call them comprehensive schools "Mark I," for they have to be distinguished from a second form of Catholic comprehensive, "Mark II." For reasons that have yet to be explained the government decided not to found any more Mark I comprehensives and instead to group together existing institutions to form comprehensives. These Mark I comprehensives were managed by a board consisting of representatives of the vocational educational committee (because the local vocational school was taken over by the new comprehensive) and the representatives of the managers of the other merged institutions, meaning the Catholic secondary schools. Almost all expenses were to be borne by the state.

Obviously neither the Mark I nor Mark II comprehensives interfered greatly with the existing power balance in education. Mark I schools filled a gap in the education network but did not rival the existing academic secondary schools or undercut the ideal of denominational schooling. Moreover, given the usual situation wherein the local clergyman was the dominant power on the vocational education committee, the church automatically dominated the Mark I management committees by a two-to-one margin over the state's representative. This explains why the Mark I comprehensive schools were welcomed by the hierarchy from the first.[35] The Mark II schools were even more decidedly in denominational hands. Indeed, one meets the extraordinary situation of a "Jesuit comprehensive" which takes only boys, streams students according to ability and implicitly practices selection before admission, and the equally noteworthy case of a convent school with a lay principal, but still firmly under private denominational management, yet which, for some reason, is now called a comprehensive school and funded as such by the state.

Clearly, "comprehensive" in the Irish sense did not mean that the schools would be religiously ecumenical. In his original statement of 1963, Hillery had tacitly admitted that the new schools would be denominational and suggested "that a proposal for the provision of a comprehensive school of this kind for Protestants, if related to a suitable region, would be welcomed by me."[36] In September 1970, after it had become clear that the comprehensive schools were a permanent part of the educational system—and that the free post-primary education scheme was far from completely adequate to meet Protestant needs—the Department of Education suggested to the Protestant secondary education committee that it form two comprehensives in Dublin and one in Cork. The Protestant committee responded by suggesting three schools in Dublin as well as one in Cork.[37] Ultimately two comprehensives in Dublin and one in Cork were opened. Hence, by 1970 there were in operation or proposed three different sorts of institutions operating under the title of comprehensive schools: the Mark I and Mark II Catholic comprehensives and the Protestant comprehensives.

But more complications were to follow. In October 1970, the Minister for Education, Padraig Faulkner, sent a document to the Catholic bishops proposing that a new type of school be established, the "community school," by merging in many areas existing vocational and academic secondary schools.[38] This new school would be managed by a committee of interested parties four of whose six members would be appointed by the bishops (this procedure was not spelled out in the original document but later evidence made clear that it was accepted implicitly both by the bishops and the Minister for Education). Not surprisingly, the bishops endorsed the plan, for it delivered into their hands control of the troublesome vocational schools, direct control of many secondary schools presently run by religious orders, and a state capital construction grant of ninety percent of all costs.

Yet despite the backing of both ministers and Catholic hierarchy, the proposals were publicly treated with contempt. It is, therefore, tempting to suggest that some kind of watershed had been reached in Irish education and that the principle of denominational control of individual schools and the practice of ever-greater bureaucratic influence from the centre had, simultaneously, been rejected. I think, however, that such a conclusion would be overreading the situation, for in reality the plan appears to have failed for several reasons, none of which relate to a major change in the Irish polity. In my view these reasons are, first, that Faulkner handled the entire affair ineptly. The October 1970 document was discovered by journalists in November and from that moment onwards he was off balance. Second, from even the most charitable viewpoint, the fundamental premises of the plan were administratively unworkable as a national plan. The original document set 400 as the minimum size for a viable post-primary institution which would have meant that, at minimum, amalgamation would have had to take place in 118 towns, involving 329 schools. Even then there were eight areas where, after amalgamation of all nearby schools, including boys and girls schools, the new schools would be below the 400 minimum. Third, although the Catholic bishops stood to gain by the plan, the teaching orders which operated many secondary schools would lose. Hence, the orders for the most part fought the proposals which threatened their control over schools they had founded and built through their own efforts. In other words conflict within the Catholic church was involved. Fourth, individual vocational education authorities throughout the Republic, well organized grass-roots bodies, strongly opposed the take-over of their schools and brought great pressure to bear on their Dail representatives.

Fifth, the plan was highly discriminatory against Protestants, both in origin and substance. The Minister for Education formulated it and negotiated details with the Catholic bishops but did not contact the Protestants. More important, the proposal to hand over the vocational schools to the control of a committee dominated by direct nominees of the Catholic church meant that the Protestants would lose access to a previously undenominational set of institutions. Therefore they vigorously fought the Faulkner plan (why they had not raised the same objections against the Mark II comprehensives is unclear). The response to the Protestant opposition was interesting for two reasons. The first of these is that the minister of education showed an unusual incapacity for comprehending the idea of cultural pluralism and, since many vocational schools had few Protestant children in them, did not see why the Protestants would object to these institutions being transferred from civic management to Catholic denominational control. Second, for one of the first times in the history of independent Ireland the Protestant and Catholic authorities clashed head-on. Understandably the Catholic hierarchy was piqued that the Protestants would feel that they had a right to block a bishop's taking over, say, in the west of Ireland a boys and a girls secondary school and a vocational school in which all but one or two students were Catholic. Equally understandable was the Protestant position that it was objectionable to hand over state institutions to clerical control and that in any case more and more Protestant children would be attending vocational schools in the future and that the transfer of such schools to the Catholic church would close this form of education to Protestants thus leaving the Protestant children at an educational disadvantage.

Out of the matrix of conflicting pressures came a revised plan for community schools at least minimally acceptable to the parties involved. In the usual case the community schools were to have a six-member management committee consisting of two representatives of the merged secondary schools, two of the merged vocational school, and two elected parents. Under this scheme the interests of the Catholic teaching orders were protected against encroachment by the Catholic bishops; the objections of the Protestants were stilled because the Catholic church was not given de jure control over the former vocational schools; the bishops agreed because in most cases Catholics would control the new schools de facto, for in the usual case the two merged schools would be Catholic (guaranteeing two representatives), the majority of parents electing representatives would be Catholic and in addition there usually was heavy clerical influence over the vocational education committee which would also be choosing two members. In essence, the community schools which are projected under these rubrics (forty are planned within the next five years) are a redefining of the Mark II comprehensives of the late 1960s. If one wishes to describe the Department of Education's present policy in a single phrase, it is the implementation of comprehensive education through community schools.

Inevitably the development of the comprehensive-community schools will increase the number of co-educational institutions for adolescents, since in the usual case a boys and a girls academic secondary school will be merged as components of the new community school. Whether or not this increase reflects a significant shift in Irish attitudes toward relations between the sexes is not yet clear, but probably it does. The marriage age has been dropping since World War II as has the incidence of bachelor–spinsterhood. And if the pattern of other western nations is followed, the next stage probably will be a female rights movement, which, among other things, will press for full co-education in the schools on the grounds that sexually segregated schools are inherently discriminatory against women.[39]

From the viewpoint of the curriculum, the most controversial development of the 'sixties and 'seventies was the announcement in April 1973 by the minister for education, Richard Burke, that the recently elected Fine Gael–Labour coalition government had decided to drop Irish as a compulsory subject for the intermediate and leaving certificate. But here, as in the introduction of comprehensive and community schools, the change was much less radical than it appeared. Pupils did not have to offer Irish as an examination subject, but their schools would not earn grants unless the pupils followed the approved curriculum, which included Irish. Undoubtedly most pupils, having studied Irish for their entire secondary school career, will continue to take the examination in Irish. Further, the bonus-points for writing various papers in the medium of Irish are to continue and, more important, for the purpose of university entrance grants, honours in the Irish paper on the leaving certificate are to count as honours in two subjects.[40]

If chronicling events in Irish education which occurred within the last decade is hazardous, speculation about the future is potentially self–destructive; but let me try.

It seems to me that in all probability the following major trends will characterize educational development in the Irish Republic during the 'seventies and 'eighties:

1. The costs of education will rise more quickly than will the financial resources of the religious bodies, most especially the Catholic church. The only viable alternative source of incremental funds will be the state and local government agencies.

2. The number of children in post-primary education will continue to grow rapidly and the proportionally greatest increment will be among Catholics.

3. Unless there is a religious revival of astounding proportions and traditional dimensions, the number of Catholic teachers in religious orders will fall considerably in absolute numbers and drastically as a percentage of the total teaching force (the total number of teachers will have to grow to meet the increase of students in post-primary institutions).[41]

This will mean:

1. that the bargaining power of the Catholic religious authorities will become less vis à vis the state; and

2. that, in counter-current, the educational problems of the Catholic and Protestant religious authorities will become much closer. (Previously the teaching orders cushioned the Catholic schools against the financial pressures that the Protestant schools experienced.) Presumably an educational-political alliance of sorts will evolve, the effective combination of Catholic and Protestant forces at least partially offsetting the decrease in bargaining power of the Catholic church as sole agent.

From the interaction of state and religious forces there seem to me to be only two possible results. The first is that the governmental authorities effectively win the field and the religious authorities of both denominations become peripheral figures in education, ones who will be treated always deferentially, but rarely seriously. If the government prevails at the expense of the religious two options are open:

1. the power lost by the religious will be assumed directly by the central government, in particular the Department of Education; or,

2. the newly-acquired powers will be divided between the Department of Education and local or regional civic agencies. The recent statements of the secretary of the Department of Education, Sean O'Connor, are suggestive in this regard, pointing to a two-tier structure comprising county and regional units of educational management.[42]

The other possible result is that the religious authorities will succeed in holding their position by manipulating the new agencies of educational management that the state is demanding in exchange for its increased financial support. The religious authorities' dexterity in protecting themselves against the threat to their powers which might have been implied by the comprehensive and community schools was remarkable and argues well for their future adaptability. In particular, if the churches are able to guarantee the perpetuation of "transferors rights" in the control of institutions which are formed from pre-existing schools, then their powers will be guaranteed for at least another generation. Conceivably, in the 1980s one could have a situation similar to that which presently exists in Northern Ireland, where the power of the clergy over the schools reflects not their actual power in society but their position thirty or forty years previously. In the long run such a situation would be potentially explosive, for each year the disproportion between the educational powers of the religious authorities and their contribution to the educational process would increase.

Such speculation about the possible educational conflicts in the future makes one look back, almost nostalgically, to the era before the 1960s when southern Ireland was a parochial and culturally self-contained agricultural nation in which church, state, and social practices all worked in smooth cooperation. Well may educational and social historians feel a twinge of regret when reflecting on that period: as the earlier chapters of this book suggested, Kathleen ni Houlihan was in those years sometimes callous, miserly, superstitious, and authoritarian, but she was, after all, a proud, independent, and upright lady.

APPENDIX

NOTES TO CHAPTER ONE

[1]For documentation of facts and interpretations concerning primary education in the last century, see Donald H. Akenson, *The Irish Education Experiment: the National System of Education in the Nineteenth Century* (London: Routledge & Kegan Paul; Toronto: University of Toronto Press, 1970). For a general summary, tailored to a public forum, see Donald H. Akenson, "National Education and the Realities of Irish Life 1831-1900," a paper given at a joint meeting of the American Historical Association and the American Committee for Irish Studies, in Washington, D.C. December 1969, published in *Eire-Ireland,* vol. IV, no. 4 (winter 1969), pp. 42–51.

[2]*Report of Mr. F. H. Dale, His Majesty's Inspector of Schools, Board of Education, on Primary Education in Ireland,* p. 89 [Cd. 1981], H.C. 1904, xx.

[3]See David W. Miller, "The Politics of Faith and Fatherland: the Catholic Church and Nationalism in Ireland, 1898-1918" (PhD. thesis, University of Chicago, 1968), pp. 83–85. I am grateful to Dr. Miller for providing with with a copy of this excellent dissertation.

[4]*Report of Mr. F. H. Dale,* pp. 34–40, 89–90.

[5]"Pastoral Address of the Irish Bishops on the Managership of Catholic Schools," *Irish Ecclesiastical Record,* 4 ser. vol. IV, no. 367 (July 1898), p. 75.

[6]"Control of Primary Education in Ireland," *Irish Educational Review,* vol. I, no. 12 (September 1908), pp. 730–31.

[7]See "Catholic Clerical Managers Association, Meeting of Central Council," *Irish Educational Review,* vol. II, no. 10 (July 1909), pp. 629-32.

[8]The Protestant "fantasy" is discussed in David W. Miller's "Educational Reform and the Realities of Irish Politics in the Early Twentieth Century" (unpublished paper presented to the American Historical Association, 30 December 1969), p. 13.

[9]Ibid., pp. 2–3.

[10]*A Bill to Provide for the Establishment and Functions of an Administrative Council in Ireland and for Other Purposes Connected Therewith,* H.C. 1907 (182), ii.

[11]For a thorough discussion of the agitation see Miller, "The Politics of Faith and Fatherland," pp. 111–24. Also illuminating is Leon O'Broin's *The Chief Secretary: Augustine Birrell in Ireland* (London: Chatto & Windus, 1969), pp. 13–16.

[12]*Seventy-First Report of the Commissioners of National Education in Ireland, for the Year 1904,* pp. 13–14 [Cd. 2567], H.C. 1905, xxviii.

[13]"Statements and Resolutions of the Irish Hierarchy at Maynooth Meeting June 21," *Irish Ecclesiastical Record,* 4 ser. vol. xxvii, no. 7 (July 1910), p. 92.

Despite this moralism, practical considerations forced the Catholic church to sanction co-educational schools in a great many rural areas. In 1904, for example, the church was managing 2,247 co-educational schools *(Seventy-First Report of the Commissioners of National Education in Ireland, for the year 1904),* p. 13.

[14]*Minutes and Proceedings of the Commissioners of National Education Relating to Rule 127(b) and Cognate Rules,* pp. 3–4, H.C. 1905 (184) lx; *Seventy-First Report of the Commissioners of National Education in Ireland, for the Year 1904,* pp. 9–13.

[15]Ibid., p. 13.

[16]*Minutes and Proceedings of the Commissioners of National Education Relating to Rule 127(b) and Cognate Rules,* p. 7.

[17]Ibid., p. 9.

[18]Compare *Seventy-Seventh Report of the Commissioners of National Education in Ireland, School Year 1910-1911,* p. 16 [Cd. 5903], H.C. 1911, xxi, with *Eighty-Sixth Report of the Commissioners of National Education in Ireland for the School Year 1919-20,* p. 16 [Cmd. 1476], H.C. 1921, xi.

[19]For the precise figures for the decade, which ranged from 68.9% to 72.6%, see the annual reports of the commissioners of national education.

In November 1919 the commissioners of national education raised the leaving standard for children eleven to fourteen from fifth to sixth standard *(Eighty-Sixth Report of the Commissioners of National Education in Ireland, School Year 1919–20,)* p. 7. This was not a solution to the attendance problem because the method of enforcement remained unchanged and ineffective.

[20]Unfortunately no thorough study of the intermediate system has been published. A valuable study is an unpublished thesis by T. J. McElligott, "Intermediate Education and the Work of the Commissioners, 1870-1922" (unpublished M.Litt. thesis, Trinity College, Dublin, 1969). Also useful is Seamus V. O'Suilleabhain's "Secondary Education," in the fascicle *Catholic Education* (Dublin: McGill and MacMillan, 1971), pp. 53–83, which will eventually form part of volume V of *A History of Irish Catholicism,* edited by Patrick J. Corish. Norman Atkinson's *Irish Education: a History of Educational Institutions* (Dublin: Allen Figgis, 1969) has some useful material, as does Graham Balfour's *The Educational Systems of Great Britain and Ireland* (Oxford: Clarendon Press, second ed., 1903). Attention also should be called to the historical sketch found in *Report of the Council of Education. . . . The Curriculum of the Secondary School,* drawn up by the Eire Department of Education (Dublin: The Stationery Office, 1960).

[21]41 and 42 Victoria c. 66.

22For an illuminating discussion of the flaws in the examination system see Matthew Arnold's "An Unregarded Irish Grievance," in his *Irish Essays and Others* (London: Smith, Elder & Co., 1882). Arnold makes extensive use in this essay of J. P. Mahaffy's report on the intermediate schools. The inter-play of Mahaffy's report and Arnold's commentary is fascinating.

23 63 and 64 Victoria c. 43; *Report of the Intermediate Education Board for Ireland for the Year 1903*, pp. xi-xii [Cd. 1670], H.C. 1903, xxi; *Report of the Intermediate Education Board for Ireland for the Year 1904*, pp. x-xiii [Cd. 2580], H.C. 1905, xxviii: *Report of the Intermediate Board for the Year 1906*, xi-xiv [Cd. 3544], H.C. 1907. xxii; *Report of the Intermediate Education Board for Ireland for the Year 1907*, pp. ix-xii [Cd. 4047], H.C. 1908, xxvii; *Report of the Intermediate Education Board for Ireland for the Year 1908*, p. ix-xii [Cd. 4707], H.C. 1909, xx.

24 3 and 4 Geo. 5. c. 29; McElligott, "Intermediate Education," p. 146; *Report of the Vice-Regal Committee on the Conditions of Service and Remuneration of Teachers in Intermediate Schools and the Distribution of Grants from Public Funds for Intermediate Education in Ireland*, pp. 8–9 [Cmd. 66], H.C. 1919, xxi.

25Eire, Department of Education, *Report of the Council of Education. . . . . The Curriculum of the Secondary School* (Dublin: The Stationery Office, 1960), p. 60.

26*Report of the Vice-Regal Committee on the Conditions of Service and Remuneration of Teachers in Intermediate Schools and the Distribution of Grants from Public Funds for Intermediate Education in Ireland*, pp. 32-33.

27*Report of the Intermediate Education Board for Ireland for the Year 1904*, p. x.

28*Report of Messrs. F. H. Dale and T. A. Stephens, His Majesty's Inspectors of Schools, Board of Education, on Intermediate Education in Ireland*, p. 85 [Cd. 2546], H.C. 1905, xxviii.

29*Report of Messrs. F. H. Dale and T. A. Stephens, His Majesty's Inspectors of Schools, Board of Education, on Intermediate Education in Ireland*, p. 85.

30Derived from *Report of the Intermediate Education Board for Ireland under the Intermediate Education (Ireland) Act, 1914, as to the Application of the Teachers' Salaries Grant*, p. 3 [Cd. 8724], HC.. 1917-18, xi.

31*Report of the Intermediate Education Board for Ireland for the Year 1910*, p. iv [Cd. 5768], H.C. 1911, xxi.

32See B. R. Mitchell, with Phyllis Deane, *Abstract of British Historical Statistics* (Cambridge: Cambridge University Press, 1962), p. 476.

33*Report of the Vice-Regal Committee on the Conditions of Service and Remuneration of Teachers in Intermediate Schools and on the Distribution of Grants from Public Funds for Intermediate Education in Ireland*, p. 11.

34Ibid., p. 11; *Parliamentary Debates, Northern Ireland House of Commons*, I: 513–515.

[35]*Report of the Intermediate Education Board for Ireland for the Year 1920*, p. x [Cmd. 1398], H.C. 1921, xi.

[36]Balfour, p. 202. The grant had been as high as £9,271 in 1871.

[37]See *A bill for Establishing a Department of Agriculture and Other Industries and Technical Instruction in Ireland, and for other purposes connected therewith*, H.C. 1899 (180), i; 62 and 63 Victoria c. 50; *Department of Agriculture and Technical Instruction (Ireland). Report of the Departmental Committee of Inquiry*, pp. 1–6 [Cd. 3572], H.C. 1907, xvii.

[38]See *First Annual General Report of the Department of Agriculture and Technical Instruction for Ireland, 1900-1901*, pp. 21–25 [Cd. 838], H.C. 1902, xx; *Second Annual General Report of the Department of Agriculture and Technical Instruction for Ireland, 1901-02*, pp. 18–28, 35–65 [Cd. 1314], H.C. 1902, xx; *Regulations under Section Twenty-Four of the Agriculture and Technical Instruction (Ireland) Act, 1899*, H.C. 1900 (132), lxvii; *Report of the Vice-Regal Committee on the Conditions of Service and Remuneration of Teachers in Intermediate Schools and on the Distribution of Grants from Public Funds for Intermediate Education in Ireland*, pp. 9–10.

[39]*Second Annual General Report of the Department of Agriculture and Technical Instruction for Ireland, 1901-02*, p. 19.

[40]*Agriculture and Technical Instruction: Nineteenth Annual General Report of the Department, 1918-19*, p. 97 [Cmd. 929], H.C. 1920, ix.

[41]*Second Annual General Report of the Department of Agriculture and Technical Instruction for Ireland 1901–02*, pp. 65–68.

[42]*Agriculture and Technical Instruction: Nineteenth Annual General Report of the Department, 1918–19*, pp. 2–3.

[43]See *Department of Agriculture and Technical Instruction (Ireland), Report of the Departmental Committee of Inquiry*, p. 10.
    See also Horace Plunkett to T. P. Gill, 20 October 1903. National Library of Ireland (hereafter "NLI"), MSS 13,478–13,526.

[44] See *Agricultural and Technical Instruction Schemes (Ireland). Returns to an Order of the Honourable the House of Commons dated 27th June 1904*, pp. 2–11, H.C. 1905 (70), lxvii.

[45]On the negotiations between the department and local authorities see *Department of Agriculture and Technical Instruction (Ireland). Report of the Departmental Committee of Inquiry*, pp. 32–33, 94–97.

[46]*Agricultural and Technical Instruction (Ireland), Local contributions (Ireland)*, pp. 2–4, H.C. 1914–16 (343), liii.

[47]For clear evidence that power lay in the hands of Plunkett and Gill, see *Department of Agriculture and Technical Instruction (Ireland). Report of the Departmental Com-*

mittee of Inquiry, pp. 8–9, 11, 13, 19, 120–23. The magnitude of the establishment under their control is indicated in the eighteen printed pages entitled *Department of Agriculture and Technical Instruction for Ireland. Returns Showing Names of Permanent Officials on 1st May 1903 with Description of Office, Salary, Scale of Travelling Expenses, Date of Appointment, Previous Employment, and Tenure of Office,* H.C. 1904 (21), lxxix. A useful biography of Plunkett is Margaret Digby's *Horace Plunkett, an Anglo–American Irishman* (Oxford: Basil Blackwell, 1949). Some biographical data on Gill, and revealing material on the Plunkett-Gill partnership, is found in the National Library of Ireland, MSS 13,478–13,526. This is a collection of about 5,000 items. Unfortunately many have been partially burned.

48Arnold F. Graves, "On the Reorganisation of Irish Education Departments and the Appointment of a Minister of Education," *Journal of the Statistical and Social Inquiry Society of Ireland,* vol. VIII, part 60 (August 1882), p. 358.

49*Report of the Vice-Regal Committee on the Conditions of Service and Remuneration of Teachers in Intermediate Schools and on the Distribution of Grants from Public Funds for Intermediate Education in Ireland,* p. 21.

50Ibid., p. 29; McElligott, "Intermediate Education," p. 142.

51For the views of T. P. Gill on this situation see the *Times Educational Supplement,* 30 November 1916.

52See *Report of the Vice-Regal Committee on the Conditions of Service and Remuneration of Teachers in Intermediate Schools and on the Distribution of Grants from Public Funds for Intermediate Education in Ireland,* passim.

53See *Report of the Vice-Regal Committee of Inquiry into Primary Education (Ireland), 1918,* passim [Cmd. 60], H.C. 1919, xxi.

54McElligott, "Intermediate Education," p. 172.

55*A Bill to Make Further Provision with Respect to Education in Ireland and for other purposes connected therewith,* H.C. 1919 (214), i.

56Typescript of speech by T. P. Gill delivered 5 June 1919, in NLI MSS 13,478–13,526.

57*Journal of Education and School World,* January 1920, pp. 43–44.

58*Eighty-Fifth Report of the Commissioners of National Education in Ireland, School Year 1918–19,* p. 8.

59McElligott, "Intermediate Education," p. 173.

60"Statement of the Standing Committee of the Irish Bishops on the Proposed Education Bill for Ireland," *Irish Ecclesiastical Record,* 5 ser. vol. XIV, no. 12 (December 1919), p. 507; *Irish News,* 10 December 1919.

61Ibid., 25 December 1919. In June of 1920 when a bill nearly identical to the ill-fated 1919 bill was under parliamentary consideration the general assembly of the Presbyterian church resolved that "it is hoped that it will find its way to the statute book at an early date and come into operation immediately." (Presbyterian Church in Ireland, *Minutes of the General Assembly of the Presbyterian Church in Ireland, January and June 1920),* p. 1165.

62 5 Hansard 123; 1234.

63 5 Hansard 125: 1508 *A Bill to make Further Provision with Respect to Education in Ireland, and for other purposes connected therewith,* H.C. 1920 (35), i.

64 *Journal of Education and School World,* March 1920, p. 163; "Pronouncement of the Irish Hierarchy at a General Meeting held at Maynooth on Tuesday January 27th," *Irish Ecclesiastical Record,* 5 ser. vol. xv, no. 2 (February 1920), pp. 150–52.

65 *Irish News,* 16 February 1920.

66 McElligott, "Intermediate Education," p. 175.

67 (Copy), T. P. Gill to W. Young, 15 May 1920. NLI MSS 13,478–13,526.

68 5 Hansard 136: 213.

69 A. N. Bonaparte Wyse, "The Irish Educational Position," 10 May 1920. NLI PC 647.

70 5 Hansard 138: 1118-1119, 24 February 1921.

NOTES TO CHAPTER TWO

[1]T. J. McElligott, "Some Thoughts on our Educational Discontents," *University Review*, vol. I, no. 5 (summer 1955), p. 27.

[2]The constitution is reproduced in Dorothy Macardle, *The Irish Republic* (New York: Farrar Straus & Giroux, 1965), pp. 923–24.

[3]*Dail Eireann. Minutes of Proceedings of the First Parliament of the Republic of Ireland, 1919–1921. Official Report,* pp. 162–63, 27 October 1919.

[4]Ibid., pp. 162–63.

[5]For example, see the mimeo reports of the language ministry, National Library of Ireland, MS 8424 and MS 15,440.

[6]*Dail Eireann. Minutes of Proceedings of the First Parliament of the Republic of Ireland, 1919–1921. Official Report,* 17 September 1920, p. 227 and 11 March 1921, p. 265.

[7]Ibid., p. 227.

[8]*Dail Eireann, Official Report for Periods 16 August 1921 to 26th August 1921 and 28th February 1922 to 8th June 1922,* 26 August 1921, p. 83.

[9]*Official report. Debate on the Treaty between Great Britain and Ireland,* 7 January 1922, p. 345.

[10]For evidence that effective power was assumed by the provisional government minister see *Irish Independent*, 19 January 1922; *Irish Times*, 1 February 1922.

T. J. O'Connell, in his *History of the Irish National Teachers' Organization 1868–1968* (Dublin: privately printed, n.d.), p. 464, says that although there was no formal separate allotment of duties to the two ministers, there was a mutual agreement that Lynch would be responsible for the primary branch and Hayes for the secondary (technical education was still controlled at this time by the Department of Agriculture and Technical Instruction). I have found no other evidence of this informal arrangement, but, assuming for the moment that the report is accurate, it does not change the basic fact that the most important functions, in this case those relating to primary education, were under provisional government control. Further, it should be added that whatever the informal arrangement, Lynch, the provisional government minister, was officially in charge of secondary education (see *Irish Independent*, 19 January 1922).

[11]*Irish Independent,* 19 April 1922; *Irish Times,* 19 April 1922.

[12]For a study of the formulation of the constitution see D. H. Akenson and J. F. Fallin, "The Irish Civil War and the Drafting of the Free State Constitution," a series of articles in *Eire-Ireland,* vol. v, no. 1 (spring 1970), pp. 10–26; vol. v, no. 2 (summer 1970), pp. 42–43; vol. v, no. 4 (winter 1970), pp. 28–70.

[13]*Irish Times,* 14 July 1922.

[14]*Times Educational Supplement,* 19 August 1922.

[15]For a discussion of the establishment of the northern ministry, see Donald H. Akenson, *Education & Enmity: the Control of Schooling in Northern Ireland 1922–1950* (Newton Abbot: published for the Institute of Irish Studies, The Queen's University, Belfast, by David & Charles Ltd., 1973), pp. 40–48.

[16]Basil Chubb, *The Government and Politics of Ireland* (Stanford: Stanford University Press, 1970), p. 221; *Irish Independent,* 19 January 1922.

[17]*Irish Independent,* 5 April 1922; *Iris Oifigiuil,* 4 April 1922; *Irish Times,* 3 April 1922; *Report of the Department of Education for the School Year 1924–25 and the Financial and Administrative Years 1924–25–26* (Dublin: Stationery Office, 1926), p. 5.

The transfer in April of power to the ministers for education and for agriculture followed lines which had been drawn by the January order. See *Irish Independent,* 19 January 1922.

[18]*Times Educational Supplement,* 20 January 1921.

[19]*Irish Times,* 1 February 1922. See also *Irish Independent,* 1 February 1922. Bradley was not himself an experienced educationist. He was on temporary loan from the Health Insurance Commission. His chief qualification seems to have been that he was an enthusiast in the Gaelic league, and was for a time president of the Celtic literary society. He had served as a publicity agent for the Reverend Dr. Hickey in the fight for compulsory Irish at the national university. An ardent student of modern Irish, he also had studied middle Irish and Irish paleography under Kuno Meyer.

[20]*Irish Times,* 1 February 1922.

[21]5 Dail Eireann, 446–47, 31 October 1923; *Report of the Department of Education for the School Year 1924–25 and the Financial and Administrative Years 1924–25–26,* p. 6.

[22]Despite the educational partition of 1 February 1922, many Catholic schools in the north sat for the intermediate examinations as set by the Dublin commissioners rather than by the northern ministry.

Also, the full financial settlement between north and south was not completed until early November 1922. See Thomas J. McElligott, "Intermediate Education and the Work of the Commissioners, 1870-1922," (unpublished M.Litt. thesis, Trinity College, Dublin, 1969), pp. 177–80.

[23]Department of Education, *Report of the Intermediate Education Commissioners for the Year 1923* (Dublin: Stationery Office, 1924), p. viii; *Iris Oifigiuil,* 15 June 1923.

[24]In his late-January 1922 meeting with the commissioners of national education, Bradley had stated that the board was largely representative of "minority" (read: Protestant) interests *(Irish Times,* 1 February 1922). This was inaccurate as the majority of southern members were Catholic. Even before partition, the Catholics had comprised at least half the board and as the single largest denomination had dominated its proceedings. My own guess is that the real problem was that the Catholics on the two boards were chiefly gentlemen and successful professional men who were less than wholeheartedly enthusiastic about the new regime.

[25]*Times Educational Supplement,* 10 November 1923 and 17 November 1923.

[26]Ibid., 30 May 1931.

[27]See for example the I.N.T.O.'s *A Plan for Education* (Dublin: I.N.T.O., 1947), pp. 19–22.

[28]Commission on Vocational Organisation, *Report* [P. 6743], pp. 331–35.

[29]*Report of Public Services Organisation Review Group, 1966–1969* [Prl. 792], p. 11.

[30]*Report of the Commission of Inquiry into the Civil Service 1932–35* [P. 1296], vol. I, p. 73.

[31]Let me emphasize that the phrase "available evidence" is used advisedly. Until the Irish government opens its archives to historians it will be impossible to adjudge precisely MacNeill's departmental activities. My opinion is based partly on a full reading of his Dail speeches on education and partly on personal interviews.

[32]9 *Dail Eireann:* 286–89, 28 October 1924.

[33]A large number of examples could be given. A useful summary of the situation is Thomas Johnson's statement in 13 *Dail Eireann:* 27–28, 3 November 1925.

Recently, a set of essays on MacNeill, edited by F. X. Martin and J. F. Byrne, has appeared: *The Scholar Revolutionary: Eoin MacNeill, 1867–1945, and the Making of the New Ireland* (Shannon: Irish University Press, 1973). There are several excellent essays in the book, but almost nothing about his performance as minister for education.

[34]Act 16/1924. Under the act the department of education also had control over various peripheral institutions such as the reformatory schools, the geological survey and the national gallery and library.

[35]A useful, independent summary of the Free State system in the mid-1920s is *Education in the Irish Free State,* published by the United States Department of the Interior, Bureau of Education (Washington D.C., 1925).

[36]Department of Education, *Report of the Council of Education. . . . . The Curriculum of the Secondary School* [Pr. 5996], p. 64.

[37]Act 17/1926.

[38]Act 29/1930. The act was modelled on the recommendations of the Committee on Technical Education which had reported in 1927. This committee, although not strictly speaking an intra-departmental committee, was chaired by a senior inspector of technical instruction and the Department of Education was so strongly represented that there was no great difficulty in obtaining the government's backing for the bill.

NOTES TO CHAPTER THREE

[1]Central Statistics Office, *Census of Population of Ireland, 1961,* vol. IX, *Irish Language* [Pr. 8669], p. 2. (For convenience of reference I have cited a recent source; the same figures are available in each of Ireland's earlier census reports).

These figures, based on United Kingdom census data, probably understate somewhat the number of Irish speakers, but there is no question about the direction of the trend.

[2]W. T. Cosgrave to Richard Mulcahy, 4 March 1925, reproduced in Coimisiun na Gaeltachta. *Report* (Dublin: Stationery Office, 1926), p. 3.

[3]*Times Educational Supplement,* 13 August 1921.

[4]Ibid., 30 October 1925.

[5]*The Restoration of the Irish Language* [Pr. 8061], p. 6.

[6]For a perhaps unnecessarily acerbic discussion of this point ("their hearts were full, but their minds were vacant: into the vacuum there swept the first exciting idea at hand") see [Sean O'Faolain], "The Gaelic Cult," *The Bell,* vol. IX, no. 3 (December 1944), pp. 185–96.

[7]The following statement taken from the 1965 white paper on *The Restoration of the Irish Language* [PR 8061] (p. 6) indicates the extraordinary longevity of this sense of debt: "Our present position as an independent state derives in large measure from the idealism evoked by the Irish language movement. The need for this idealism is now as great as ever."

[8]Sean O'Faolain, "The Death of Nationalism," *The Bell,* vol. XVII, no. 2 (May 1951), p. 48.

[9]Article by Mairtin O'Cadhain in the *Irish Independent,* 10 February 1964.

[10]An influential school inspector stated in 1934 that had he the power he would issue a fiat which would make Irish the language of business throughout the country in five years' time. He did not, he said, desire a bilingual people, and he would drive English out of every primary school. *Times Educational Supplement,* 21 April 1934.

[11]This was the position at which de Valera eventually arrived. See his speech at Athlone reported in *Irish Times,* 12 October 1924.

[12]For a concise discussion of the reasons for the breakdown see Maureen Wall, "The

Decline of the Irish Language," in Brian O'Cuiv (ed.), *A View of the Irish Language* (Dublin: Stationery Office, 1969), 81–90.

[13]Michael P. Hickey, *Gaelic League Pamphlets—no. 29* [sic. no. 28], *The Irish Language Movement, its Genesis, Growth, and Progress* (Dublin: Gaelic league, 1902), p. 2.

[14]Douglas Hyde, *A Literary History of Ireland from Earliest Times to the Present Day* (London: Ernst Benn Ltd., new ed. 1967, originally published 1899), p. 630.

[15]Donald H. Akenson, *The Irish Education Experiment: the National System of Education in the Nineteenth Century* (London: Routledge & Kegan Paul; Toronto: University of Toronto Press, 1970), pp. 378–84.

[16]*Irish Statesman,* 24 October 1925.

[17]*Dail Eireann:* 187, 11 November 1925.

[18]*Irish Catholic Directory, 1933,* entry for 21 December 1931.

[19]For a discussion of the extreme attitudes see O'Faolain, "The Gaelic Cult," pp. 83–85.

[20]Daniel Corkery, *Synge and Anglo-Irish literature* (Cork: Mercier Press Edition, 1966, originally published 1931), pp. 4–5.

[21]Conor Malone, "English Literature in Ireland: a Comment on School Courses," *Catholic Bulletin,* vol. xxv. no. 3 (March 1933), p. 200.

[22]W. T. Cosgrave to Richard Mulcahy, 4 March 1925, reproduced in Coimisiun na Gaeltachta, *Report,* p. 3.

[23]87 *Dail Eireann:* 761–62, 2 June 1942.

[24]Donal McCartney, "Education and Language, 1938–51," in Keven B. Nowlan & T. Desmond Williams (eds.), *Ireland in the War Years and After 1939–51* (Dublin: Gill and MacMillan, 1969), p. 80.

[25]Granted, it was sometimes argued that every child should learn Irish so that he could know first-hand the Irish language culture, but this too in reality was a collectivist rather than an individualist argument, since the implied middle term in the argument was that every child should experience the Irish language culture because he was part of the Irish nation. This is very different from arguing, on individualistic grounds, that children should have an opportunity to be exposed to the culture because it would help bring out their potentialities as individual human beings.

[26]For a convenient summary of the national commissioners' Irish language policy see: *Report of the Department of Education for the School Year 1924–25 and for the Financial and Administrative Years 1924–25–26* (Dublin: Stationery Office 1926), pp. 27–30.

[27]The text of the 1917 constitution is given in full in Dorothy Macardle, *The Irish Republic* (New York: Farrar, Straus & Giroux, 1965), pp. 233, 915–16.

[28]Brian O'Cuiv, "Education and Language," in Desmond Williams (ed.), *The Irish Struggle 1916–1926* (London: Routledge & Kegan Paul), p. 160.

[29]*Dail Eireann. Minutes of Proceedings of the First Parliament of the Republic of Ireland, 1919–21. Official Report,* p. 259, 25 January 1921.

[30]Ibid., p. 227, 17 September 1920.

[31]*Iris Oifigiuil,* 10 March 1922. The order also is reproduced in *Irish Times,* 6 February 1922.

[32]This is clearly implied in T.J. O'Connell, *History of the Irish National Teachers' Organization 1868–1968* (Dublin: privately printed, n.d.), pp. 342–43. O'Connell was the honorary secretary of the programme conference and his book is the most useful single source of information thereon.

[33]Ibid., pp. 343–45. The unofficial Dail representative was Frank Fahy, assistant secretary to the Department of the Irish Language, who was receiving the salary (and presumably exercising the power) of a full ministership while J.J. O'Kelly, the minister, was on the run. See *Dail Eireann. Minutes of Proceedings of the First Parliament of the Republic of Ireland, 1919–21. Official Report,* p. 227, 17 September 1920.

[34]O'Connell, p. 344. See also National Programme Conference, *National Programme of Primary Instruction* (Dublin: Educational Company of Ireland Ltd., 1922), p. 4. This report is now extremely rare, both the Department of Education and the National Library of Ireland having lost their copies. I am very grateful to Dr. T. O'Raifeartaigh for finding me a copy in private hands.

[35]*National Programme of Primary Instruction,* pp. 4, 6–8, 13–14.

[36]See ibid., pp. 15–16.

[37]O'Connell, pp. 347–49.

[38]See obituaries by Dermot Gleeson, Joseph O'Neill and Maureen Beaumont, "Father T. Corcoran, S.J.," *Studies,* vol. xxxii (June 1943), pp. 153-62.

[39]"Reverend Dr. Timothy Corcoran," *Analecta Hibernica,* no. 16 (March 1946), p. 386.

[40]See my comments in *Irish Historical Studies,* vol xvi, no. 2 (September 1968), pp. 227–28. A bibliography of Corcoran's most important articles on Irish educational history is found in my *Irish Education Experiment.*

[41]*Irish Historical Studies,* vol. iii, no. 11 (March 1943), pp. 404–405.

[42]*Irish Monthly,* vol. li (June 1923), pp. 26–34.

[43]O'Connell, pp. 347–48.

[44]Ibid., pp. 348–51. See also *National Programme of Primary Instruction,* pp. 30–32. Also see *Irish School Weekly,* 10 January 1925, report of O'Connell's speech at Thurles, 13 December 1924.

[45]O'Connell, pp. 351–52.

[46]*Report of the Second National Programme Conference (1925–26) made for the Information of the Minister for Education* (Dublin: Stationery Office, 1926), pp. 9–10.

[47]O'Connell, pp. 354–55.

[48]Ibid., pp. 357–58.

[49]*Report of the Second National Programme Conference (1925–26) made for the Information of the Minister for Education*, pp. 8–9.

[50]Ibid., pp. 22–24.

[51]63 *Dail Eireann:* 1458, 21 July 1936.

[52]"Minority Report," in Department of Education, *Report of the Council of Education ... The Function of the Primary School* [Pr. 2583], pp. 297–98.

[53]*Second National Programme Conference (1925–26) made for the Information of the Minister for Education*, p. 28. The entire course is found on pp. 27–52. Even Reverend Professor Corcoran refused to accept the "I + E = a constant" formula as too vague to be valid. See *Studies*, vol. xv (June 1926), p. 331.

[54]15 *Dail Eireann:* 1313, 7 May 1926.

[55]Cited in 150 *Dail Eireann:* 1494, 17 May 1955.

[56]O'Connell, p. 362. The changes were the result of a report drawn up, in 1928, by the Reverend Lambert McKenna, who had been the chairman of the second programme conference. The administrative circulars which followed upon the report are found in *Report of the Department of Education for the School Years 1925–26–27 and the Financial and Administrative Year 1926–27* (Dublin: Stationery Office, 1928), pp. 9–17.

[57]26 *Dail Eireann:* 1132, 31 October 1928.

[58]33 *Dail Eireann:* 1686, 21 May 1931.

[59]The circular is reproduced in full in Department of Education, *Report of the Council of Education ... The Function of the Primary School*, pp. 330–34.

[60]O'Connell, pp. 208–209.

[61]55 *Dail Eireann:* 1746, 3 April 1935; 150 *Dail Eireann:* 1494, 17 May 1955, O'Connell, pp. 363–65; *Times Educational Supplement*, 6 October 1934.

The negotiations are covered in the weekly articles on Free State education in the *Times Educational Supplement* for the period.

Until the government opens its archives it will be impossible to know to what degree Eamon de Valera was the guiding force behind the 1934 changes. He was personally very concerned both with education and the language revival. O'Connell, who as executive secretary of the I.N.T.O. was well-informed, notes in another context that de Valera often intervened in the affairs of Derrig's department. See O'Connell, p. 239.

---

[62]*Times Educational Supplement,* 14 January 1939.

---

[63]The official circular of March 1928 introducing the new certificate is found in *Report of the Department of Education 1928–29* [P. 207], pp. 21–23.

---

[64]*Report of the Department of Education 1937–38* [P. 3588], p. 153.
A few of the pupils in the sixth standard and above had previously taken the tests, so the percentage slightly understated the degree of voluntary compliance.

---

[65]*Report of the Department of Education 1942–43* [P. 6567], pp. 18–19.
Here I should call the reader's attention to my use of the phrases "predominantly Irish-speaking" and "partially Irish-speaking" in reference to geographical areas. Strangely, in view of the emphasis placed upon the Irish language, the Irish government did not define precisely the criteria by which a given area was listed as being Irish-speaking. Different government agencies used different criteria. (Indeed, even "Irish-speaker" was an undefined term.) The 1926 report of the Gaeltacht commission defined as predominantly Irish-speaking those areas where eighty percent of the population was Irish-speaking and as partially Irish-speaking those areas where twenty-five to seventy-nine percent were Irish speakers. I have rendered the phrase "Breac-Ghaeltacht" used in educational reports as "partially Irish-speaking" and the phrase "Fíor-Ghaeltacht" as "predominantly Irish-speaking." This usage and its equation with the percentages of the 1926 Gaeltacht commission report is clearly justified by the Department of Education's practices as implied in *Report of the Department of Education 1930–31* [P. 733], pp. 24–26.

If the reader is delving into educational records and reports, he should be aware of the extraordinary flexibility with which the department employed the word "Gaeltacht." It was fully capable in an annual report of using the word to mean the Fíor-Ghaeltacht and also to mean the area encompassing both the Fíor- and the Breac-Ghaeltacht, within a single paragraph! (See Ibid., p. 24.) Then a few years later it would use "Gaeltacht" to refer to an arbitrarily defined area coterminous neither with the Fíor- nor Breac-Ghaeltacht, but comprising much less than their totality (see *Report of the Department of Education 1933–34* [P. 1693], p. 128). The department thought nothing of jumping its definition of the word within the space of a single year (compare *Report of the Department of Education 1955–56* [P. 4137], p. 62 and *An Roinn Oideachais, Tuarascail 1956–57* [Pr. 4642], p. 62).

All of this explains why I have chosen to translate educational directives into the English vocabulary of the 1926 commission — "predominantly and partially Irish-speaking" — instead of using those Irish words whose meaning has been so bewilderingly protean.

---

[66]Patrick O'Callaghan, "Irish in Schools," *The Bell,* vol. xiv, no. 1 (April 1947), p. 65.

---

[67]*Report of the Council of Education. . . . The Function of the Primary School,* pp. 158–60; *Report of the Department of Education 1951–52* [Pr. 2450], pp. 64, 70.

[68]*Report of the Council of Education. . . . The Function of the Primary School,* pp. 168–70, 274.

In 1948 it had again been made permissible to teach infants English for half an hour a day. During the late 1950s it appears that the school inspectors pressed less hard on the teachers about the Irish language. In 1959 the minister for education, Dr. Patrick Hillery, circularised the national school teachers telling *them* to decide which medium of instruction should be used in junior classes. See *Irish Times,* 29 January 1963.

[69]*Report of the Department of Education 1933–34* [P. 1693], p. 2.

[70]*Report of the Department of Education 1945–46* [P. 8508], p. 9.

[71]83*Dail Eireann:* 985–86, 27 May 1941.

[72]*Report of the Department of Education 1949–50* [Pr. 571], p. 10.

[73]Timothy Corcoran, "The Irish Language in the Irish Schools," *Studies,* vol. XIV (September 1925), p. 383.

[74]*Times Educational Supplement,* 18 June 1927.

[75]Seamus Fenton, *It All Happened* (Dublin: M.H. Gill & Son Ltd., 1949), p. 268.

[76]*Times Educational Supplement,* 23 January 1932.

[77]Ibid., 13 August 1938.

[78]Ibid., 15 July 1933.

[79]Ibid., 5 May 1934.

[80]*An Roinn Oideachais Tuarascail 1959–60* [Pr. 6218], p. 38.

[81]21 *Dail Eireann:* 1176, 10 November 1927.

[82]*Report of the Council of Education. . . . The Function of the Primary School,* p. 72.

[83]*National Programme of Primary Instruction,* p. 23.

[84]5 *Dail Eireann:* 144, 3 October 1923; *Irish Times,* 13 October 1961; *Report of the Council of Education. . . . The Function of the Primary School,* p. 68

[85]*Report of the Department of Education 1928–29* [P. 207], pp. 20–21.

[86]*Report of the Department of Education for the School Year 1924–25 and the Financial and Administrative Years 1924–25–26,* p. 31.

[87]*Report of the Department of Education 1936–37* [P. 3144], p. 159.

[88]*Times Educational Supplement,* 4 February 1922.

[89]*Report of the Council of Education. . . . The Curriculum of the Secondary School* [Pr. 5996], p. 62.

[90]*Report of the Department of Education for the School Year 1924–25 and the Financial and Administrative Years 1924–25–26,* p. 51.

The *Report of the Council of Education. . . . The Curriculum of the Secondary School* states (p. 64) that the 1924 programme was based on the findings of a commission constituted by the Dail in 1921. Unhappily, neither the Department of Education nor the National Library of Ireland is presently able to find a copy of the report.

[91]*Report of the Department of Education for the School Years 1925–26–27 and the Financial and Administrative Years 1926–27,* p. 51.

[92]*Report of the Department of Education 1933–34* [P. 1693], p. 54.

[93]177 *Dail Eireann:* 66, 21 October 1959.

[94]*The Restoration of the Irish Language* [Pr. 8061], pp. 116–20.

[95]Department of Education, *Rules and Programme for Secondary Schools, 1948–49* [P. 8910], pp. 9, 12.

[96]177 *Dail Eireann:* 360, 28 October 1959.

[97]*Times Educational Supplement,* 11 August 1928.

[98]21 *Dail Eireann:* 1724, 23 November 1927.

[99]*Times Educational Supplement,* 9 July 1932 and 16 July 1932.

[100]*Report of the Council of Education. . . . The Curriculum of the Secondary School,* pp. 76–78.

[101]*Report of the Department of Education for the School Years 1925–26–27 and the Financial and Administrative Year 1926–27,* pp. 189–90.

[102]*Report of the Department of Education 1934–35* [P. 2155], p. 55.

[103]*Report of the Department of Education 1954–55* [Pr. 3622], p. 80.

[104]*Census of Population of Ireland, 1961,* vol. ix, *Irish Language,* p. 2.

Believing the census is, of course, the problem. It is reasonable to suppose that the censuses taken before 1922 by the United Kingdom government somewhat underestimated the number of Irish speakers. After 1922 the opposite happened. In 1961 the director of the Central Statistics Office, speaking on the 1961 census, doubted if the Irish-speaking figures were of any value at all. In a partial census of the Gaeltacht in 1956 the police, who served as census-takers, overcounted Irish speakers by about thirty percent. The £5 per child annual bonus for each Irish-speaking child probably was at least a partial cause of this exaggeration. See *Irish Times,* 29 January 1963.

[105]That in both the predominantly and the partially Irish-speaking areas the number of Irish speakers, as well as the total population, was declining (the Irish-speaking

population proportionately more quickly than the total population) no reputable source denies. But precise comparable figures are unattainable because of the Irish government's unreliable statistical techniques. If one wants to be caught in a statistician's nightmare, study the methods used by the Gaeltacht commission of 1925-26 and then try to compare them to the methods used in the various census reports.

[106]On this point see R. A. Breatnach, "Irish Revival Reconsidered," *Studies,* vol. LIII (Spring 1964), pp. 20–22.

[107]29 *Dail Eireann:* 905-911, 25 April 1929.

[108]*Report of the Department of Education 1928–29,* p. 164.

[109]*Investment in Education. Annexes and Appendices* [Pr. 8527], p. 353.

[110]For an indication that many expert witnesses had contested Corcoran's views see 63 *Dail Eireann:* 532–33, 30 June 1926, and the I.N.T.O.'s *Report of Committee of Inquiry into the Use of Irish as a Teaching Medium to Children whose Home Language is English* (Dublin: I.N.T.O., 1941), pp. 9–10.

[111]*Report of the Council of Education.... The Function of the Primary School,* p. 144.

[112]See *Report of the Council of Education. . . . The Curriculum of the Secondary School,* pp. 116–30, passim.

[113]For a devastating criticism of the restoration report and a review of the actual state of the literature on the second-language question, see John MacNamara, "The Commission on Irish: Psychological Aspects," *Studies,* vol. LIII (Summer 1964), pp. 164–72.

[114]*The Restoration of the Irish Language,* p. 106.

[115]*Report of Committee of Inquiry into the Use of Irish as a Teaching Medium to Children whose Home Language is English,* pp. 15–25.

[116]Compiled from Ibid., pp. 28, 34–35, 39–40, 42, 47, 53, 54.

[117]83 *Dail Eireann:* 1094–95, 27 May 1941.

[118]MacNamara, *Bilingualism,* p. 134.

[119]Ibid., pp. 132–34.

[120]Ibid., p. 113.

[121]Martin Brennan, "The Restoration of Irish," *Studies,* vol. LIII (Autumn 1964), p. 269.

[122]A "language attitudes research committee" was set up in September 1970, but it is too early yet to evaluate its proposed research. Quarrels among the research team

make it unlikely that a significant document will emerge. See *Hibernia,* 17 November 1972 and 1 December 1972.

[123]89 *Dail Eireann:* 2380, 5 May 1943.

[124]*Report of Committee of Inquiry into the Use of Irish as a Teaching Medium to Children whose Home Language is English,* p. 60.

[125]59 *Dail Eireann:* 2197, 10 December 1935.

[126]Ibid., "I am, I think, in possession of greater knowledge and greater experience of the matter since I have occupied the position of minister for education, than any other group."

NOTES TO CHAPTER FOUR

[1]"Resolutions of the Assembled Archbishops and Bishops of Ireland on the Education Bill," *Irish Ecclesiastical Record*, 3 ser. vol. XIII (May 1892), pp. 474–77.

[2]National Programme Conference, *National Programme of Primary Instruction* (Dublin: Educational Company of Ireland Ltd., 1922), p. 24.

[3]Ibid., p. 24.

[4]*Times Educational Supplement*, 10 June 1922.

[5]6 *Seanad Eireann:* 519, 24 March 1926.

[6]Ibid., col. 542.

[7]12 *Dail Eireann:* 793–96, 11 June 1925.

[8]Act 17/1926.

[9]Compiled from Department of Education, *Report of the Department of Education for the School Years 1925–26–27 and the Financial and Administrative Year 1926–27* (Dublin: Stationery Office, 1928), p. 106; *Investment in Education. Annexes and Appendices* [Pr. 8527], p. 633.

[10]Act 29/1930, part v.

[11]Notably from the I.N.T.O. and from the Trades Union Congress. See *Times Educational Supplement,* 6 August 1932.

[12]The extracts are most easily available in Department of Education, *Report of the Council of Education . . . . The Function of the Primary School* [Pr. 2583], pp. 338–39. The same extracts, with additional information on the composition of the committee, are in Thomas J. McElligott, *Education in Ireland* (Dublin: Institute of Public Administration, 1966), pp. 53–54. Other direct quotations are found in the department's report for 1934–35, pp. 90–92.

[13]Department of Education, *Report of the Department of Education 1934–35* [P. 2155], p. 91.

[14]Department of Education, *Report of the Department of Education 1942–43* [P. 6567], pp. 41–45; Department of Education, *Report of the Department of Education 1947–48* [P. 9662], pp. 35–39.

[15]McElligott, *Education in Ireland*, p. 41.

[16]*Report of the Council of Education* . . . .*The Function of the Primary School*, pp. 260–62; *Times Educational Supplement*, 26 October 1951.

[17]*Times Educational Supplement*, 25 April 1952.

[18]*Report of the Council of Education*. . . .*The Function of the Primary School*, pp. 262–266.

[19]Ibid., p. 264.

[20]*Investment in Education* [Pr. 8311], p. 20.

[21]Ibid., p. 150.

NOTES TO CHAPTER FIVE

[1]*Irish Education* (London: Tuairim [c. 1962]) , p. 2.

[2]H. R. Chillingworth, "Examinations in the Irish Free State," *The Year Book of Education, 1938* (London: Evans Brothers Ltd., 1938), pp. 241–42.

[3]Department of Education, *Report of the Department of Education for the School Year 1924–25 and the Financial and Administrative Years 1924–25–26* (Dublin: Stationery Office, 1926), pp. 50–53.

[4]Department of Education, *Rules and Programme for Secondary Schools, 1948–49* [P. 8910], pp. 8–9.

In passing, note that each school had to provide English as a subject, but that no pupil had to take it as an examination subject.

[5]Peter Birch, "Secondary School English," *Irish Ecclesiastical Record*, 5 ser. vol. LXII, no. 6 (June 1944), p. 392.

[6]*Irish Education*, p. 7.

[7]*Irish School Weekly*, 21 June 1924; *Report of the Department of Education for the School Year 1924–25 and the Financial and Administrative Years 1924–25–26*, pp. 51–52.

[8]Sean O'Cathain, "Education in the New Ireland," in Francis MacManus (ed.), *The Years of the Great Test, 1926–39* (Cork: Mercier Press, 1967), p. 107.

[9]Department of Education, *Report of the Council of Education . . . .The Curriculum of the Secondary School* [Pr. 5996], p. 66, note 30.

[10]Patrick Pearse, *The Murder Machine* in, *Political Writings and Speeches* (Dublin: Talbot Press, 1966), p. 13.

[11]Ibid., p. 34.

[12]Ibid., pp. 12–13.

[13]*Irish Education*, p. 3.

[14]*Rules and Programme for Secondary Schools, 1948–49*, p. 8.

[15]F. S. L. Lyons, *Ireland since the Famine* (London: Weidenfeld and Nicolson, 1971), p. 640.

[16]In 1964 the Irish government decided to initiate capital grants to the academic secondary schools, but that is beyond the time boundary of the present chapter.

[17]In point of fact the teachers' incremental salary grants, which originally had been six to ten percent increments, became consistently larger until they were actually larger than the basic salaries paid by the schools and were the largest category of state grants to secondary schools. Compare *Report of the Department of Education for the School Year 1924–25 and the Financial and Administrative Years 1924–25–26*, pp. 53–54, to *Investment in Education* [Pr. 8311], pp. 10 and 85.

[18]*Investment in Education*, p. 85.

[19]Department of Education, *Report and Statistics Relating to National Education in Saorstat for the Year 1924–25* (Dublin: Stationery Office, 1926), pp. 6–7.

[20]Department of Education, *Report of the Department of Education 1944–45* [P. 7761], pp. 21–22.

[21]*Report of the Council of Education . . . .The Curriculum of the Secondary School*, p. 228.

The state intermediate scholarship system seems to have been above reproach as far as its operations were concerned. The pre-treaty Dail had voted to refuse public scholarships to children of ex-royal Irish constabulary members and others formerly in the service of the crown, but this policy was repudiated even before the intermediate scholarship system came into operation. (*Times Educational Supplement*, 30 June 1923.) The county and county borough schemes, however, seem to have been open to local pressures and vulnerable to local political and cultural idiocyncracies. For example, in 1930, the Galway county council decided that any student who played "foreign games" (i.e. soccer football, field hockey, or cricket) would be ineligible for a county council scholarship (*Times Educational Supplement*, 25 October 1930). Evidently this super-nationalism did not last forever, for in 1936 the request of a county council scholarship winner to study at a school which countenanced the foreign game of rugby football was approved – by a vote of nine to three! (*Times Educational Supplement*, 10 October 1936.)

[22]Derived from *Investment in Education. Annexes and Appendices* [Pr. 8527], 634, 649, 651, 652, with corrections for 1925–26, from the department's annual report for 1925–26–27.

These figures, it should be noted, do not include those children who were receiving an academic secondary schooling in the so-called "secondary tops," that is by paying a nominal fee and staying on for an extended time in the primary schools. Their numbers were not great: 119 pupils from secondary tops sat for the intermediate certificate in 1926, and fifteen for the leaving certificate. The corresponding numbers for 1961 were 1,330 and 355. (Source: *Investment in Education. Annexes and Appendices*, p. 658.)

Three comments about the scholarship statistics. First, one should realize that the county and county borough scholarship could be used at vocational schools, although in actual fact they were almost always taken at academic secondary schools. Second, in addition to these state scholarships, there were numerous private awards made by individual schools, whether formally from endowment or other funds, or informally through reducing the tuition for deserving poor students. Third, it can be argued that all students in Catholic secondary schools in which members of religious communities taught received an invisible scholarship because the religious did not draw their full salaries and thus implicitly underwrote the cost of the schooling.

[23]*Report of the Department of Education 1944–45,* p. 22.

[24]Department of Education, *Report of the Department of Education 1927–28* [P. 19], pp. 46–47.

[25]*Investment in Education,* p. 309; *Report of the Council of Education . . . .The Curriculum of the Secondary School,* p. 228.

[26]See *Investment in Education,* p. 309.

[27]See map and statistics in the *Irish Times,* 6 July 1963, based on 1960–61 academic year.

[28]*Report of the Council of Education . . . .The Curriculum of the Secondary School,* pp. 252–54.

NOTES TO CHAPTER SIX

[1]Basil Chubb, *The Government and Politics of Ireland* (Stanford: Stanford University Press, 1970), p. 270.

[2]*Investment in Education. Annexes and Appendices* [Pr. 8527], p. 353.

[3]Michael O'Donnell, "Irish Education Today," *Iris Hibernia,* vol. v, no. 1 (1963), p. 20.
O'Donnell's source was U.N.E.S.C.O. data published in 1962. Usually U.N.E.S.C.O. data should be taken as indicative rather than definitive.

[4]Ibid., p. 20.

[5]Private investment in Irish education was, in 1961–62, slightly less than one-third of public investment (see *Investment in Education* [Pr. 8311], p. 105; estimates vary according to the accounting system employed). In all probability the proportion of Irish private investment in education was higher than in most other developed countries, but that makes little difference to our conclusion about the actual per capita educational expenditure as compared to that of other nations. Even if one incorporates Irish voluntary expenditure in the estimate while assuming *none* in other countries, Ireland still comes out ahead only of Italy.

[6]*Investment in Education. Annexes and Appendices,* p. 353. A low of 8.5% was reached in 1954.

[7]See 133 *Dail Eireann:* 1504, 23 July 1952.

[8]*Investment in Education,* p. 304.

[9]*Times Educational Supplement,* 23 March 1951.

[10]*Investment in Education,* p. 254.

[11]Ibid., p. 247.

[12]Ibid., p. 261.

[13]Ibid., p. 261.

[14]129 *Dail Eireann:* 921, 21 February 1952.

[15]*Investment in Education,* p. 248.
"Dry latrines" were found in 49.4% of the primary schools, a euphemism for no facilities at all. One shudders to think what the 3.1% "other" category represented.

[16]*Irish Times,* 28 January 1964.

---

[17]*Investment in Education,* p. 249.

---

[18]Ibid., p. 250.

---

[19]Thomas J. McElligott, *Education in Ireland* (Dublin: Institute of Public Administration, 1966), p. 52.

A departmental committee on the matter had been appointed in 1932. (*Times Educational Supplement,* 2 July 1932.)

---

[20]*Irish Education* (London: Tuairim [c. 1962]), p. 5.

---

[21]*Investment in Education. Annexes and Appendices,* p. 265.

---

[22]Ibid., p. 558.

---

[23]183 *Dail Eireann:* 422, 28 June 1960.

In response to a similar Dublin situation in the late 'thirties, James Larkin had declared it was "a crucifixion of the children," to force the children of the ill-provided Dublin suburbs to be transported to schools in the centre of the city. (*Times Education Supplement,* 12 August 1939.)

---

[24]*Investment in Education,* p. 78.

---

[25]See Conrad M. Arensberg, *The Irish Countryman: an Anthropological Study* (New York: MacMillan Co. 1937) and Conrad M. Arensberg and Solon T. Kimball, *Family and Community in Ireland* (Cambridge, Mass.: Harvard University Press, second ed., 1968).

NOTES TO CHAPTER SEVEN

[1]The following statement by Sean O'Faolain is relevant: "The Celt's sense of the Otherworld has dominated his imagination and affected his literature from the beginning. So I see him at any rate struggling, through century after century, with this imaginative domination, seeking for a synthesis between dream and reality, aspiration and experience, a shrewd knowledge of the world and a strange reluctance to cope with it, and tending always to find the balance not in an intellectual synthesis but in the rhythm of a perpetual emotional oscillation." From: *The Irish. A Character Study* (New York: Devin-Adair Co., 1956), pp. 3–4.

[2]Jean Blanchard, *The Church in Contemporary Ireland* (Dublin: Clonmore & Reynolds Ltd., 1963; original French edition, 1960), p. 17.

[3]*Irish Catholic Directory 1936,* entry for 6 January 1935, p. 578. The reader will note that throughout this book I have shortened clerical titles. This is a practical matter. No disrespect is intended.

[4]*Irish Catholic Directory 1934,* entry for 1 January 1933, p. 572.

[5]*Irish Catholic Directory 1952,* entry for 10 October 1951, p. 709.

[6]*Irish Catholic Directory 1953,* entry for 6 May 1952, p. 641.

[7]The best account of this affair is found in J.H. Whyte's *Church and State in Modern Ireland 1923–1970* (Dublin: Gill & MacMillan, 1971). Whyte's excellent work is indispensable for the student of modern Ireland.

[8]125 *Dail Eireann:* 781; quoted in Whyte, p. 232.

[9]The bishops' lenten pastorals for 1922 are especially interesting. See *Irish Catholic Directory 1923,* entries for 26 February 1922, pp. 551–55.

A little later, the bishops issued a collective statement favouring the treaty. See Ibid., entry for 26 April 1922, pp. 598-602.

[10]For a study illustrating the point see Alexander J. Humphrey's *New Dubliners: Urbanization and the Irish Family* (London: Routledge & Kegan Paul, 1966).

[11]Roman Catholic Church in Ireland, *Acta et Decreta Concillii Plenarii Episcoporum Hiberniae ... 1927* (Dublin: Brown & Nolan, 1929) , pp. 155–56.

[12]*Irish Catholic Directory 1945,* entry for 20 February 1944, p. 674.

[13]*Divini Illius Magistri,* quoted in John Mescal, *Religion in the Irish System of Education* (Dublin: Clonmore & Reynolds Ltd., 1957), p. 23.

[14]*Irish Catholic Directory 1935*, entry for 10 December 1933, p. 572.

[15]Martin Brennan, "The Catholic School System of Ireland," *Irish Ecclesiastical Record*, 5 ser. vol. LIII, no. 9 (September 1938), p. 259. In the original the words quoted were italicized.

[16]Roman Catholic Church in Ireland, *Acta et Decreta Concillii Plenarii . . . 1956* (Dublin: M.H. Gill, 1970), p. 96.

[17]*Report of the Second National Programme Conference (1925–26) made for the Information of the Minister for Education* (Dublin: Stationery Office, 1926), p. 21.

Admittedly, the conference was presided over by the Reverend Lambert McKenna, S.J., but the great majority of members were lay (see p. 4).

[18]Brennan, "Catholic School System," p. 263.

[19]Department of Education, *Report of the Council of Education. . . . The Function of the Primary School* [Pr. 2583], pp. 94, 130.

Like the Second National Programme Conference, the Council of Education was chaired by a cleric but constituted chiefly of laymen.

[20]*Irish Catholic Directory 1956*, entry for 21 August 1955, p. 656.

[21]Department of Education, *Report of the Council of Education. . . . The Curriculum of the Secondary School* [Pr. 5996], p. 80.

To the examples of lay attitudes cited in the text (which are limited to the post-independence period) one should add the archtypal words of the nationalist politician Timothy Healy, who was destined to become Governor General of the Irish Free State, spoken in the United Kingdom parliament in 1902: "I would rather have my children learn to say 'Our Father' than learn the use of the Globes. I would rather they understood their religion so as to prepare them for the eternity that is to come than that they should become rich and prosperous and educated in the things of this world." Quoted in P.J. Dowling, *A History of Irish Education. A Study in Conflicting Loyalties* (Cork: Mercier Press, 1971), p. 127.

[22]I do not have space here to discuss the substance and style of religious instruction. A useful study is *Religious Education in Ireland* by J.D. King (Dublin: Fallons, 1970). Three periodical articles are of special interest: Sean C. O'Mordha's, "The Origin of the Written Examination in Religious Knowledge in Irish Secondary Schools," *Irish Ecclesiastical Record*, 5 ser. vol. CIV, no. 5 (October-November 1965), pp. 278–85, and two articles entitled "Religious Instruction in Primary Schools," *Irish Ecclesiastical Record*, 5 ser. vol. LXVI, no. 1 (July 1945), pp. 1–10 and no. 2 (August 1945), pp. 120–28, written by "a lay teacher."

[23]Jeremiah Newman, "The Priests of Ireland: A Socio-Religious Survey — II — Patterns of Vocations," *Irish Ecclesiastical Record*, 5 ser. vol. XCVIII, no. 2 (August 1962), pp. 66–69.

Newman's figures include schools in Northern Ireland, but these are not so many as to make it improper to apply his conclusion to this study of the southern situation.

[24]Source: Jeremiah Newman, "The Priests of Ireland: A Socio-Religious Survey — 1 — Numbers and Distribution," *Irish Ecclesiastical Record*, 5 ser. vol. xcviii, no. 1 (July 1962), p. 6.

The figures include Northern Ireland, but this does not invalidate the basic point made in the text. Actually, because Ireland "exported" so many priests to other countries, the increasing ratio of priests to people within Ireland is only a pale reflection of the extraordinary ability of the Irish schools to produce priestly vocations.

[25]John J. O'Meara, *Reform in Education* (Blackrock: Mount Salus Press Ltd., 1958), p. 3.

[26]*Acta et Decreta Concilii Plenarii Episcoporum Hiberniae . . . 1927*, p. 156.

[27]John Charles McQuaid, *Catholic Education: Its Function and Scope* (Dublin: Catholic Truth Society of Ireland [1942], p. 18.

[28]Denis Fahey, "The Introduction of Scholastic Philosophy into Irish Secondary Education," *Irish Ecclesiastical Record*, 5 ser. vol. xxii, no. 8 (August 1923), p. 177.

[29]*Irish Catholic Directory 1959*, entry for 7 October 1958, p. 700.

[30]After World War ii the bishops were sensitive to the threats posed by both right- and left-wing movements, but prior to the war they were much more concerned with communism than fascism. The following statement from a Lenten pastoral of Michael Fogarty, bishop of Killaloe, is representative of their view: "The heart of Catholic Ireland is with the noble Spanish nation that under General Franco are now fighting, at tremendous cost to themselves, the sacred cause of Christianity against the anti-God ferocity of the Reds from all over the world; and may Heaven bless their crusading valour with success." Source: *Irish Catholic Directory 1939*, entry for 27 February 1938, p. 625.

[31]Whyte, p. 301.

[32]*Irish Catholic Directory 1952*, entry for 12 November 1951, p. 716.

[33]For examples see Whyte, pp. 307–308.

[34]*Irish Catholic Directory 1927*, entry for 26 May 1926, pp. 586–87.

[35]*Irish Catholic Directory 1946*, entry for 3 April 1945, p. 681.

[36]Information on the course of the agitation from the 1920s onward is found in T. J. O'Connell, *History of the Irish National Teachers' Organization 1868–1968* (Dublin: privately printed, n.d.), pp. 437–42.

[37]*Times Educational Supplement*, 8 February 1952.

[38]Ibid., 13 June 1952.

[39]O'Connell, pp. 440–41.

[40]*Seventy-First Report of the Commissioners of National Education in Ireland for the Year 1904*, pp. 13–14 [Cd. 2567], H.C. 1905, xxviii.

⁴¹Department of Education, *Report of the Department of Education for the School Years 1925–26–27 and the Financial and Administrative Year 1926–27* (Dublin: Stationery Office, 1928), p. 107.

⁴²*Times Educational Supplement,* 27 March 1926.

⁴³Department of Education, *Report of the Department of Education 1927–28* [P. 19], pp. 10–12.

⁴⁴47 *Dail Eireann:* 91, 26 April 1933.

⁴⁵Compare *Report of the Department of Education for the School Years 1925–26–27 and the Financial and Administrative Years 1926–27,* p. 107, with *Report of the Department of Education 1953–54* [Pr. 3153], p. 50.

⁴⁶Whyte, p. 38.

⁴⁷Quoted in "Correspondence. The Vocational Schools," *Irish Ecclesiastical Record,* 5 ser. vol. LVII, no. 4 (May 1941), p. 369.

⁴⁸Martin Brenan, "The Vocational Schools," *Irish Ecclesiastical Record,* 5 ser. vol. LVII, no. 2 (February 1941), pp. 13–27.

⁴⁹Whyte, p. 38, n. 52.

⁵⁰*Times Educational Supplement,* 24 December 1938. On combined state-clerical opposition see also Ibid., 18 November 1939.

⁵¹Whyte, p. 67ff.

⁵²Cornelius Lucey, "A Guild for Education," *Irish Ecclesiastical Record,* 5 ser. vol. LI, no. 6 (June 1938), pp. 582–92. See also pp. 416–17 of Lucey's article, "Making the School System of Ireland Catholic," *Irish Ecclesiastical Record,* 5 ser. vol. LII, no. 10 (October 1938).

⁵³Commission on Vocational Organisation, *Report* [P. 6743]. For a summary of the commissions' appointment and results see Whyte, pp. 87–88, 96–119.

⁵⁴*Times Educational Supplement,* 23 June 1950. See also Ibid., 10 April 1948.

NOTES TO CHAPTER EIGHT

[1]Since this book is an educational history, not a general history of modern Ireland, I do not have space to develop the point that southern Irish legislation on birth control, divorce, censorship, and, for a long time, the adoption of children, was perceived by most Protestants as being in violation of their own civil rights. In each case, Catholic canon law was replicated in Irish civil law with no exceptions being made for those whose religious traditions made it impossible for them to accept these pieces of Catholic social legislation.

For a discussion of the interpretation of religion and social and moral legislation see chapter "Religion and Values" in my *The United States and Ireland* (Cambridge: Harvard University Press, and London: Oxford University Press, 1973), pp. 130–67.

[2]Conor Cruise O'Brien, "1891-1916" in Conor Cruise O'Brien (ed.), *The Shaping of Modern Ireland* (London: Routledge & Kegan Paul, 1960), p. 16.

[3]Myles Dillon, "Douglas Hyde," in Ibid., pp. 53–54.

[4]Even after having read scores of revolutionary nationalist pamphlets wherein these equations are implicitly made, I am still unsure to what extent they were conscious and intentional. In any case, a very useful scholarly article could be written analyzing nationalist rhetoric from the viewpoint of Protestant sensibilities. My impression is that very few nationalist pamphleteers and orators made any serious attempt to soothe Protestant fears in a vocabulary the Protestants would understand. Indeed, many efforts seemed perfectly, if perhaps unintentionally, designed to encourage the Ulster Protestants to resist and the southern Protestants to emigrate.

[5]Patrick J. Buckland, "Southern Unionism, 1885–1922," (Ph.D. thesis, Queen's University, Belfast, 1969), pp. 585, 589.

For reports of outrages see the *Church of Ireland Gazette* for the entire period and especially for 16 June 1922, 1 December 1922, and 12 January 1923. See also the condemnation of the murder of Protestants in the western part of his diocese by Daniel Cohalan, bishop of Cork, in the *Irish Catholic Directory 1923*, entry for 30 April 1922, p. 566.

[6]*Church of Ireland Gazette*, 26 May 1922.

[7]A fascinating example of the efforts of some Protestants to hide from the reality of what had happened was the argument by John Henry Barnard, provost of Trinity College, Dublin, and formerly archbishop of Dublin, who said in 1924 that "there have, indeed, been outbursts of violence directed against loyalist minorities, but for

the most part it has been *qua* loyalists, and not *qua* Protestants that the members of the Church of Ireland have suffered" (*Church of Ireland Gazette*, 18 January 1924). This argument must have been scant comfort to the outrage victims.

[8]*Church of Ireland Gazette*, 12 May 1922.

[9]Direct quotation, in Buckland, p. 591.

[10]*Church of Ireland Gazette*, 19 May 1922.

[11]Memorandum of 25 May 1922, quoted in Buckland, p. 584.

[12]F. S. L. Lyons, *Ireland since the Famine* (London: Weidenfeld and Nicholson, 1971), p. 468.
On the political agreements see, D. H. Akenson and J. F. Fallin, "The Irish Civil War and the Drafting of the Free State Constitution," *Eire–Ireland*, vol. 1, no. 4 (Winter 1970), pp. 31–32, 61–62.

[13]8 December 1922.

[14]Buckland, pp. 583, 587.

[15]Source: Central Statistics Office, *Census of Population of Ireland, 1946*, vol. III, *Religions, Birthplaces* [Pr. 158], p. 1; Central Statistics Office, *Statistical Abstract of Ireland 1966* [Pr. 8950], p. 53.

[16]For the 1946-61 period see the excellent study *Religion and Demographic Behaviour in Ireland* by Brendan M. Walsh (Dublin: The Economic and Social Research Institute, 1970).

[17]F. S. L. Lyons, "The Minority Problem in the Twenty-Six Counties," in Francis MacManus (ed.), *The Years of the Great Test 1926–39* (Cork: Mercier Press, 1967), pp. 99–100.

[18]Compiled from Department of Education, *Report of the Department of Education for the School Years 1925–26–27 and the Financial and Administrative Year 1926-27* (Dublin: Stationery Office, 1928), p. 108; *Report of the Department of Education 1935–36* [P. 2656], pp. 148–49; *Report of the Department of Education 1945–46* [P. 8508], p. 109; *An Roinn Oideachais Tuarascail 1960–61* [Pr. 6718], p. 107.

[19]*Investment in Education. Annexes and Appendices* [Pr. 8527], p. 640. Rounding of the figures precludes the totals equalling precisely 100.00% in all cases.

[20]9 May 1930.

[21]John Mescal, *Religion in the Irish System of Education* (Dublin: Clonmore & Reynolds Ltd., 1957), p. 112.

[22]Ibid., p. 112.

[23]*Investment in Education* [Pr. 8311], pp. 230–32.

[24]Act 17/1926, section 4.

[25]Compare *Church of Ireland Gazette,* 19 May 1933 and Church of Ireland, *Sixty-First Report of Proceedings of the Representative Body laid before the General Synod of the Church of Ireland . . . 1931,* p. 238.

[26]*Times Educational Supplement,* 21 May 1932.

[27]See Church of Ireland, *Fifty-Ninth Report of Proceedings of the Representative Body laid before the General Synod of the Church of Ireland . . . 1929,* pp. 229–30; *Journal of the Session of the General Synod of the Church of Ireland . . . 1930,* p. lxxiii.

[28]*Sixtieth Report of Proceedings of the Representative Body laid before the General Synod of the Church of Ireland. . . 1930,* p. 227.

[29]For the Anglican Board of Education's summary of the conclusion of the negotiations see *Sixty-Fifth Report of Proceedings of the Representative Body laid before the General Synod of the Church of Ireland . . . 1935,* pp. 226–27.

[30]Department of Education, *Report of the Department of Education 1934–35* [P. 2155], pp. 8–9.

[31]*Times Educational Supplement,* 18 May 1940.
   By 1963/64 the government grant had risen to £14 for each pupil or 50% of the total cost of the scheme, whichever was smaller. For details see *Investment in Education. Annexes and Appendices,* pp. 608–09.

[32]*Times Educational Supplement,* 9 July 1939.

[33]J.H. Whyte, "Political Life in the South," in Michael Hurley (ed.) , *Irish Anglicanism 1869–1964* (Dublin: Allen Figgis Ltd., 1970), p. 144.

[34]Church of Ireland, *Eightieth Report of Proceedings of the Representative Church Body laid before the General Synod of the Church of Ireland . . . 1950,* p. 188.

[35]*Church of Ireland Gazette,* 5 November 1926.

[36]Ibid., 3 December 1926.

[37]Matthew Arnold, *Irish Essays and Others* (London: Smith, Elder & Co., 1882) , p. 87.

[38]*Gaelic League Pamphlets — no. 12. The Irish Language and Irish Intermediate Education* (Dublin: Gaelic League, 1901) , pp. 1–2. I have clarified somewhat the identity of the speakers; otherwise the dialogue is as published by the League.

[39]*Church of Ireland Gazette,* 6 July 1923, article by the Reverend Dudley Fletcher.

[40]*Times Educational Supplement,* 1 January 1938.

[41]22 October 1926.
   Threats against the Protestants came even from Catholic clergy in Northern Ireland At one clerical meeting the Reverend Canon John McCafferty referred to the Protestant apprehensions and said that no consideration should be shown to someone who set himself in opposition to the preservation, revival, spread, and cultivation

of Irish as the mother tongue (Irish Catholic Directory 1930, entry for 15 August 1929), p. 598.

42Church of Ireland Gazette, 5 November 1926.

43Church of Ireland, Sixtieth Report of Proceedings of the Representative Body laid before the General Synod of the Church of Ireland . . . 1930, p. 228.

44Church of Ireland Gazette, 25 January 1929, article by the Reverend R.I. Ford.

45Church of Ireland Gazette, 3 December 1926, letter originally published in Irish Times, 17 November 1926.

46Church of Ireland Gazette, 10 December 1926.

47Church of Ireland, Report of Proceedings of the Representative Body laid before the General Synod of the Church of Ireland . . . 1922, pp. 213–14.

48Presbyterian Church in Ireland, Report and Accounts, June 1924, p. 101.

49Church of Ireland, Eighty-First Report of Proceedings of the Representative Church Body . . . 1951, p. 178.

The board's reference to problems of books in English as well as in Irish raises a point tangential to my main argument about the Irish language. From the very beginning of the Free State there were serious Protestant objections to the English language texts, especially those in history. The following extract is from the report of the Presbyterian Board of Education found in the Report and Accounts, June 1924 of the Presbyterian Church in Ireland and indicates both the problem and the government's sympathetic response (p. 101): "In the histories of Ireland available for our schools, references to the past relations between Ireland and England occur, which in the judgment of competent authorities are incorrect and unfair. The committee understand that any history which, judged by Protestant scholarship, gives as far as possible an unbiased account of events and personalities as to which opinion is divided will be sufficiently recognised."

That such problems were unavoidable seems obvious when one reads the views on history held by that most influential of Irish educationalists, the Reverend Father Corcoran: "[The] main object of attention in the school treatment of history must be national rather than international. The proper corrective, which will keep this basis of treatment sound and healthy, is the linkage of Irish history with Catholic history, rather than with European. The Catholic standpoint will not fail to give our race and its work its due and ample credit from the time of O'Connell, through the period of the Vatican council, and in the missionary enterprises of constructive Catholicity in both hemispheres." (Timothy Corcoran, "The Teaching of Modern Irish History," Irish Monthly, vol. li [October 1923], pp. 494–95.)

The following is from a recent analysis by a Catholic teacher from Northern Ireland:

It is understandable that a new state, itself the creation of the physical force tradition and the Gaelic cultural revival, should want to emphasise its national identity and to inculcate a respect for the history and tradition of the people.

In practice, however, the policy had a restrictive and illiberal tendency. In the primary schools only Irish history was taught, and, although in the secondary schools the programme was widened to include some aspects of the history of Western Europe, Britain, with whom Ireland had been linked for so long, was deemed not to exist at all. The textbooks used in Irish history were impregnated with a spirit of exaggerated nationalism, with its stress on war and hatred of the enemy. (John Magee, "The Teaching of Irish History in Irish Schools," reprinted from *The Northern Teacher*, vol. x, no. 1 [winter 1970], p. 2.)

Similarly, Mark Tierney, O.S.B., a history teacher in the Irish Republic, notes: "Because Ireland was a British colony for so long, her history is necessarily linked to that of England. Yet there has been a tendency since 1922 to neglect English history in Irish schools. What is worse, many teachers and textbook authors have approached Irish history with a definite bias. They have taken sides, believing that the Irish were always 'the goodies,' while the English were 'the badies.' They have blamed England for all Ireland's ills. This has given our history a lop-sidedness and has created many unfortunate distortions of the truth." (Mark Tierney, "History in Education," in Michael Murphy [ed.], *Education in Ireland* II, *What Sould Students Learn?* [Cork: Mercier Press, 1971], p. 41.)

50 *Times Educational Supplement,* 24 December 1926.

51 Ibid., 20 May 1939.

52 *Church of Ireland Gazette,* 10 March 1922.

53 Ibid., 12 November 1926.

54 Ibid., 15 October 1926.

55 Presbyterian Church in Ireland, *Reports and Accounts, June 1925,* p. 79.

56 Church of Ireland, *Journal of the Third Session of the Twenty-Fourth General Synod of the Church of Ireland . . . 1936,* p. lxviii.

This resolution was an endorsement of the action of the church's Board of Education which had presented their opinion to the minister for education in person in January 1935. See Church of Ireland, *Sixty-Sixth Report of Proceedings of the Representative Body laid before the General Synod of the Church of Ireland . . . 1936,* p. 232.

57 *Church of Ireland Gazette,* 20 May 1938.

58 Church of Ireland, *Sixty-Ninth Report of Proceeding of the Representative Body laid before the General Synod of the Church of Ireland . . . 1939,* p. 232.

59 Whether these British antecedents were real or not in individual cases is irrelevant: it is the belief in their reality that determined Protestant reactions to the compulsory Irish revival.

60 See Church of Ireland, *Eightieth Report of Proceedings of the Representative*

Church Body laid before the General Synod of the Church of Ireland . . . 1950, pp. 188–89; *Eighty-Fifth Report of Proceedings of the Representative Church Body . . . 1955,* pp. 114–21; *Ninety-Third Report of Proceedings of the Representative Church Body to be laid before the General Synod of the Church of Ireland . . . 1963,* p. 111.

61Church of Ireland, *Seventy-Second Report of Proceedings of the Representative Body laid before the General Synod of the Church of Ireland . . . 1942,* p. 211.

62For the board's submission of 16 February 1955, see, Church of Ireland, *Eighty-Sixth Report of Proceedings of the Representative Church Body to be laid before the General Synod of the Church of Ireland . . . 1956,* p. 119.

63Church of Ireland, *Ninety-Third Report of Proceedings of the Representative Church Body to be laid before the General Synod of the Church of Ireland . . . 1963,* p. 111.

64W.B. Stanford and R.B. McDowell, *Mahaffy. A Biography of an Anglo–Irishman* (London: Routledge and Kegan Paul, 1971), p. 235.

65Act 17/1926, section 4 (1).

66Ibid., section 5 (1).

67*Times Educational Supplement,* 27 October 1934.

68Ibid., 17 November 1934.

69Ibid., 8 December 1934.

7088*Dail Eireann:* 2118–19, 18 November 1942.

71See General Mulcahy's comments in Ibid: 2523, 26, November 1942.

72Ibid: 2122, 18 November 1942.

73Ibid: 2122–23, 18 November 1942.

74Ibid: 2521, 26 November 1942. Obviously Mulcahy was exaggerating, for rhetorical effect, but his basic point, that the law offended against the civil right of free circulation of the person, is valid.

7527 *Seanad Eireann:* 1533, 10 March 1943.

76Ibid: 1845, 20 April 1943.

77Editorial in the *Church of Ireland Gazette,* 3 February 1922.

78Bradley said, "The members of the board, being largely representative of what has hitherto been known as the minority will be all the more useful to the ministry in advising as to how far schemes of education which may fully commend themselves to the majority of the population will, in their application to the schools under the control of other sections of the community, require further consideration from the point of view of the latter." *(Irish Times,* 1 February 1922.)

As I have noted earlier, Bradley was wrong in implying there was a Protestant majority among the Free State primary education commissioners. But in any case, neither in intention nor practice did the Department of Education wish any advice from its former commissioners.

[79]*Church of Ireland Gazette,* 6 July 1923.

[80]Ibid., 12 October 1923.

[81]*Times Educational Supplement,* 1 December 1923.

[82]*Church of Ireland Gazette,* 15 May 1931.

[83]*Times Educational Supplement,* 13 July 1935.

[84]Norman Atkinson, *Irish Education: a History of Educational Institutions* (Dublin: Allen Figgis, 1969), p. 198. One should perhaps add that the underdeveloped African and South American areas historically were associated with the missionary activities of the Catholic church.

[85]Presbyterian Church in Ireland, *Annual Reports 1953,* p. 75.

[86]Church of Ireland, *Careers in Ireland* (Dublin: Sparsely Populated Areas Commission of the Church of Ireland, n.d. [1957]).

[87]For sample statements see *Church of Ireland Gazette,* 31 May 1935; Church of Ireland, *Eighty-Fourth Report of Proceedings of the Representative Church Body to be laid before the General Synod of the Church of Ireland . . . 1954,* p. 116; Presbyterian Church in Ireland, *Annual Reports 1954,* p. 82, and *Annual Reports 1956,* p. 84.

[88]Church of Ireland, *Ninety-Fifth Report of Proceedings of the Representative Church Body to be laid before the General Synod of the Church of Ireland . . . 1965,* p. 144.

The full document also was published separately as *Report on Secondary Education, 1965* (Dublin: Dublin University Press Ltd., 1965).

[89]Presbyterian Church in Ireland, *Annual Report 1970,* p. 196.

[90]The phrase is Donal McCartney's. See his review of *Irish Anglicanism 1869–1969* in *Eire-Ireland,* vol. v, no. 4 (Winter 1970), pp. 135–37.

NOTES TO CHAPTER NINE

[1]Compiled from: *Report of the Department of Education for the School Year 1924–25 and the Financial and Administrative Years 1924–25–26* (Dublin: Stationery Office, 1926), p. 100; *Report of the Department of Education 1930–31* [P. 733], p. 127; *Report of the Department of Education 1940–41* [P. 5529], p. 94; *Report of the Department of Education 1950–51* [Pr. 1609], p. 92; *An Roinn Oideachais Tuarascail 1960–61* [Pr. 6718], p. 126.

[2]Here I am projecting backward in time statistics given by T.J. McElligott in the *Irish Times*, 26 January 1965. This is necessary because of lacunae in the Department of Education's statistical reports.

In the discussion which follows in the text I am talking about the dominant Catholic culture and not that of the Protestant minority.

[3]*Investment in Education* [Pr. 8311], p. 230.

[4]Ibid., p. 232.

[5]See *Investment in Education. Annexes and Appendices* [Pr. 8527], p. 635.

[6]See *Investment in Education*, p. 230.

[7]On the varying attitudes of the bishops I am relying on private information provided by two high ranking individuals each of whom, understandably, prefers to remain anonymous.

[8]"Statements and Resolutions of the Irish Hierarchy at Maynooth Meeting June 21," *Irish Ecclesiastical Record*, 4 ser. vol. xxvii, no. 7 (July 1910), p. 92.

[9]Quoted in *Acta et Decreta Concilii Plenarii. . . 1956*, p. 207.

[10]For a discussion of this anti-sex campaign see J. H. Whyte's *Church and State in Modern Ireland 1923–1970* (Dublin: Gill and MacMillan, 1971), pp. 24–30.

[11]*Irish Catholic Directory 1925*, entry for 2 March 1924, p. 562.

[12]Ibid., entry for 8 April 1924, p. 563.

[13]Ibid., entry for 2 March 1924, p. 560.

[14]*Irish Catholic Directory 1926*, entry for 22 February 1925, p. 561.

[15]"Statement of the Archbishops and Bishops of Ireland on the Evils of Dancing,

Issued at their Meeting, Held in Maynooth, on 6th October 1925," *Irish Ecclesiastical Record,* 5 ser. vol. xxvii, no. 1 (January 1926), p. 91.

16Ibid., p. 92.

17Reported by C.B. Murphy, "Sex, Censorship and the Church," *The Bell,* vol. ii, no. 6 (September 1941), p. 71.

18Whyte, pp. 28–29.

19*Irish Catholic Directory 1929,* entry for 4 January 1928, p. 560.

20The classic work in the field has been done by Conrad M. Arensberg and Solon T. Kimball, *Family and Community in Ireland* (Cambridge: Harvard University Press, second edition. 1968). See also Conrad M. Arensberg, *The Irish Countryman: an Anthropological Study* (New York: MacMillan, 1937).

An uncontrolled, but often informative, set of essays is *The Vanishing Irish* (London: W.H. Allen, 1954), edited by John A. O'Brien.

21Statistics from census data cited by Alexander J. Humphreys, *New Dubliners: Urbanization and the Irish Family* (London: Routledge and Kegan Paul, 1966), pp. 66–68.

22Two especially valuable essays on the relationship between social and religious influences and the Irish sexual code are: "Catholicism and Marriage in the Century after the Famine," by K.H. Connell in his *Irish Peasant Society. Four Historical Essays* (Oxford: Clarendon Press, 1958), pp. 113–61, and "Sex and Repression in an Irish Folk Community," by John C. Messenger in *Human Sexual Behaviour. Variations in the Ethnographic Spectrum,* edited by Donald S. Marshall and Robert C. Suggs (New York and London: Basic Books Inc., 1971), pp. 3–37.

23Humphreys, p. 259; Brendan M. Walsh, *Religion and Demographic Behaviour in Ireland* (Dublin: The Economic and Social Research Institute, 1970), p. 11.

24Paradoxically, the censuses indicated that non-Catholics married even later than did Catholics. This fact was in part a function of social class determinants, however, for the higher one's social class, the older one was apt to be before marrying, and Protestants were found in relatively large numbers in the middle and upper classes (Humphreys, pp. 259–60; Walsh, p. 13). It was also partially accounted for by distortions resulting from the statistical procedures employed (Walsh, p. 27).

25A thorough investigation of the literary censorship system is Michael Adams' *Censorship: The Irish Experience* (Dublin: Scepter Books, 1968).

On other matters discussed in the text Whyte's book provides the most complete and illuminating discussion.

26Commission of Inquiry on Mental Illness, *Report* [Pr. 9181], p. xiii.

27*The Guardian,* 24 August 1972.

NOTES TO CHAPTER TEN

[1]Two quotations from articles by T. J. McElligott, a leading educational critic of the period, are apposite: "Education is today blinking in the searchlight trained upon it not alone by educationists, but by economists and industrialists as well." (*Irish Times,* 11 December 1962). "Danger is a great bringer of repentance. The fear of being rejected by the common market or of being classed as backwards or under-developed has made us very conscious of the role of education in our national life." (*Irish Times,* 4 March 1963.)

[2]Two volumes, Pr. 8311 and Pr. 8527.

[3]*An Roinn Oideachais Tuarascal, Tablai Staitistic 1966–67* [Prl. 1121], p. 8. In this case the statistical year ends on 31 March of each year, so the 1958 figures are for the 1957-58 academic year and so on, for each year.

[4]*Irish Times,* 14 February 1964.

[5]*Times Educational Supplement,* 15 May 1964.
Approximately one half of the Republic's academic secondary schools had under 150 pupils (*Irish Times,* 19 May 1964).

[6]J.H. Whyte, *Church and State in Modern Ireland 1923–1970* (Dublin: Gill and MacMillan, 1971), p. 341.

[7]For a convenient précis of the economic plan see the *Weekly Bulletin of the Department of External Affairs,* no. 668: 13-VII-1964.

[8]*Hibernia* 7 January 1972.

[9]*An Roinn Oideachais Tuarascail 1960–61* [Pr. 6718], p. 50.
The act, it should be noted, provided that up to one third of the budget of each local authority could be allocated to university scholarships. For an extended summary of the measure see Thomas J. McElligott, *Education in Ireland* (Dublin: Institute of Public Administration, 1966), pp. 25–27.

[10]Compare *An Roinn Oideachais Tuarascail 1960–61,* p. 136 with *An Roinn Oideachais Tuarascail, Tsablai Staitistic 1966–67,* p. 50.

[11]Donogh O'Malley [untitled] Transcript of speech, 10 September 1966 (Dublin: Mimeo., 1966), p. 5.

[12]Ibid., p. 6.

[13]Sean O'Connor, "Post-Primary Education Now and in the Future," *Studies,* vol. LVII (Autumn 1968), p. 234. The article is reprinted in Robert Bell, Gerald Fowler and Ken Little (eds.), *Education in Great Britain and Ireland: A Source Book* (London: Routledge and Kegan Paul, 1973), pp. 146–55.

[14]*Irish Times* 9 January 1970.

[15]Church of Ireland, *Ninety-Sixth Report of Proceedings of the Representative Church Body. . . 1966,* pp. 133–34.

[16]Kenneth Milne, "A Church of Ireland View," *Studies,* vol. LVII (Autumn 1968), p. 262.

[17]Milne (ibid., p. 263) gives the higher figure, the *Irish Times* (12 May 1967), the lower.

[18]See Milne, pp. 263–65, and, Secondary Education Committee for Protestant Schools, *1967 Report* (Dublin: n.p., 1968).

[19]*Irish Times,* 12 May 1967.

[20]Norman Atkinson, *Irish Education: a History of Educational Institutions* (Dublin: Allen Figgis, 1969), p. 176.

[21]*Irish Times* 12 and 13 April 1968 (dual issue).

[22]For an elaboration of this argument see, Secondary Education Committee for Protestant Schools, *Public Statement with Regard to Grants for Protestant Secondary School Pupils* (Dublin: Mimeo. 1967, revised 1969).

[23]See article by John Horgan in the *Irish Times* 15 June 1971.

[24]Church of Ireland, *One Hundredth Report of Proceedings of the Representative Church Body . . . 1970,* p. 133; Secondary Education Committee for Protestant Schools, *1970 Report* (Dublin: n.p. 1971).

[25]In 1971 the Church of Ireland bishops called once again for a government re-assessment of the O'Malley scheme (*Irish Times* 2 April 1971).

[26]*Irish Times* 18 June 1971.

[27]Whyte, p. 341.

[28]Article by John Horgan, "What about the parents?" *Irish Times* 8 June 1971.
  In 1969 a "national parent-schools movement" was founded with the Catholic hierarchy's approval. Its activities centered on Dublin-area academic secondary schools (*Irish Times* 20 January 1970).

[29]Whyte, p. 352.

[30]O'Connor, p. 249.

[31]Patrick J. Hillery, *Statement by Dr. P.J. Hillery, T.D., Minister for Education, in Regard to Post-Primary Education* (Dublin: Mimeo. 1963), pp. 7–11. See also *Irish Times* 21 May 1963.

[32]See Hillery, p. 8.

[33]Atkinson, p. 171.

[34]Hillery, p. 9.

[35]Whyte, p. 341.

[36]Hillery, p. 9.

[37]*Irish Times* 2 February 1971 and 23 September 1971.

[38]In the discussion which follows I have relied on private interviews plus the following printed material: "Community Schools," in *Studies* vol. LIX (Winter 1970) , pp. 341–76. This contains both the original document and cogent observations thereon. The best journalistic coverage was done by the *Irish Times* which originally broke the story. See especially the issues of: 12 November 1970; 12 January 1971; 10 February 1971; 23 February 1971; 16 March 1971; 11 May 1971; 16 May 1971; 17 May 1971; 27 May 1971; 31 May 1971; 2 June 1971; 3 June 1971; 4 June 1971; 18 June 1971; 21 June 1971; 24 June 1971; 1 September 1972.

There are useful discussions in *Fortnight,* 28 May 1971, in *Hibernia,* 28 May 1971, and in *Times Educational Supplement,* 2 June 1972. From April 1973 onwards *The Education Times,* newly founded, becomes the fullest source of information.

See also: John Horgan, "Education in the Republic of Ireland," in Bell, Fowler & Little (eds.), esp. pp. 36–37; Secondary Education Committee for Protestant Schools, *1972 Report* (Dublin: n.p. 1972).

[39]This argument already has been made in the *Report,* published in the spring of 1973 of the Commission on the status of Women [Prl. 2760]. For a summary see *The Education Times,* 10 May 1973.

[40]*Fortnight,* 13 April 1973; *Hibernia,* 13 April 1973; *Irish Times,* 5 April 1973.

[41]For evidence that the religious authorities are very much concerned with the decline of the traditional teaching orders see the report on the conference of major religious superiors, reported in *The Education Times,* 31 May 1973.

[42]*The Education Times,* 14 June 1973.

NOTES TO APPENDIX

(a) *Dail Eireann ... 16th August 1921 ... 8th June 1922,* 2 August 1921.

(b) Ibid., p. 523.

(c) Basil Chubb, *The Government and Politics of Ireland* (Stanford: Stanford University Press, 1970), p. 338.

(d) *Iris Oifigiuil,* 12 September 1922.

(e) 1 *Dail Eireann*:10, 9 September 1922.

(f) *Iris Oifigiuil,* 30 December 1922.

(g) 14 *Dail Eireann*:326, 3 February 1926; *Iris Oifigiuil,* 2 February 1926.

(h) 41 *Dail Eireann*:38, 9 March 1932; Iris Oifigiuil, 11 March 1932.

(i) *Iris Oifigiuil,* 15 September 1939.

(j) Ibid., 29 September 1939.

(k) Ibid., 21 June 1940.

(l) Ibid., 20 February 1948.

(m) 126 *Dail Eireann*:81, 13 June 1951.

(n) *Iris Oifigiuil,* 4 June 1954.

(o) 161 *Dail Eireann*:29, 20 March 1957.

(p) *Iris Oifigiuil,* 26 June 1959.

(q) Ibid., 23 April 1965.

(r) 224 *Dail Eireann*:p.iii.

(s) 233 *Dail Eireann*:p.iii.

(t) Ibid., p.iii.

(u) *Iris Oifigiuil,* 4 July 1969.

(v) *Bulletin of the Department of External Affairs,* no.885, 30 March 1973.

BIBLIOGRAPHY

Probably the reader will have noticed in the footnotes to this study that for the period after 1921 almost no manuscript material is cited. This fact points to an unusual attitude held by successive southern Irish governments, namely that public records are not to be examined by the public. Thus the individual scholar is forced to glean what he can from the occasional private interview and to treat published governmental documents as palimpsests, approaching them with an eye for shading and with the realization that a point or a line missing in an oblique and confusing text often is more important than what is clearly visible.

Of course the most useful official documents are the annual reports of the Department of Education. A full series of these reports is surprisingly difficult to find, so I am listing the entire series with proper title and publication number of each volume, in the hope that this will make finding individual items easier for future researchers. Because the Department of Education habitually runs four to five years behind on its statistical reports and almost a full decade in arrears on the associated verbal text, the series is of no value on recent events.

The debates of the Irish legislature contain a good deal of material on education, but most of it is found scattered in questiontime response. Actual debates on education were remarkably rare, a reflection of the political unimportance of the topic. Dail and Seanad material is cited in footnotes but for reasons of space is not collated in the bibliography.

Newspapers and periodicals which ran education stories as regular, short news items, not as substantive articles, also are cited in the notes to the text, but are not here collated. Of the newspapers the *Irish Times* is by far the most revealing. Not only is it Ireland's only newspaper-of-record, but in the 'fifties it began a tradition of by-lined interpretative reporting on educational issues, with the articles of T.J. McElligott, a tradition which has flowered in the more recent work of John Horgan and Michael Heney. In April 1973 the parent firm began a new publication, *The Education Times* which is edited by John Horgan. The substantive articles listed below are those which were of direct value to me. There are many, many more which might aid those interested in other aspects of Irish education. A reasonably full listing can most conveniently be found by consulting *Sources for the History of Irish Civilisation: Articles in Irish Periodicals* (Boston: G.K. Hall & Co., 1970), compiled by the National Library of Ireland, under the editorship of Richard J. Hayes.

SYNOPSIS
I. Official publications of United Kingdom government, prior to Irish independence.
II. Official Irish government publications:
   A. Annual education reports.
   B. Occasional education publications.
   C. Other government publications.
III. Books and Pamphlets.
IV. Articles.
V. Unpublished papers and theses.

I. OFFICIAL PUBLICATIONS OF UNITED KINGDOM GOVERNMENT, PRIOR TO IRISH INDEPENDENCE (chronological order).

A Bill for Establishing a Department of Agriculture and Other Industries and Technical Instruction in Ireland, and for other purposes connected therewith, H.C. 1899 (180), i.

Regulations under Section Twenty-Four of the Agriculture and Technical Instruction (Ireland) Act 1899, H.C. 1900 (132), lxvii.

First Annual General Report of the Department of Agriculture and Technical Instruction for Ireland, 1900–1901 [Cd. 838], H.C. 1902, xx.

Second Annual General Report of the Department of Agriculture and Technical Instruction for Ireland, 1901–02 [Cd. 1314], H.C. 1902, xx.

Report of the Intermediate Education Board for Ireland for the Year 1903 [Cd. 1670], H.C. 1903, xxi.

Report of Mr. F. H. Dale, His Majesty's Inspector of Schools, Board of Education, on Primary Education in Ireland [Cd. 1981], H.C. 1904, xx.

Department of Agriculture and Technical Instruction for Ireland. Returns Showing Names of Permanent Officials on 1st May 1903 with Description of Office, Salary, Scale of Travelling Expenses, Data of Appointment, Previous Employment and Tenure of Office, H.C. 1904 (21), lxxix.

Report of Messrs. F. H. Dale and T. A. Stephens, His Majesty's Inspectors of Schools, Board of Education, on Intermediate Education in Ireland [Cd. 2546], H.C. 1905, xxviii.

Seventy-First Report of the Commissioners of National Education in Ireland, for the Year 1904 [Cd. 2567], H.C. 1905, xxviii.

Report of the Intermediate Education Board for Ireland for the Year 1904 [Cd. 2580], H.C. 1905, xxviii.

Minutes and Proceedings of the Commissioners of National Education Relating to Rule 127 (b) and Cognate Rules, H.C. 1905 (184), lx.

Agricultural and Technical Instruction Schemes (Ireland). Returns to an Order of the Honourable the House of Commons dated 27 June 1904, H.C. 1905 (70), lxvii.

A Bill to Provide for the Establishment and Functions of an Administrative Council in Ireland and for other purposes connected therewith, H.C. 1907 (182), ii.

Department of Agriculture and Technical Instruction (Ireland). Report of the Departmental Committee of Inquiry [Cd. 3572], H.C. 1907, xvii.

Report of the Intermediate Education Board for Ireland for the Year 1906 [Cd. 3544], H.C. 1907, xxii.

Report of the Intermediate Education Board for Ireland for the Year 1907 [Cd. 4047], H.C. 1908, xxvii.

Report of the Intermediate Education Board for Ireland for the Year 1908 [Cd. 4707], H.C. 1909, xx.

Report of the Intermediate Education Board for Ireland for the Year 1910 [Cd. 5768], H.C. 1911, xxi.

Seventy-Seventh Report of the Commissioners of National Education in Ireland, School Year 1910–1911 [Cd. 5903], H.C. 1911, xxi.

Agricultural and Technical Instruction (Ireland). Local Contributions (Ireland), H.C. 1914–16 (343), liii.

Report of the Intermediate Education Board for Ireland under the Intermediate Education (Ireland) Act, 1914, as to the Application of the Teachers' Salaries Grant [Cd. 8724], H.C. 1917–18, xi.

A Bill to make Further Provision with respect to Education in Ireland and for other purposes connected therewith, H.C. 1919 (214), i.

Report of the Vice-Regal Committee of Inquiry into Primary Education (Ireland), 1918 [Cmd. 60], H.C. 1919, xxi.

Report of the Vice-Regal Committee on the Conditions of Service and Remuneration of Teachers in Intermediate Schools and the Distribution of Grants from Public Funds for Intermediate Education in Ireland [Cmd. 66], H.C. 1919, xxi.

A Bill to make Further Provision with respect to Education in Ireland, and for other purposes connected therewith, H.C. 1920 (35), i.

Agriculture and Technical Instruction: Nineteenth Annual General Report of the Department, 1918–19 [Cmd. 929], H.C. 1920, ix.

Report of the Intermediate Education Board for Ireland for the Year 1920 [Cmd. 1398], H.C. 1921, xi.

Eighty-Sixth Report of the Commissioners of National Education in Ireland for the School Year 1919–1920 [Cmd. 1476], H.C. 1921, xi.

II. OFFICIAL IRISH GOVERNMENT PUBLICATIONS
A. ANNUAL EDUCATION REPORTS

Report of the Intermediate Education Commissioners for the Year 1922 (Dublin: Stationery Office, 1923).

Report of the Intermediate Education Commissioners for the Year 1923 (Dublin: Stationery Office, 1924).

Report and Statistics relating to National Education in Saorstat for the Year 1924–25 (Dublin: Stationery Office, 1926).

Report of the Department of Education for the School Year 1924–25 and the Financial and Administrative Years 1924–25–26 (Dublin: Stationery Office, 1926).

Report of the Department of Education for the School Years 1925–26–27 and the Financial and Administrative Year 1926–27 (Dublin: Stationery Office, 1928).
Report of the Department of Education 1927–28 [P. 19].

1928–29 [P. 207].
1929–30 [P. 490].
1930–31 [P. 733].
1931–32 [P. 962].
1932–33 [P. 1263].
1933–34 [P. 1693].
1934–35 [P. 2155].
1935–36 [P. 2656].
1936–37 [P. 3144].
1937–38 [P.3588].
1938–39 [P. 4281].
1939–40 [P. 4649].
1940–41 [P. 5529].
1941–42 [P. 6041].
1942–43 [P. 6567].
1943–44 [P. 7070].
1944–45 [P. 7761].
1945–46 [P. 8508].
1946–47 [P. 9274].
1947–48 [P. 9662].
1948–49 [Pr. 136].
1949–50 [Pr. 571].
1950–51 [Pr. 1609].
1051–52 [Pr. 2450].
1952–53 [Pr. 2626].
1953–54 [Pr. 3153].
1954–55 [Pr. 3622].
1955–56 [Pr. 4137].

An Roinn Oideachais Tuarascail 1956–57 [Pr. 4642].

1957–58 [Pr. 5118].
1958–59 [Pr. 5905].
1959–60 [Pr. 6218].
1960–61 [Pr. 6718].
1961–62 [Pr. 7066].
1962–63 [Pr. 7734].
1963–64 [Pr. 8487].

An Roinn Oideachais Tuarascail, Tablai Staitistic 1964–65 [Pr. 8982].

1965–66 [Prl. 31].
1966–67 [Prl. 1121].

B. OCCASIONAL EDUCATION PUBLICATIONS
Commission on Higher Education, 1960–67, vol. I. *Presentation and*

Summary of Report [Pr. 9326]; vol. II. *Report, chapters 1–19* [Pr. 9389]; vol. II. *Report, chapters 20–32* [Pr. 9588].

Commission on Technical Education, *Report* (Dublin: Stationery Office, 1927).

Committee on National Teachers' Salaries, *Reports and Appendices of the Committee on National Teachers' Salaries, etc., presented to the Minister for Education 18th May 1949* [P. 9634].

Department of Education, *Report on the Council of Education. . . . The Curriculum of the Secondary School* [Pr. 5996].

———, *Report of the Council of Education. . . . The Function of the Primary School. . . .* [Pr. 2583].

———, *National Adult Education Survey. Interim Report* [Prl. 1343].

———, *Notes for Teachers. English* (Dublin: Stationery Office, 1968).

———, *Notes for Teachers. Geography* (Dublin: Stationery Office, 1968).

———, *Rules and Programme for Secondary Schools, 1948–49* [P. 8910].

———, *Rules and Programme for Secondary Schools, 1970–71* [Pr. 1288].

———, Teachers' Salaries Committee, *Reports and Appendices presented to the Minister for Education 29th July 1960* [Pr. 5694].

Higher Education Authority, *Report on Teacher Education* (Dublin: Stationery Office, 1970).

Investment in Education [Pr. 8311].

Investment in Education. Annexes and Appendices [Pr. 8527].

National Programme Conference, *National Programme of Primary Instruction* (Dublin: Educational Company of Ireland, Ltd., 1922).

Reformatory and Industrial Schools [Prl. 1342].

Report of the Second National Programme Conference (1925–26) made for the information of the Minister for Education (Dublin: Stationery Office, 1926).

Steering Committee on Technical Education, *Report to the Minister for Education on Regional Technical Colleges* [Prl. 371].

Tribunal on Teachers' Salaries, *Report Presented to the Minister for Education* [Prl. 37].

C. OTHER GOVERNMENT PUBLICATIONS

Censorship Board, *Register of Prohibited Publications* (Dublin: Stationery Office, 1968).

Central Statistics Office, *Census of Population of Ireland, 1946.* vol. III, *Religions, Birthplaces* [Pr. 158].

———, *Census of Population of Ireland, 1946.* vol. VIII, *Irish Language* [Pr. 439].

———, *Census of Population of Ireland, 1961.* vol. VII, *Religions, Birthplaces* [Pr. 8097].

———, *Census of Population of Ireland, 1961.* vol. IX, *Irish Language* [Pr. 8669].

———, *Census of Population of Ireland, 1966,* vol. VII, *Education* [Prl. 1195].

———, *Statistical Abstract of Ireland, 1966* [Pr. 8950].

The Child Health Services [Prl. 171].

Coimisiun na Gaeltachta, *Report* (Dublin: Stationery Office, 1926).

Comhairle na Gaeilge, *Language and Community* (Dublin: Stationery Office, 1970).

———, *Local Government and Development Institutions for the Gaeltacht* (Dublin: Stationery Office [1971]).

———, *Submission to Higher Education Authority* (Dublin: Stationery Office, 1971).

———, *Towards a Language Policy* (Dublin: Stationery Office, 1971).

Commission of Inquiry on Mental Illness, *Report* [Pr. 9181].

Commission on Vocational Organisation, *Report* [P. 6743].

Department of Industry and Commerce, *Census of Population 1926*, vol. III, *Religions, Birthplaces* (Dublin: Stationery Office, 1929).

Report of the Commission of Inquiry into the Civil Service, 1932–35, vol. I [P. 1296].

Report of Public Services Organisation Review Group, 1966–1969 [Prl. 792].

The Restoration of the Irish Language [Pr. 8061].

Third Programme. Economic and Social Development 1969–72 [Prl. 431].

White Paper on the Restoration of the Irish Language: Progress Report for the Period ended 31 March 1966 [Pr. 9088].

III. BOOKS AND PAMPHLETS

Michael Adams, *Censorship: the Irish Experience* (Dublin: Scepter Books, 1968).

Donald H. Akenson, *Education and Enmity: the Control of Schooling in Northern Ireland 1922–1950* (Newton Abbot: published for the Institute of Irish Studies, the Queen's University of Belfast, by David and Charles Ltd., 1973).

———, *The Irish Education Experiment: the National System of Education in the Nineteenth Century* (London: Routledge & Kegan Paul; Toronto: University of Toronto Press, 1970).

———, *The United States and Ireland* (Cambridge: Harvard University Press, and London: Oxford University Press, 1973).

Conrad M. Arensberg, *The Irish Countryman: an Anthropological Study* (New York: MacMillan, 1937).

Conrad M. Arensberg and Solon T. Kimball, *Family and Community in Ireland* (Cambridge: Harvard University Press, second edition, 1968).

Matthew Arnold, *Irish Essays and Others* (London: Smith, Elder and Co., 1882).

Norman Atkinson, *Irish Education: a History of Educational Institutions* (Dublin: Allen Figgis, 1969).

Graham Balfour: *The Educational Systems of Great Britain and Ireland* (Oxford: Clarendon Press, second edition, 1903).

Robert Bell, Gerald Fowler and Ken Little (eds.), *Education in Great Britain and Ireland: a Source Book* (London: Routledge and Kegan Paul, 1973).

Jean Blanchard, *The Church in Contemporary Ireland* (Dublin: Clonmore and Reynolds, 1963, original French edition, 1960).

Basil Chubb, *The Government and Politics of Ireland* (Stanford: Stanford University Press, 1970).

Church of Ireland, *Careers in Ireland* (Dublin: Sparsely Populated Areas Commission of the Church of Ireland [1959]).

———, *Report on Secondary Education, 1965* (Dublin: Dublin University Press, 1965).

———, *Journals of the General Synod of the Church of Ireland, 1920* and following.

———, *Report of Proceedings of the Representative Body laid before the General Synod of the Church of Ireland. . . 1920* and following.

K. H. Connell, *Irish Peasant Society. Four Historical Essays* (Oxford: Clarendon Press, 1958).

Timothy P. Coogan, *Ireland since the Rising* (London: Pall Mall Press, 1966).

Daniel Corkery, *The Fortunes of the Irish Language* (Cork: Mercier Press, 1968, original ed., 1954).

———, *The Hidden Ireland. A Study of Gaelic Munster in the Eighteenth Century* (Dublin: Gill and Son, 1967, original ed., 1924).

———, *Synge and Anglo-Irish Literature* (Cork: Mercier Press, 1966, original ed., 1931).

Margaret Digby, *Horace Plunkett, an Anglo-American Irishman* (Oxford: Basil Blackwell, 1949).

P. J. Dowling, *A History of Irish Education. A Study in Conflicting Loyalties* (Cork: Mercier Press, 1971).

Patrick S. Duffy, *The Lay Teacher: a Study of the Position of the Lay Teacher in an Irish Catholic Environment* (Dublin: Fallons [1968]).

Desmond Fennell (ed.), *The Changing Face of Catholic Ireland* (London: Geoffrey Chapman, 1968).

Federation of Irish Secondary Schools, *Investment in Education in the Republic of Ireland, with some Comparative Statistics* (Dublin: Federation of Irish Secondary Schools, 1962).

Seamus Fenton, *It All Happened* (Dublin: M. H. Gill and Son Ltd., 1949).

Garret Fitzgerald, *Towards a New Ireland* (Dublin: Torc Books edition, 1973).

T. W. Freeman, *Ireland, a General and Regional Geography* (London: Methuen and Co., third ed., 1965).

Gaelic League Pamphlets—no. 12. The Irish Language and Irish Intermediate Education (Dublin: Gaelic League, 1901).

M. W. Heslinga, *The Irish Border as a Cultural Divide: A Contribution to the Study of Regionalism in the British Isles* (Assen: Van Gorcum and Co., 1962).

Michael P. Hickey, *Gaelic League Pamphlets—no. 29* [sic. no. 28]. *The Irish Language Movement, its Genesis, Growth, and Progress* (Dublin: Gaelic League, 1902).

Patrick J. Hillery, *Statement of Dr. P. J. Hillery, T.D., Minister for Education, in Regard to Post-Primary Education* (Dublin: Mimeo., 1963).

Alexander J. Humphreys, *New Dubliners: Urbanization and the Irish Family* (London: Routledge and Kegan Paul, 1966).

Douglas Hyde, *A Literary History of Ireland from Earliest Times to the Present Day* (London: Ernest Benn, new edition 1967, original ed., 1899).

Brian Inglis, *West Briton* (London: Faber and Faber, 1962).

Irish Education (London: Tuairim [c. 1962]).

Irish National Teachers' Organization, *A Plan for Education* (Dublin: I.N.T.O., 1947).

———, *Report of Committee of Inquiry into the Use of Irish as a Teaching Medium to Children Whose Home Language is English* (Dublin: I.N.T.O., 1941).

J. M. Kelly, *Fundamental Rights in the Irish Law and Constitution* (Dublin: Allen Figgis and Co. Ltd., second ed., 1967).

J. D. King, *Religious Education in Ireland* (Dublin: Fallons, 1970).

Earl of Longford and Thomas P. O'Neill, *Eamon de Valera* (London: Hutchinson, 1970).

F. S. L. Lyons, *Ireland Since the Famine* (London: Weidenfeld and Nicolson, 1971).

J. L. McCracken, *Representative Government in Ireland: a Study of Dail Eireann 1914–48* (London: Oxford University Press, 1958).

Thomas J. McElligott, *Education in Ireland* (Dublin: Institute of Public Administration, 1966).

John MacNamara, *Bilingualism and Primary Education: a Study of Irish Experience* (Edinburgh: Edinburgh University Press, 1966).

John Charles McQuaid, *Catholic Education: its Function and Scope* (Dublin: Catholic Truth Society of Ireland [1942]).

John Mescal, *Religion in the Irish System of Education* (Dublin: Clonmore and Reynolds, 1957).

B. R. Mitchell, with Phyllis Deane, *Abstract of British Historical Statistics* (Cambridge: Cambridge University Press, 1962).

Michael W. Murphy (ed.), *Education in Ireland: Now and the Future* (Cork: Mercier Press, 1970).

———, *Education in Ireland II. What Should Students Learn?* (Cork: Mercier Press, 1971).

Conor Cruise O'Brien (ed.), *The Shaping of Modern Ireland* (London: Routledge and Kegan, 1960).

John A. O'Brien (ed.), *The Vanishing Irish* (London: W. H. Allen, 1954).

Leon O'Broin, *The Chief Secretary: Augustine Birrell in Ireland* (London: Chatto and Windus, 1969).

Sean O'Cathain, *Secondary Education in Ireland* (Dublin: Talbot Press [1958]).

T. J. O'Connell, *History of the Irish National Teachers' Organization 1868–1968* (Dublin: privately printed, n.d.).

Brian O'Cuiv (ed.), *A View of the Irish Language* (Dublin: Stationery Office, 1969).

Sean O'Faolain, *The Irish. A Character Study* (New York: Devin-Adair Co., 1956).

Donogh O'Malley [Untitled] *Transcript of Speech 10 September 1966* (Dublin: Mimeo., 1966).

John J. O'Meara, *Reform in Education* (Blackrock: Mount Salus Press, 1958).

Donal O'Sullivan, *The Irish Free State and its Senate: a Study in Contemporary Politics* (London: Faber and Faber Ltd., 1940).

Sean O'Tuama, *Facts about Irish* (Naas: Leinster Leader, new ed., 1970).

Patrick Pearse, *The Murder Machine*, in, *Political Writings and Speeches* (Dublin: Talbot Press, 1966), pp. 5–50.

Presbyterian Church in Ireland, General Assembly, *Reports and Accounts, 1924*, and following.

Dorine Rohan, *Marriage Irish Style* (Cork: Mercier Press, 1969).

Roman Catholic Church in Ireland, *Acta et Decreta Concillii Plenarii. . . . 1956* (Dublin: M. H. Gill, 1970).

———, *Acta et Decreta Synodi Plenariae Episcoporum Hiberniae. . . . MDCCCC* (Dublin: Browne and Nolan, 1906).

———, *Acta et Decreta Concillii Plenarii Episcoporum Hiberniae. . . . 1927* (Dublin: Browne and Nolan, 1929).

———, *Irish Catholic Directory, 1920*, and following.

Desmond Ryan, *The Sword of Light* (London: Arthur Barker, 1939).

George Seaver, *John Allen Fitzgerald Gregg, Archbishop* (Dublin: Allen Figgis, 1963).

Secondary Education Committee for Protestant Schools, *Public Statement with Regard to Grants for Protestant Secondary School Pupils* (Dublin: mimeo., 1967, revised 1969).

———, *1967* Report (Dublin: n.p., 1968).

———, *1970 Report* (Dublin: n.p., 1971).

———, *1972 Report* (Dublin: n.p., 1972).

Michael Sheehy, *Is Ireland Dying? Culture and the Church in Modern Ireland* (London: Hollis and Carter, 1968).

W. B. Stanford, *A Recognised Church: the Church of Ireland in Eire* (Dublin and Belfast: A.P.C.K., 1944).

W. B. Stanford, and R. B. McDowell, *Mahaffy. A Biography of an Anglo–Irishman* (London: Routledge and Kegan Paul, 1971).

Michael Tierney, *Education in a Free Ireland* (Dublin: Martin Lester Ltd. [1920]).

Honor Tracy, *Mind you, I've said nothing! Forays in the Irish Republic* (London: Methuen and Co. Ltd., 1953).

United States Department of the Interior, Bureau of Education, *Education in the Irish Free State* (Washington, D.C., 1925).

Brendan M. Walsh, *Religion and Demographic Behaviour in Ireland* (Dublin: The Economic and Social Research Institute, 1970).

J. H. Whyte, *Church and State in Modern Ireland 1923–1970* (Dublin: Gill and MacMillan, 1971).

IV. ARTICLES

Donald H. Akenson, "National Education and the Realities of Irish Life, 1831–1900," *Eire–Ireland*, vol. IV, no. 4 (winter 1969), pp. 42–51.

Donald H. Akenson and J. F. Fallin, "The Irish Civil War and the Drafting of the Free State Constitution," *Eire–Ireland*, vol. V, no. 1 (spring 1970), pp. 10–26; vol. V, no. 2 (summer 1970), pp. 42–93; vol. V, no. 4 (winter 1970), pp. 28–70.

T. J. Barrington, "Public Administration 1927–1936," in Francis Mac-Manus (ed.), *The Years of the Great Test 1926–39* (Cork: Mercier Press, 1967), pp. 80–91.

Peter Birch, "Secondary School English," *Irish Ecclesiastical Record*, 5 ser. vol. LXII, no. 6 (June 1944), pp. 391–95.

R. A. Breatnach, "Irish Revival Reconsidered," *Studies*, vol. LIII (Spring 1964), pp. 18–30.

Martin Brenan, "The Catholic School System of Ireland," *Irish Ecclesiastical Record*, 5 ser. vol. LIII, no. 9 (September 1938), pp. 257–71.

———, "The Restoration of Irish," *Studies*, vol. LIII (Autumn 1964), pp. 263–77.

———, "The Vocational Schools," *Irish Ecclesiastical Record*, 5 ser. vol. LVII, no. 2 (February 1941), pp. 13–27.

"Catholic Clerical Managers Association, Meeting of Central Council," *Irish Educational Review*, vol. II, no. 10 (July 1909), pp. 629–32.

H. R. Chillingworth, "The Education of the Adolescent in the Irish Free State," *The Year Book of Education 1937* (London: Evans Brothers, 1937), pp. 239–46.

———, "Examinations in the Irish Free State," *The Year Book of Education 1938* (London: Evans Brothers, 1938), pp. 241–48.

———, "Irish Free State," *The Year Book of Education 1934* (London: Evans Brothers, 1934), pp. 350–56.

"Community Schools," *Studies*, vol. LIX (winter 1970), pp. 341–76.

"Control of Primary Education in Ireland," *Irish Educational Review*, vol. I, no. 12 (September 1908), pp. 729–36.

Timothy Corcoran, "How the Irish Language can be Revived," *Irish Monthly*, vol. LI (June 1923), pp. 26–34.

———, "The Irish Language in the Irish Schools," *Studies*, vol. XIV (September 1925), pp. 377–88.

———, "The Teaching of Modern Irish History," *Irish Monthly*, vol. LI (October 1923), pp. 491–96.

Correspondence. The Vocational Schools," *Irish Ecclesiastical Record*, 5 ser. vol. LVII, no. 4 (May 1941), pp. 368–75.

Terence P. Cunningham, "Church Reorganization," *The Church since Emancipation*, Patrick J. Corish (ed.) (Dublin: Gill and MacMillan, 1970), pp. 1–32.

[Eamon de Valera] "Address of an Taoiseach to the Teachers' Congress, Killarney, Easter, 1940," *Capuchin Annual, 1941*, pp. 183–88.

P. J. Dowling, "Eire," *The Year Book of Education 1948* (London: Evans Brothers, 1948), pp. 204–11.

Denis Fahey, "The Introduction of Scholastic Philosophy into Irish Secondary Education," *Irish Ecclesiastical Record*, 5 ser. vol. XXII, no. 8 (August 1923), pp. 177–93.

Dermot F. Gleeson, Joseph O'Neill, and Maureen Beaumont, "Father T. Corcoran, S. J.," *Studies*, vol. XXXII (June 1943), pp. 153–62.

Arnold F. Graves, "On the Reorganisation of Irish Education Departments and the Appointment of a Minister of Education," *Journal of the Statistical and Social Inquiry Society of Ireland*, vol. VIII, part 60 (August 1882), pp. 350–59.

"Lay Teacher," "Religious Instruction in Primary Schools," *Irish Ecclesiastical Record*, 5 ser. vol. LXVI, no. 1 (July 1945), pp. 1–10.

———, "Religious Instruction in Primary Schools," *Irish Ecclesiastical Record*, 5 ser. vol. LXVI, no. 2 (August 1945), pp. 120–28.

M. P. Linehan, "The Irish Republic," *The Year Book of Education 1953* (London: Evans Brothers, 1953), pp. 193–202.

Cornelius Lucey, "A Guild for Education," *Irish Ecclesiastical Record*, 5 ser. vol. LI, no. 6 (June 1938), pp. 582–92.

———, "Making the School System of Ireland Catholic," *Irish Ecclesiastical Record*, 5 ser. vol. LII, no. 10 (October 1938), pp. 405–17.

F. S. L. Lyons, "The Minority Problem in the 26 Counties," in Francis MacManus (ed.), *The Years of the Great Test, 1926–39* (Cork: Mercier Press, 1967), pp. 92–103.

Donal McCartney, "Education and Language, 1938–51," in Kevin B. Nowlan and T. Desmond Williams (eds.), *Ireland in the War Years and After, 1939–51* (Dublin: Gill and MacMillan, 1969).

T. J. McElligott, "Some Thoughts on our Educational Discontents," *University Review*, vol. I, no. 5 (summer 1955), pp. 27–36.

John MacNamara, "The Commission on Irish: Psychological Aspects," *Studies,* vol. LIII (summer 1964), pp. 164–72.

John Magee, "The Teaching of Irish History in Irish Schools," reprinted from *The Northern Teacher,* vol. x, no. 1 (winter 1970).

Conor Malone, "English Literature in Ireland: a Comment on School Courses," *Catholic Bulletin* vol. XXV, no. 3 (March 1953), pp. 199–204.

John C. Messenger, "Sex and Repression in an Irish Folk Community," in Donald S. Marshall and Robert C. Suggs (eds.), *Human Sexual Behaviour. Variations in the Ethnographic Spectrum* (New York: and London: Basic Books Inc., 1971), pp. 3–37.

Kenneth Milne, "A Church of Ireland View," *Studies,* vol. LVII (Autumn 1968), pp. 261–69.

C. B. Murphy, "Sex, Censorship and the Church," *The Bell,* vol. II, no. 6 (September 1941), pp. 65–75.

Gerard Murphy, "Irish in our Schools, 1922–1945," *Studies,* vol. XXXVII (December 1948), pp. 421–28.

Jeremiah Newman, "The Priests of Ireland: a Socio-Religious Survey—I—Numbers and Distribution," *Irish Ecclesiastical Record,* 5 ser. vol. XCVIII, no. 1 (July 1962), pp. 1–23.

———, "The Priests of Ireland: a Socio-Religious Survey—II—Pattern of Vocations," *Irish Ecclesiastical Record,* 5 ser. vol. XCVIII, no. 2 (August 1962), pp. 65–91.

Patrick O'Callaghan, "Irish in Schools," *The Bell,* vol. XIV, no. 1 (April 1947), pp. 62–68.

Sean O'Cathain, "Education in the New Ireland," in Francis MacManus (ed.), *The Years of the Great Test, 1926–39* (Cork: Mercier Press, 1967), pp. 104–14.

Sean O'Connor, "Post-Primary Education Now and in the Future," *Studies,* vol. LVII (autumn 1968), pp. 233–51.

Brian O'Cuiv, "Education and Language," in Desmond Williams (ed.), *The Irish Struggle 1916–1926* (London: Routledge and Kegan Paul, 1966), pp. 153–66.

Diarmaid P. O'Donnabhain, "Curriculum Planning in the Comprehensive Schools: the Junior Cycle," *Oideas,* no. 3 (autumn 1969) pp. 13–19.

Michael O'Donnell, "Irish Education Today," *Irish Hibernia,* vol. V, no. 1 (1963), pp. 18–26.

Peadar O'Donnell, "Teachers Vote Strike," *The Bell,* vol. XI, no. 2 (November 1945), pp. 669–72.

Sean O'Faolain, "The Death of Nationalism," *The Bell,* vol. XVII, no. 2 (May 1951), pp. 44–53.

[Sean O'Faolain], "The Gaelic Cult," *The Bell,* vol. IX, no. 3 (December 1944), pp. 185–96.

[Sean O'Faolain], "The Gaelic League," *The Bell,* vol. IV, no. 2 (May 1942), pp. 77–86.

[Sean O'Faolain], "On State Control," *The Bell,* vol. VI, no. 1 (April 1943), pp. 1–6.

[Sean O'Faolain], "The Senate and Censorship," *The Bell,* vol. V, no. 4 (January 1943), pp. 247–52.

[Sean O'Faolain], "The Stuffed-Shirts," *The Bell,* vol. VI, no. 3 (June 1943), pp. 181–92.

Sean C. O'Mordha, "The Origin of the Written Examination in Religious Knowledge in Irish Secondary Schools," *Irish Ecclesiastical Record,* 5 ser. vol. CIV, no. 5 (October-November 1965), pp. 278–85.

Alfred O'Rahilly, "The Republic of Ireland," *The Year Book of Education, 1951* (London: Evans Brothers, 1951), pp. 345–54.

Seamus V. O'Suilleabhain, "Secondary Education," *Catholic Education,* Patrick J. Corish (ed.) (Dublin: Gill and MacMillan, 1971).

"Outis," "Compulsory Irish and the Secondary Schools Programme," *Irish Monthly,* vol. LV, (February 1927), pp. 68–79.

"Pastoral Address of the Irish Bishops on the Managership of Catholic Schools," *Irish Ecclesiastical Record,* 4 ser. vol. IV, no. 367 (July 1898), pp. 75–78.

"Pronouncement of the Irish Hierarchy at a General Meeting Held at Maynooth on Tuesday January 27th," *Irish Ecclesiastical Record,* 5 ser. vol. XV, no. 2 (February 1920), pp. 150–52.

"Resolutions of the Assembled Archbishops and Bishops of Ireland on the Education Bill," *Irish Ecclesiastical Record,* 3 ser. vol. XIII (May 1892), pp. 472–77.

"Rev. Brother Philip," "The Gael and the Gaeltacht," *Irish Ecclesiastical Record,* 5 ser. vol. XXX, no. 7 (August 1927), pp. 140–53.

"Rev. Dr. Timothy Corcoran," *Analecta Hibernica,* no. 16 (March 1946), p. 386.

P. Ivers Rigney, "Local Aid in Education," *Irish Monthly,* vol. LIII (December 1925), pp. 624–27.

W. B. Stanford, et. al., "Protestantism since the Treaty," *The Bell,* vol. VIII, no. 3 (June 1944), pp. 219–32.

"Statement of the Archbishops and Bishops of Ireland on the Evils of Dancing, Issued at their Meeting, Held in Maynooth, on 6th October, 1925," *Irish Ecclesiastical Record,* 5 ser. vol. XXVII, no. 1 (January 1926), pp. 91–92.

"Statement of the Standing Committee of the Irish Bishops on the Proposed Education Bill for Ireland, *Irish Ecclesiastical Record,* 5 ser. vol. XIV, no. 12 (December 1919), pp. 504–507.

"Statements and Resolutions of the Irish Hierarchy at Maynooth Meeting June 21," *Irish Ecclesiastical Record,* 4 ser. vol. XXVII, no. 7 (July 1910), pp. 91–93.

J. H. Whyte, "Political Life in the South," Michael Hurley (ed.), *Irish*

Anglicanism 1869–1969 (Dublin: Allen Figgis Ltd., 1970), pp. 143–53.

V. UNPUBLISHED PAPERS AND THESES

Patrick J. Buckland, "Southern Unionism, 1885–1922" (Ph.D. thesis, Queen's University, Belfast, 1969), 2 vols.

Thomas J. McElligott, "Intermediate Education and the Work of the Commissioners, 1870–1922" (M. Litt. thesis, Trinity College, Dublin, 1969).

David W. Miller, "Educational Reform and the Realities of Irish Politics in the Early Twentieth Century" (paper presented to the American Historical Association, 30 December 1969).

David W. Miller, "The Politics of Faith and Fatherland: the Catholic Church and Nationalism in Ireland, 1898–1915" (Ph.D. thesis, University of Chicago, 1968).

John W. Musson, "The Training of Teachers in Ireland from 1811 to the Present Day" (Ph.D. thesis, Queen's University, Belfast, 1955).

Patrick K. O'Leary, "The Development of Post-Primary Education in Eire since 1922, with Special Reference to Vocational Education" (Ph.D. thesis, Queen's University, Belfast, 1962), 2 vols.

INDEX